D0948719

HOW

TO SUCCEED

ON YOUR OWN

HOW
TO SUCCEED
ON YOUR OWN

OVERCOMING THE EMOTIONAL
ROADBLOCKS ON THE WAY FROM
CORPORATION TO COTTAGE,
FROM EMPLOYEE TO ENTREPRENEUR

KARIN ABARBANEL

THE NATIONAL ASSOCIATION FOR
FEMALE EXECUTIVES PROFESSIONAL LIBRARY
HENRY HOLT AND COMPANY   NEW YORK

The chart on p. 114 is reprinted here courtesy of the designers,
Jordana Simpson and Terry Protheroe,
from a concept by Karin Abarbanel.

Henry Holt and Company, Inc.
Publishers since 1866
115 West 18th Street
New York, New York 10011

Henry Holt® is a registered
trademark of Henry Holt and Company, Inc.

Library of Congress Cataloging-in-Publication Data
Abarbanel, Karin.
How to succeed on your own : overcoming the emotional roadblocks
on the way from corporation to cottage, from employee to
entrepreneur / Karin Abarbanel.
p.   cm.—(The National Association for Female Executives
professional library)
Includes index.
1. New business enterprises.   2. Women-owned business enterprises—
Management.   3. Small business—Management.   4. Cottage industries.
5. Success in business.   I. Title.   II. Series.
HD62.5.A28   1994   93-25490
658′.041—dc20   CIP

ISBN 0-8050-1381-4

Henry Holt books are available for special promotions and
premiums. For details contact: Director, Special Markets.

First Edition—1994

Book design by Claire Naylon Vaccaro

Printed in the United States of America
All first editions are printed on acid-free paper. ∞

1   3   5   7   9   10   8   6   4   2

A New Chapter Press Book

To my family,
without whose loving support and patience
this book would still be a dream:
Dorothy, David, Alexander,
Stephanie, Judy, Peter, Joan, and Luis.
And to my father, Albert, who first showed me
the joys and demands of working on your own.
And to emerging entrepreneurs:
May this book give wings to
your desire!

CONTENTS

ACKNOWLEDGMENTS

I am grateful to my family, my friends, and especially the many gifted entrepreneurs and experts who share their lives, dreams, and advice here. Their enthusiasm and interest sustained me over many long months of research and writing. My deepest thanks must go to my mother, Dorothy Abarbanel, for her loving inspiration and help; to my husband, David Grossman, for his wonderful support and encouragement; to my son, Alexander, for his joyfulness; to my insightful sisters, Stephanie and Judy Abarbanel; and to my inspiring brother, Peter. A special thank you to Wendy Reid Crisp for all her advice and encouragement. Thanks also to Lonah Birch, Barbara Brabec, Jackie Farley, Karen Fried, Edward Hallowell, Caroline Hull, Barbara Mackoff, Joyce McClure, Debra Oppenheim, Jordana Simpson, and Cheryl Williams.

ENTREPRENEURS AND BUSINESS ADVISORS INTERVIEWED

Jane Adams, author of *Wake Up, Sleeping Beauty*; *Women on Top: Success Patterns and Personal Growth*; and *I'm Still Your Mother: A Modern Woman's Guide to Post-Parenting*, Seattle, Washington

Jan Berg, strategic planner, prosperity counselor, and founder of The Center for Business Advancement, Port Townsend, Washington

Lonah Birch, assistant regional administrator, Public Affairs and Communications, U.S. Small Business Administration, Kansas City, Missouri

Barbara Brabec, publisher and editor of the quarterly newsletter *National Home Business Report*, and author of *Homemade Money: How to Select, Start, Manage, Market, and Multiply the Profits of a Business at Home*, Naperville, Illinois

Alison Cross, screenwriter and producer, Los Angeles, California

Jackie Farley, television talk-show host, corporate wellness consultant, and founder and president of CenterPoint in Aspen, which offers retreats for women, Aspen, Colorado

Kathryn Frazier, outplacement counselor, Drake Beam Morin; manager of the General Electric Career Center, Mount Vernon, Indiana; former assistant district director for business development, U.S. Small Business Administration; and entrepreneur, St. Louis, Missouri

Karen J. Fried, game creator and entrepreneur, Think-It Link-It, New York, New York

Lorraine Gerstein, owner and president, Rehab Inc., a private rehabilitation consulting company, Bedford, New Hampshire

Edward Hallowell, M.D., psychiatrist, instructor at Harvard Medical School and Massachusetts Mental Health Center, and coauthor of *What Are You Worth?*, Cambridge, Massachusetts

Sara Harrell, advertising marketing consultant and writer, Phoenix, Arizona

Ann Hull, founder and president, MeetingWorks International, an independent meeting planning company, New York, New York

Caroline Hull, founder and editor of *ConneXions*, a newsletter and resource for home-based working mothers and professionals, and The ConneXus Group, a consulting firm on alternative work options, Manassas, Virginia

Sue Laris-Eastin, founder and publisher, the *Downtown News Group*, Los Angeles, California

Kathy Lloyd-Williams, founder and president of xoxo international, inc., a manufacturer of innovative products that help children learn through fun, discovery-oriented creative play, Huntington Beach, California

Barbara Mackoff, Ph.D., management psychologist, seminar leader, and author of *Leaving the Office Behind, What Mona Lisa Knew, The Art of Self-Renewal*, and *Lessons from a Caterpillar*, Seattle, Washington

Joyce McClure, marketing consultant, small business advisor, and vice-president for institutional advancement, Thomas College, Waterville, Maine

Pamela Mauney, confectioner, Pam's Blue Ribbon Toffee, Ferndale, California

Susan O'Hara-Brill, owner, desktop publishing and typing service, Chapel Hill, North Carolina

Debra Oppenheim, cofounder and partner, The Phillips Oppenheim Group, not-for-profit search consultants, New York, New York

Judith Grant Palma, aesthetician and owner of Grant Palma, Upper Montclair, New Jersey

Melinda Pancoast, cofounder of Milestone Management Consulting Services, a company specializing in organizational transformation, Burlington, Vermont

Myrna Ruskin, president, Myrna Ruskin Associates, stress management consulting, New York, New York

Brian Schwartz, Ph.D., career management consultant and psychologist, The Greenwich Consortium, Greenwich, Connecticut, and New York, New York

Jordana Simpson, graphic designer and creator of fine home furnishing products and accessories, Forest Hills, New York

Jayne Tear, The Jayne Tear Group, gender dynamics consultant, New York, New York

After lying awake worrying about cash flow from 11:01 P.M. to 4:36 A.M. (aren't digital clocks helpful?), you stagger into a cold, dark office, rinse out yesterday's mug, and make coffee. The answering machine light is blinking; it's all the other entrepreneurs calling during off-hours to get you to pick up the tab for the callback. There are bills to pay, plants to water, marketing plans to complete, distribution channels to develop, and bookshelves to dust. Your in basket is full—you filled it—and when the work is done, you'll be the one who scurries around and empties the out basket. Congratulations! You've started your own business. Are we having fun yet?

Some days you feel the triumphant *yes!* gesture of the tennis pros; other days you let the phone ring because your voice is too low and quavering to answer. You wonder, What was I thinking of? Am I alone out here?

Well, the statistical answer to the latter question is no. The most recent government surveys say that nearly seven million women have started their own businesses. And this figure includes only those women who have sole proprietorships; it has no way to count the women who have corporations or partnerships. And another study, by the National Association of Women Business Owners (NAWBO), reports that female-owned businesses employ more people in the United States than do all of the Fortune 500 companies combined.

In your own beginnings, when the only employee is you—or maybe you and your Cousin Lois—these figures are not encouraging. How did everyone else make it? you wonder.

The question is not necessarily directed at the business aspects of entrepreneurships, it is a question of emotional stamina—enduring the roller coaster ride of elation and despair, the stretches of loneliness, the awareness that no one cares much about your good news and sympathy is short for the bad news.

The answers to questions about the personal aspects of starting your own business have not been available: the entrepreneurial revolution has been sudden (the number of female-owned businesses has increased tenfold since 1978), and while heralded, it has been largely unexamined. We cannot anticipate the effect that millions of cottage industries—a quaint term—coupled with twenty-first-century electronics will have on our economy, and until Karin Abarbanel came along we were not able to delineate the psychological effects of going it alone.

What we do know is that the wide-open opportunities already have begun to change the structure of our work lives. For many women, this means working two or three jobs in order to plant the seeds of a new business in soil enriched by another income. At every event of the National Association for Female Executives that I have attended, members have handed me more than one business card, saying, "This is what I really do, and this is what I'm starting." "I'm a cop," one woman told me, "but I've started a construction company on my days off."

It is as if for the first time, the quest for the American dream has admitted women unconditionally. We are behaving in the classic style of new immigrants who have just reached the land of hope and opportunity. However, because we are, with the exception of our gender, as diverse a group of humans as has ever been assembled into one special interest group, there is no precedent by which to measure the changes our striving will fuel.

One thing we know as surely as we know our patriotic anthems:

whatever the risks, however long coming the rewards, there is no life as full as the one that is free and independent.

"It's the busy brain," a very old man told me on a plane trip from Minneapolis. "There's something the brain releases when it's busy. It makes you happier than anything else you can imagine. Men have known this for years. Now women know it, too. Their brains are busy. They're happy. And nothing will ever be the same again."

Amen.

Wendy Reid Crisp
National Director
National Association for Female Executives

*It is never too late to be what
you might have been.*

—*George Eliot*

W hat is there about the classic cottage that so captures our imagination? Perhaps it's the sense of style and simplicity it conveys. If well crafted, its dimensions are pleasing and of human scale. If we're lucky (and why not!), our cottage commands a sweeping view, refreshing the mind and eye and giving scope to the work within. That work, when it's going well, tumbles through our cottage door to meet the world and take its measure. And in our most perfect fantasy, our cottage is a green and growing place—a safe and joyous haven where we are free to explore and create.

"The time is so ripe," one expert told me, "for women to leave corporations and start cottage industries—to create a home for their business, a nest. To nurture it and make it grow." How true this is! Yet embracing the cottage life and crafting an independent, self-structured work style isn't easy. It demands time and energy, creativity, emotional stamina, and a healthy dose of humor and optimism. When you make the move from employee to entrepreneur and start your own business, you are not just changing your job, or changing your life-style, or changing careers. *You are changing your identity.*

At a stroke, your office, your title, the camaraderie of colleagues, the security of a regular paycheck, the rhythm of your workday, the deadlines, business lunches, and secretarial help are gone. Suddenly you're all alone; everything begins and ends with you. And if you're no longer director of marketing or manager of special events, then who are you? As one woman entrepreneur asked, "Do I really exist if I don't have six phone messages by noon?" Helping you find the answer to this question—and redefine your identity, what you want to achieve, and how you want to work—is at the heart of this book.

How to Succeed on Your Own is not a traditional guide to starting a small business. It won't tell you how to write a marketing plan, choose an accountant, or talk to your banker. Instead, through the advice and firsthand experience of female entrepreneurs and experts, you'll learn exactly what you can expect, both personally and professionally, if you decide to forgo a corporate career and launch a small business. *How to Succeed on Your Own* explores exciting new territory by charting the emotional and psychological changes you'll face if you choose to pursue greater control over your time, energy, and talent as an entrepreneur.

Starting a business is exhilarating, but it's also the stuff of sleepless nights. It can make you feel alive and energized, but it also can make you feel uprooted and at odds with yourself. Without the emotional and practical tools to tap your strengths and manage your fears, the best business plan, the biggest bank account in town, and the savviest marketing strategy won't help you when the going gets tough. And as the women in this book will tell you, it *will* get tough—suppliers and trusted clients will fail you, the phone won't ring for days, and for weeks on end, your bank balance will look more like Mother Teresa's than Madonna's. At the same time, surviving and triumphing over the odds will give you newfound strength and confidence. It also will reveal the wellspring of energy and creativity needed to nurture your success. Learning how to weather the storms you'll face and enjoy your days of calm takes practice and persistence. But with a little help, like other seasoned voyagers, you too can become skilled at knowing when to pull out your emotional rain gear and when to leave it at home.

The goal of this book is threefold. My first aim is to help you decide if the cottage life really makes sense for you. Can you handle its emotional demands? Do you have the inner resources to succeed? What are the hidden payoffs and pitfalls of this work style—the ones you tend not to hear about? These are some of the questions we'll explore together honestly and openly. My second goal is to provide you with an upbeat and supportive "emotional road map" to the first eighteen months of your venture. It's designed to help you master the intense feelings and challenges you'll face during the peak start-up period, when the demands of creating a new work life make you most vulnerable. And finally, this book will serve as a small business survival kit: it will arm you with tools for success by offering frontline advice from a wide range of female entrepreneurs.

In the course of my research, I had long conversations with many inspiring and creative women all across the country. I also spoke with experts in psychology, money, stress management, and small business counseling, all of whom shared their insights and advice with great generosity and enthusiasm. With their help, we'll discuss timing your move, outline the emotional stages you can expect to go through, pinpoint the biggest traps you'll face, and probe key aspects of money and self-motivation. Along the way, we'll also explore the rich rewards you'll reap in creating a work style all your own, one that reflects your experience, talents, and dreams.

Writing this book has taken me on a fascinating journey. As a seasoned moonlighter, new entrepreneur, and mother coping with the demands of work and family, I've often been inspired by women who left corporate life to strike out on their own. At the same time, I've found myself asking questions most books never seem to answer: When should you make your move? Do you need some mysterious risk-taking gene to take this step, or do you find the strength by doing instead of dreaming, by committing yourself and taking the plunge? Can your money style affect your chances of success? Does the fear of failure ever go away? Can you have a personal life and still make a small business work? You'll find the answers to all of these questions and more in this book. I know the advice it offers will be helpful and encouraging as you think through your plans and dreams.

"Starting your own business is really about being your own hero."

That's how one woman expressed her personal quest for independence. After talking to many talented female entrepreneurs about their trials and triumphs, I've learned how right she is. What bold adventurers they are! And if there is one thing the world needs today, it surely is more heroes—and heroines. I hope one of them is you. Good luck!

1

IS THE "COTTAGE LIFE" FOR YOU?

*I have this wonderful feeling of freedom and exhilaration
in taking charge of my own life. I wouldn't trade it, even
with all the anxiety that comes with it. The word is
overused, but it's true: there's a feeling of empowerment.
It's more than rewarding, this new sense of independence
I've discovered.*

—Debra Oppenheim

The fantasy is a familiar one: wouldn't it be wonderful to throw all caution to the wind, strike out on your own, do work that you really love, and make more money? Think about it. No more corporate politics. No more useless meetings. No pink slips. No glass ceiling, burnout, or career plateaus. Instead, an altogether different life- and work style that gives you greater independence and control over your time and talent. The chance to create a product or service you're passionate about, from start to finish, in a way that reflects your personal goals and values. The opportunity to master new skills and reach new levels of personal growth. The freedom to work alone or with self-chosen teams of people you admire and respect. The challenge of leveraging your time and money to achieve your goals. The ability to continually motivate yourself and others. The resources to create a work environment attuned to your personality and pace.

From time to time, just about everyone indulges in his or her private fantasy about launching a business. For most of us, however, this fantasy remains out of reach—a castle in the air. But achieving the independence and rewarding life-style a small business can offer *isn't* an impossible dream. Each year, all across the country, hundreds of thousands of women are eagerly transforming their personal visions into fulfilling work. Many of them have either left or lost their jobs, and their drive for advancement in the corporate arena has diminished or been abruptly short-circuited. Often they are compelled to make a major change, radically alter their work style, and discover the sense of scale and intimacy a small business can offer.

You'll meet some of these women in the pages of this book, scattered across the country, from California to New York, Vermont to Virginia. Some of them were in their twenties when they began their businesses; others didn't take the plunge until they were well past fifty. Some of the women work alone; others have teamed up with a partner. And a few have already burst through their cottage doors and run businesses that employ anywhere from two to twenty people or more. For some, their "cottage" is a room in an old Victorian house, a garage, or a corner of their apartment with a view of the sea. For others, it's a small office on Fifth Avenue in New York or a suburb of Seattle.

Still, the cottage image seems appropriate because it captures the major reasons why the women I interviewed chose to leave the corporate world and reshape their work lives: the desire to operate on a scale small enough to provide personalized attention and service to clients, the need to be at the center of the decisions they make about their businesses, and the chance to fully tap their time, energy, and talents. As the women I spoke with know all too well, achieving these goals by moving from corporation to cottage requires far more than adapting to a new environment. It involves a new mind-set, new ways of working, and an unquenchable desire for greater freedom.

The entrepreneurs profiled in this book are still working, day by day, to realize their own unique visions of the "cottage life." You'll meet Jordana Simpson, a graphic designer; Melinda Pancoast, an expert in transformational dynamics; Debra Oppenheim, a not-for-profit search consultant; and Ann Hull, a meetings planner—all of whom chose to strike out on their own in the same industry in which they had begun their corporate careers. You'll also meet women who changed fields, including Karen Fried, a real estate executive–turned–game creator; Sue Laris-Eastin, a teacher-turned-publisher; and Joyce McClure, a public relations executive who left her job, moved to Maine, and became a small business advisor. Debra, Jordana, Karen, Joyce, and the other women interviewed here come from different backgrounds and traveled different roads in building their businesses. Yet I found four key themes running through most of their stories: seizing the moment, the desire for personal growth, a need for greater balance in their lives, and the drive to fulfill a personal vision.

Almost all of the women I met experienced a sense of urgency about "seizing the moment" once they committed themselves emotionally to making a radical change in their work lives. When the drive to strike out on their own surfaced and gathered force—even if it took years to emerge—it pushed them forward almost in spite of themselves. Something cracked, something clicked, something sprang inside them and they simply had to make a move. For some, the decision was triggered by a layoff or corporate reorganization; others simply found themselves hitting the glass ceiling or feeling burned out. Child-care, family, and life-style preferences were key motivators for a handful of the women—they wanted more flexibility over their time and work flow. And for several of the women, age was a factor, especially as they approached forty or fifty. In their view, it was now or never: if they waited a year or two, they might be too comfortable to take on the risks and financial burdens of starting a new venture.

Most of the women attached great importance to satisfying their needs for personal growth through their work; they felt they had earned the right to learn more and acquire new skills. When opportunities for growth didn't exist on the job, their work quickly lost its luster, even if it was quite lucrative. In reaction to the stagnation and lack of advancement these women experienced, they felt almost compelled to challenge and stretch themselves in new ways, often to the point of discomfort and even stress. It was this need, in part, that drove them to put themselves on the line by starting a business.

Many of the women, too, expressed a strong desire to achieve greater emotional balance by working toward a blending of values in their business and personal lives. Some of them felt work was consuming all their energy, leaving little or no time for friends, family, or taking part in their communities. Others became disenchanted with their industries and employers and the way they were forced to handle clients and do business—their own values and those of the organizations they worked for were out of synch. At some point, the need to translate their own values into action overcame their fears about going into business for themselves.

And finally, nearly all of the women I spoke with are building their new lives around a defining principle or vision of the kind of work they want to do and how they want to work. In some cases, that vision is clear and easily described: creating a community newspaper or offering high-level executive search services to nonprofit organizations. For others, pinpointing exactly what they wanted to do has been a greater challenge. Circumstances, rather than a clearly defined goal, pushed them through the cottage gate. In either case, as we'll see, the original vision that inspired their decision often proves to be a moving target, clarifying and redefining itself as time goes on.

DANCING WITH REALITY

The desire for personal growth, the drive to achieve balance between one's professional and personal lives, and the need for some sort of sustaining vision or goal—these are some of the building blocks of what I call a "self-structured" work life. Starting a business on a small scale often can be the means to make that life a reality. Throughout these pages, I use the terms *cottage industry*, *small business*, *entrepreneurial venture*, and *home-based business* almost interchangeably. Whatever term is used to describe the means, the end remains the same: an independent, more satisfying, and flexible work style. But what else does the self-structured life involve?

The word *structure* provides at least a partial answer. Defined most basically, it means the way in which something is built. It also involves patterns—the manner in which the elements of anything are organized or interrelated. And finally, structure often involves a systematic framework. Building, organizing, creating patterns, working within a self-imposed framework—all of these concepts are encompassed in the word *structure*. With this in mind, we can begin to clarify the key facets of a self-structured life: it is a life in which you establish your own guidelines for working, create an environment geared to your professional needs and personal style, and deliver the product or services you value to the markets and clients you select. It does *not* mean exercising *total* control over your time and resources. As any entrepreneur will tell you, especially during its start-up stage, your business controls you, you don't control the business. But at its best, a self-structured life can offer you the freedom to orchestrate all of the elements of your work in a way that expresses values you believe in while earning a living. And if you're like many of the women in this book, at the heart of this vision of the independent life is the desire to achieve some degree of harmony between who you are, what you want to produce and market, and how you want to work.

As most of us have learned all too well, achieving self-fulfillment while meeting our family and financial needs involves quite a balancing act. And rearranging the different pieces of our lives so that we can find greater satisfaction and happiness often forces us to make major, and sometimes very painful, changes in the way in which we live and work. This is especially true for women, who continue to feel greater pressure than men to play many more roles and to integrate their personal and professional lives more fully at a time when it is increasingly difficult to do so.

Mary Catherine Bateson addresses the special challenges facing women in *Composing a Life*, a book in which she explores "that act of creation that engages us all—the composition of our lives." In the book, Bateson, a professor of English and anthropology, examines her own life and those of four other women in an effort to discover "a set of metaphors for looking at the discontinuities that are forced on people." The central image she focuses on is that of the composer. Each person, says Bateson, acts as a composer in her own life and is engaged in creative improvisation, a process in which "we combine familiar and unfamiliar components in response to new situations . . . as the choices and rhythms of life change." "Improvisation," she adds, "is a dance with reality."

Viewing ourselves and the work we do as an act of improvisation takes both bravery and imagination, says Bateson, as we must begin to think of all the elements and events shaping our lives as part of a single, harmonious musical composition, "just as the orchestra conductor conducting a symphony knows that every instrument is valuable in its place." Bateson's academic ivory tower may be a long way from the drafty garage in which a small publisher stores her inventory or the shared kitchen a postmaster uses to make candy in her off hours. Yet, despite this distance, many of the images in *Composing a Life* vividly capture the demands of crafting a self-structured life. Flexibility and the ability to improvise are certainly key survival skills in a small business. But beyond this, it does indeed take both bravery and imagination to see yourself as a composer creating a harmonious, integrated life out of the fragmented events, disruptions, and emotional intensity this work style involves.

Making the Move from Employee to Entrepreneur: Is the Grass Really Greener?

Just about all of us find some aspect of the independent life enormously appealing. Yet, to quote an old proverb, "There's many a slip between the cup and the lip." When you make the decision to start a small business, you are not just changing jobs or changing locations or changing careers. *You are changing your identity.* This work style offers both new freedoms and new demands: the need to assume greater risks, do more with less, wear many hats, and give up the benefits and trappings of corporate success.

As Jackie Farley, founder of CenterPoint in Aspen, puts it, going into business for yourself means that you've made a decision to "give up comfort for freedom—and to sacrifice security, status, and a sense of community to follow your own voice." In addition to the identity "crisis" many people experience when they leave corporate jobs to work on their own, there's also an enormous cultural gap between working for a corporation and being an entrepreneur. One small business article called it "the great divide." In the same article, an executive whose wife runs her own direct-marketing firm commented, "It's the difference between sleeping in a house and sleeping in a tent. In a corporation, you have all the comforts: people to talk to, support from other departments, travel budgets. You can call a travel agent and order up a five-hundred-dollar ticket and off you go. You can't operate like that in a small business. You have to measure the value of every little step before you act."

Glowing visions of living the simple life aside, making the shift from corporation to cottage is one of the toughest career—and life—changes imaginable. It affects every aspect of your personal and professional well-being: your identity and self-esteem, your family, your finances, your health, your retirement plans, your children's future, your hopes and dreams, your fears. It can be mind-quaking, gut-wrenching, and exciting all at once. As we'll see, when you give up your job, you're not just giving up prestige, you're also giving up the fun and satisfaction of working as part of a team on creative projects you care about. Then there's the "one-armed paperhanger" syndrome: if you work alone, you have to do everything—even boring jobs like copying and stuffing envelopes—because you often can't afford to pay anyone else to do it.

Beyond these challenges, there's loneliness and the feeling that you're no longer a part of things. This isolation is one of the biggest obstacles many entrepreneurs find they have to overcome, especially if they are sole proprietors or free-lancers who work at home. They have to force themselves to get out, to network, to be visible—even when it's much easier and more comfortable to hide within the four walls of their home or office. Then there's the issue of money. Anxiety about holding everything together financially is all too familiar to most female entrepreneurs, who often find their savings quickly depleted and must borrow from family and friends. Most women continue to be underfinanced during their start-up phase and have to struggle to make ends meet and manage their cash flow. Although they tend to start small and keep their overhead low when they launch a business, many of them are no strangers to sleepless nights.

If you're still employed by a large corporation or even a small company, all of the concerns raised here are ones you should think long and hard about. Crafting a self-structured life may sound appealing and romantic, but will it meet your needs—both personal and professional—not just today or tomorrow, but six months from now? What about in five or ten years? Is this a life- and work style to which you can commit your time and talents? Along with all of the benefits you'll have to give up, what else do you need to succeed?

What It Really Takes
to Run a Small Business

Throughout this book, we'll be exploring in depth the inner resources and professional qualities you'll need to make the transition from corporation to cottage. To set the stage for these discussions, I've captured here in broad brush strokes some of the key changes and "pressure points" you'll face.

A Strong Commitment to the Business You Choose

Without a deeply rooted belief in the importance of the venture you are launching and the value it offers, your business will not thrive and probably won't survive. [Do what you love and love what you do.] Time and time again, this is the most important piece of advice that the women I interviewed felt they had to offer anyone just starting out. If you are lukewarm or conflicted, or if you expect to receive little encouragement and support from your family, then think twice about taking this road. Barbara Brabec is the author of a popular how-to guide called *Homemade Money: How to Select, Start, Manage, Market and Multiply the Profits of a Business at Home* and publishes a quarterly newsletter called the *National Home Business Report.* Here's how she describes the commitment you'll need: "The first word of advice that I give to budding entrepreneurs is to make sure that you love what you plan to do as a business. This becomes really critical when the business gets in trouble—and I don't know any home-based business that has not had its ups and downs. Sometimes you get so low that you are ready to throw in the towel; I've been there several times myself. There are cash flow problems, recessions, and other difficulties. You have to be very creative about pulling yourself out of them. If you really aren't dedicated to what you're doing and if you really don't care about your work, then you won't be able to motivate yourself to get through the rough times. So do what you love and what you're good at."

The Willingness to Invest Enormous Amounts of Time

The desire for more control over your time may be one of the major drives behind your decision to start a business of your own—it is for most women. Yet, in reality, you may find that the kind of control you're hoping for eludes you. During your start-up stage especially, the demands your business will make on your time are never ending; you easily can find yourself working many more hours than you did in your corporate days. As Barbara Brabec puts it, "People think they will be in control of their own time when they work at home. What usually happens, however, is that a new home-based business will demand more hours than anyone has to give it, often making a person feel as though the business is running her, instead of the other way around. Home business owners in my network report they often work sixty- to eighty-hour weeks, but they also add that they're not complaining. You may have heard the old joke about the definition of an entrepreneur—someone who will gladly work sixteen hours a day for himself to avoid working eight hours a day for an employer. There's some truth to this image."

Kathy Lloyd-Williams, the founder of xoxo international, a company that manufactures high-quality children's products (the name stands for hugs and kisses), knows firsthand just how demanding a start-up can be: "Because my company first began operating out of my garage, one of my biggest challenges has been trying to separate my business and family life. It's an ongoing struggle. Both my husband and I are type A personalities, but we operate from the notion that the family comes first. I've been putting in far more hours working on my own than I did in my corporate life. I thought I worked like a maniac then—but this has gone way beyond that! Turning it off is difficult. It takes discipline to focus on your children and your husband. The other difficult thing is figuring out how and where to find time for yourself. It has to be found, but it's the first thing to go. But you can only go so long before you crash and burn if you haven't spent some time paying attention to yourself."

As Kathy points out, these demands can place enormous strains on you, your family, and your relationships with friends. You'll have less personal time, not more. Your work schedule also may be out of synch with the rest of the world. Working at home often causes problems with neighbors and friends who don't share your ideas and work rhythms and expect you to be on call for baby-sitting duty or package delivery. If you are a mother working at home with young children, then your time and attention will be far more fragmented than you imagine. At first you'll probably be able to find only fifteen or twenty hours a week for your business—if you're lucky. You also may find that having a home-based business isn't the magic solution to child-care needs you may have been hoping for. In fact, if your venture takes off, then working for yourself can force you to seek the very child-care alternatives that you went into business to avoid. And home-based working mother guilt isn't any easier to handle than the kind you feel when you head off to a corporate job.

A Strong Desire to Operate Independently

To survive in your own business, you have to develop an entrepreneurial mind-set about working alone, motivating yourself, and measuring your achievements. This attitude is different in many ways from that of an employee. You have to be willing to take charge, make something happen, make mistakes, not be afraid to ask questions, or even have a dumb idea that you take a flier on now and then. You have to have the courage to be wrong and admit it. You have to know yourself well enough to hire to your weakness. You have to have genuine rock-bottom self-confidence in who you are and what you have to offer—or be willing to push the envelope so you can develop that confidence over time.

As Karen Fried, the creator of a successful word game called Think-It Link-It, says, "You have to be someone who believes in yourself and has the confidence and passion to move forward in a 'take charge way.' You have to have real leadership qualities and be willing to be the first one over the bridge. Confidence, leadership, passion, not being afraid—these are the qualities of a good entrepreneur. But a great entrepreneur needs more. You have to have great communication skills and know how to get the information you need."

To foster this kind of fearlessness and independence within yourself, you have to be willing to be accountable to yourself and to others for your actions to a degree that goes far beyond what's required in a corporate job. Making this kind of commitment often requires that you surrender long-held and deeply ingrained ideas about what your life could or should be like. Jane Adams, author of *Wake Up, Sleeping Beauty* and *Women on Top*, describes this process: "I think it's extremely hard for women to become entrepreneurial. To do this, they need to take responsibility for their lives and accept the fact that their lives are the result of choices they've made so far. Who they are is not the result of things that have happened to them, but choices they've made. Being an entrepreneur demands that you accept responsibility for the product or service you offer. The most important advice I think you can give someone who's thinking about becoming one is to say, Take responsibility for yourself. To do this, you need to give up lots of cherished fantasies—the kinds of fantasies I talk about in *Wake Up, Sleeping Beauty*. Fantasies like, Someone will save me. There will always be someone there for me. I will complete someone else's life rather than completing my own. All these ideas put your life on hold."

A Realistic, Clear-Eyed View of the Demands Involved

Kathryn Frazier is currently an outplacement executive with the firm of Drake Beam Morin, where she counsels displaced managers, some of whom see going into business as a career option. Frazier also has started several small ventures. While in her twenties, she started a modeling agency and a credit card company in Alaska, where she learned firsthand about the ups and downs of running a shoestring operation. More recently, she and her husband have teamed up to open a restaurant and a bed and breakfast. She also spent seven years as an advisor for the Small Business Administration (SBA). Here's what she says about making a small business work: "You have to be very directed. You have to be very motivated. You have to have a lot of confidence. You have to have vision. You have to be very objective. You have to be able to see—not just what you want to see, but what is *really* going on. Sometimes it's too late to do anything when you finally realize what's happening. You have to be multifaceted—you have to be able to do a lot of different things well. You have to be a very good time manager. You have to be a very good problem solver. You have to be extremely good at handling stress. And these qualities are just the beginning.

"I believe that most people go into small businesses very blindly. I wouldn't want to make a blanket statement about women, but in my years of counseling experience, I have found that women tend to want to just jump into something and see it as the answer to their problems, especially their financial problems. And I have to tell them, 'No, starting a business isn't the answer to your financial problems, it's the *beginning* of your financial problems.'

"A lot of women say, 'If I do this, I can make money,' but they don't know how to set goals or even the basic principles of starting a small business. I often run into the 'superwoman syndrome,' women who think they can do everything—start a business, give time to their families, have more control over their lives. They get enthusiastic. They talk to a friend about starting something and they get overwhelmed by the idea, they are going to make it happen. Sometimes the women I work with have been laid off, and that's their motivation. In outplacement, I also see many women who are really upset because their husbands have lost their jobs. When this happens, they think that now is the time to start a business. And I tell them, 'No, this is absolutely not the time to start a business.' And they say, 'Why not?' Starting a business can be a way out and it is a means to running your own show, but people think there is no work involved. They don't understand the amount of effort it takes to make it happen."

Making the move from corporation to cottage may also force you to give up some cherished values and radically redefine your notion of success. Caroline Hull, the founder and publisher of *ConneXions*, a newsletter for home-based working mothers, feels that this is a very important issue for many women. As she points out, "Women thinking about starting their own businesses often ask me the same questions again and again: 'What are the most profitable businesses?' 'How long does it take to be successful?' 'How much money can I make working at home?' What they really mean is, how quickly can they get rich? Because unless you're getting rich in our society, you're not considered successful. But we really need to rethink and expand our concept of success. There's nothing wrong with a woman who's decided to stay at home making the decision to cut back in other areas and saying, 'I'm successful because I'm here when my kids get off the school bus.' Having a realistic time frame is also important. Don't expect to make fifty thousand dollars in your first year; be reasonable about your profit-making expectations. Reaching your financial goals may take you five or even ten years, especially if you are working part-time. It's also very helpful to connect with other like-minded individuals who applaud and celebrate your definition of success. In my own kids' eyes, I'm more successful as a mother because of my work-style choice, and ultimately, that's more important to me than what my bank manager thinks."

By now you should have a pretty clear picture of some of the major emotional demands you'll face if you decide to start a small business. Launching a new venture takes enormous staying power and patience. It also takes many more hours of work than most full-time jobs require. Money is also a continuing concern. The financial sacrifices you have to make during the start-up years also are likely to be very substantial, both for you and your family. Yet many women seem to have an unrealistic view of the financial hardships they'll encounter in launching a new venture. Would-be entrepreneurs are often long on ideas and enthusiasm but short on planning.

WHAT'S REALLY AT STAKE: A "LIFE STRATEGY"

Yes, starting a new business is tough, financially, emotionally, and in terms of the time and energy it requires. Yet, despite this reality, every day, thousands of women bet on themselves and try to beat the odds. What do they want that a corporate job can't give them? Earlier we talked about the feelings of independence and exhilaration starting a business can foster; the boost it can give your self-image; and the satisfaction that comes from doing work you care about and believe will make a difference to other people. What are some of the other rewards a self-structured life offers women? What's the payoff?

"For men, self-employment is a business decision—for women, it's a life strategy." That's how the Women of Enterprise Awards program launched by Avon Products and the U.S. Small Business Administration summed up the prime motivation of successful female entrepreneurs. According to Carol Crockett, former director of the SBA's Office of Women's Business Ownership, "Women become entrepreneurs in order to define and control their success. Self-employment offers them this control plus the flexibility they need to combine financial rewards with quality time for their families. . . . It is a life decision that we believe more and more women will be making in the future."

A "life strategy"—this phrase seems to capture the essence of what most women are looking for when they make the move from employee to entrepreneur. In sharp contrast to men's pursuit of the bottom line, the desire for self-fulfillment, the need to achieve, and a concern for helping others all motivate female business owners more than the drive for profits, according to "The Avon Report: A National Attitude Survey of Successful Women Entrepreneurs." The survey, completed in the late 1980s, was conducted for Avon's Women of Enterprise Awards program and was based on in-depth questionnaires completed by over 450 female entrepreneurs.

When asked what motivated them to take action and start their businesses, the successful female entrepreneurs surveyed cited the desire for career control and flexibility; willingness to seize an opportunity that presented itself; encouragement from friends and colleagues; the desire to earn more money; and more flexibility over time spent with family. Concerning their personal definitions of success, four different measures of success emerged in the survey: happiness/self-fulfillment, a sense of challenge and achievement, helping other people, and profit/sales growth. One of the most intriguing results of the survey is that "regardless of whether a woman business owner's focus is on self-fulfillment, achievement, helping others, or simply profit, she is equally likely to own a business that earns more than $500,000 per year." In short, female entrepreneurs who don't see money as their top priority can be just as successful financially as those who do. "Women entrepreneurs may choose different paths to success, yet each path can lead to a profitable enterprise," says an expert on women in business whose firm conducted the Avon study. "In fact," she adds, "successful women entrepreneurs who pursue goals other than sales or profit are found slightly more often at the highest level of annual gross sales—$500,000 and above."

Asked to single out the most important personal quality responsible for their success, the majority cited an "internal perspective," such as attitude or perseverance, rather than an "external perspective," such as acquiring business skills. More than 75 percent of the women surveyed said staying power and a positive attitude (optimism, self-confidence, a sense of humor) are key to survival. The biggest rewards of business ownership for the women surveyed were producing a quality product or service, gaining control over their lives, and increased flexibility. Next in importance were client relationships and profitability and watching their own business's sales grow and profits increase. Increased personal income was ranked as least important.

Many of the findings in "The Avon Report" were confirmed in my interviews and in original research conducted for this book. In a special survey called "Tell Us About Your Home Business," the National Association for Female Executives (NAFE) polled its 250,000 members in the January/February 1992 issue of *Executive Female* magazine. Five questions were asked of entrepreneurs; two, the length of time in business and type of business, were direct, and three addressed feelings about motivation, risks, and rewards. The results, in percentages, are outlined below. (Asterisked questions are ones in which more than one answer could be given and the sum of percentages is more than 100.)

HOW OLD IS YOUR BUSINESS?

Six months to three years	42%
Three to five years	23
Over five years	23
Less than six months	11

WHAT KIND OF BUSINESS IS IT?

Service	78%
Sales	11
Other	7
Manufacturing	4

WHAT TRIGGERED YOUR START-UP?*

Need to explore new talents	36%
New service/product idea	21
Industry downturn/layoff	18
Need for more money	15
Family/child-care concerns	13

WHAT'S BEEN MOST CHALLENGING?*

Managing cash flow	37%
Redefining myself	29
Finding the time/energy	22
Juggling work/family	13

WHAT'S BEEN MOST SATISFYING?*

Greater freedom/control	50%
Personal growth	32
Building my own team	18
Making money	11

The powerful revelations of this survey support the "lunch with a friend" research reported by most women who start a business: not only is money the most stressful and least satisfying part of entrepreneurship, it is also a minor motivation for starting a business in the first place. The survey also, unsurprisingly, reinforces the awareness that freedom—the self-structured life the entrepreneur enjoys—is the real payoff.

Citing a need to explore new talents or develop a new idea, the survey respondents put less emphasis on economic necessities and family obligations as reasons for starting a home-based business. However, in many of the personal stories accompanying the results, an immediate need to earn more money or a perceived need to restructure one's plans for future income were mentioned as significant motivators for taking the plunge into self-employment. Overwhelmingly, in both the numbers and personal stories, the NAFE members responding to this survey told of their personal satisfaction in setting their own goals and developing their own strategies for reaching those goals—satisfaction so complete that even the occasional failure did not deter the entrepreneur from pursuing her vision.

What's the bottom line here? In a word, the answer is *happiness*. Most female entrepreneurs, regardless of the size of their business and the product or service they produce, want greater control over their lives and equate success with happiness and self-fulfillment. According to recent research, these women are on the right track. In one of the largest studies of life satisfaction ever conducted by Michael Crichton and published in *Self* magazine, Dr. Alex C. Michalos revisited a question at least as old as Socrates: What makes people happy? In his search for an answer that would make sense in today's fragmented world, Dr. Michalos surveyed more than eighteen thousand women and men in thirty-nine countries. His study explored health, friendships, family, work, and eight other "domains" of daily living. According to his findings, there are four things that give all of us, both women and men, the most satisfaction and pleasure: relationships with other people, some measure of control over our lives, total absorption in activities we care about, and enjoying new experiences. Dr. Michalos also found that women are generally happier than men because they naturally attach more value to these qualities and are more likely to actively seek to build them into both their personal and professional lives.

In a second *Self* magazine study, Dr. John W. Reich found that "happiness is being in control of the daily events in your life to the extent that you *can* be in control. . . . The more you're the cause of events in your life, the better off you are. . . . People should be exercising control over those parts of their lives where they have desires and want to get things achieved." Feeling connected and involved with other people, exercising some degree of control over the things that we care about, the desire to be totally absorbed in work we enjoy and value, and new experiences that offer personal growth— the strong desire to attain these goals reinforces and confirms the rewards of the self-structured life. These are also the key motivators pushing women out the corporate door and through the cottage gate.

WHEN IT'S GOOD, IT'S VERY GOOD

If improvisation really is a "dance with reality" and if starting a new business is largely a matter of improvising, then what's it like when the music is in tune and the dance is going well? Let's take a few moments to listen to what some women have to say about the joys of working on their own.

Debra Oppenheim left a position as a partner in an international executive search firm to offer high-level search services to not-for-profit organizations. Here's how she feels about her choice: "I felt an enormous sense of euphoria when I finally made the decision. Sometimes it helps not to think too much. It's like tumbling downhill. Once the ball gets rolling, there's a momentum and you just keep going, because underneath it all, you know it's the right thing to do. If you have self-confidence, presence, creativity, and ingenuity, then you can build a business, especially a service business, that doesn't require huge amounts of capital. Sometimes you find that you have the self-confidence but not the self-esteem to make the leap, because you haven't been valued on the job. But when you own your own business, you value yourself and you are valued by others. There's an enormous feeling of triumph. People who know me well say they can see the difference in my face. Having your own business does wonders for your self-image."

Melinda Pancoast and her husband created a training business in Vermont to help small and emerging companies increase their profitability by motivating their employees and putting "life into the hopes, dreams, and visions of people at work." Says Melinda, "I found myself desiring less structure, more independence, and more fun. I knew a lot about managing people, and about motivating people to produce results and enjoy their work. My husband Mal and I also knew that we wanted to work together and we knew where we wanted to live. Although life-style was a primary issue for us, we didn't know whether Vermont was a particularly good place to set up our training business. We just trusted that we could do this work anywhere with the information we had. And I really have found this to be true. So we made a decision to live here and work together to do something that could make a difference to other people. That's the most satisfying thing about the work we do.

"We also wanted to create a life-style that we could design around the things we enjoyed. This business has given us a lot of flexibility. We were able to move to California for a year, continue to have clients in Vermont, and then move back to Vermont again. Organizational transformation is a very exciting field, and we spent our time in California at a university, learning and educating ourselves about new research and training techniques. . . . One of the things that's been best about this business is that both my husband and I have been able to spend so much time with our daughter, Lana. It's been really special having both of us so involved as parents. We had an office in our home for several years, and while Lana was a baby, I could work at home. We've really been able to have a family life as well as a work life together."

Caroline Hull, the mother of four children, faced the challenge of meeting her family's needs while finding a way to satisfy her own desire for continued professional growth. This situation provided the inspiration for her business venture, a newsletter called *ConneXions*, aimed at home-based working mothers who share her goals. "When it's good, it's *really* good," says Caroline. "Certainly, the sense of fulfillment and gratification you get from creating something from scratch and knowing that you're responsible for all the good things that happen is terrific. I love the fact that my children see me working and are involved in my business. In fact, I gave a speech recently on Capitol Hill about working at home, and at the end I said, 'It's not unusual at my house to see my oldest son, Christopher, arranging labels in alphabetical order for me or my twins stapling newsletters. My youngest can't do much yet, but she recycles all my wastepaper for crayoning! They all have a sense of involvement, are thrilled when something good happens, and share the joys with me. It's like having my own little team.' That's a wonderful feeling."

Kathy Lloyd-Williams shares Caroline's enthusiasm for the independent work style she's created for herself and her family as the founder of xoxo international: "I've never had so much fun in my life! Most days I feel I'm the luckiest person around. I never considered myself a creative person, but I've had a lot of fun making things. It's been very satisfying to develop my company from a number of perspectives—to sell it to investors, develop the products and market them to retailers, and have people come back and say, 'You know, we really have a great time using this!' I never got this kind of satisfaction from my jobs. There's really something to be said for making things—for being a product-oriented company rather than a service-oriented one.

"There were two things integral from the beginning to both our product and corporate strategy that I also feel very good about. One was to be environmentally responsible and to be on the cutting edge in using new kinds of materials and trying to make sure that everything we do, to the extent possible, is made of recyclable materials or reusable materials. I've always felt myself to be a lucky person and I also felt it was important to give something back. And so we began using handicapped people in our manufacturing. In the early stages, this decision turned out to be good business. We don't use handicapped people today to the degree that we did in the beginning, but we've still tried to make community support part of our corporate philosophy, whether it's hosting a party or donating materials to Ronald McDonald. We also hired a group called United Mothers Against Drugs to make some sample cards for us. Giving something back in this way has been very rewarding."

And finally, a few words from Jan Berg, who spent more than thirty years in corporate life, primarily as a turnaround specialist and strategic planner, before embarking on a journey of self-discovery: "I've found that I never knew how to play. I've been working since I was a kid. When you're in school, you are under the influence of your family and authoritarian figures. And then you go into the corporate world and it's the same thing, just another game. I'm teaching myself to appreciate my free time and how to play again.

And the more I play, the more my world opens up. These are the newfound truths in my life. . . . To reach this level of understanding is priceless. The process has taught me ways to approach my life that I now use in my teaching and workshops. I've realized that I do have choices about my life. A lot of times that's the biggest thing we don't know about ourselves—that we have choices."

THE TWELVE BUILDING BLOCKS OF A SELF-STRUCTURED LIFE

1. A sense of mission and purpose about the product or service you plan to offer.

2. A compelling need to do work that is absorbing and intrinsically satisfying.

3. A strong desire to put your values into action through your work.

4. A willingness to push the boundaries of your self-image and test yourself.

5. A strong drive to exercise greater control over the work you do.

6. The ability to fantasize and set yourself adrift in a sea of desire.

7. The ability to accept and depersonalize your fears of both failure and success.

8. The desire to better balance the professional and personal sides of your life.

9. A willingness to shape a new professional image by building on the past.

10. The ability to accept the fact that running a small business means selling yourself.

11. Large reserves of emotional and physical stamina.

12. A healthy regard for money as a tool for achieving your goals.

.   .   .

FOR Debra Oppenheim, starting her own venture has given her an enormous sense of "exhilaration and freedom," and transformed her self-image. For Melinda Pancoast, it has allowed her to work with her husband and help small companies increase their profits, productivity, and employee satisfaction. Cottage life also offers her the flexibility to enjoy an appealing life-style in Vermont and spend time with her family. Through their small businesses, Caroline Hull and Kathy Lloyd-Williams have created a satisfying balance between family needs and their personal quests for growth. In Jan Berg's case, leaving corporate life opened the door to greater creativity and fresh ways of looking at the world, and it has empowered her to help other people identify and achieve their life goals.

Each of these women, in her own way, has discovered new challenges, benefits, and pleasures in pursuing a self-structured life. What about you? We all have choices, says Jan Berg, more choices than we think. Is starting a business the right choice for you?

2

TIMING YOUR MOVE

My move was the culmination of a lot of years of feeling that I could be successful as an entrepreneur. You have to have a sense of your own strength to pursue this direction, and it took me some time to feel that. I think I had the ideal combination at the time I made the move: I was pushed by the fact that I was unhappily employed and pulled by an idea that I'd had for a while.

—Lorraine Gerstein

We've all heard stories about the child who sees *Cinderella* onstage, finds stardust in her pocket on the way home, and knows at that very instant that she's destined to be an actress. Then there are those tales of the teen tycoons: the girl who designs T-shirts, for instance, puts herself through college with the profits, and then goes on to start a merchandising empire. But most of us, women and men alike, find that our work histories are less directed and more haphazard than this. The jobs we take are as much the product of accident and circumstances as they are the result of careful planning or a professional calling that dates back to childhood. As a result, timing major career moves isn't always a simple process; lightning doesn't strike and the Red Sea doesn't part. This seems to be especially true when it comes to entrepreneurship. For every one woman who satisfies the image of the classic entrepreneur—someone with a burning, passionate desire to bring a new idea or product into the world—there are at least two or three others who lack this total clarity when they commit themselves to starting a business. These women can best be described as "emerging entrepreneurs."

Emerging entrepreneurs aren't born, they're made—or rather, they create themselves. In many instances, they don't satisfy the traditional profile of both male and female business owners: They may not be first-born children, for instance, or the children of an entrepreneur. They may not even have exhibited obvious leadership skills or seemed to be very enterprising as children. Still more revealing, their paths to a more independent work style aren't straight and narrow, but winding and often filled with detours. More often than not, the ideas for their businesses don't spring into life full-blown like Athena from the head of Zeus; they emerge slowly and over time. For these women—and you may be one of them—the decision to start a business may initially be more reactive than proactive. Circumstances or events, rather than a clearly defined, compelling goal, may be the catalyst that triggers your move into entrepreneurship. If so, then you have plenty of company; many of the women profiled here and elsewhere (Catherine Hull, pages 64–67, for example) found themselves in exactly the same state of limbo: in the process of making the transition from employee to entrepreneur, they felt a growing drive to take control of their work life but lacked a blueprint to map out their next steps.

As we'll see, Lorraine Gerstein is a perfect example of this non-traditional entrepreneurship model. Her confidence in her ability to succeed as a business owner took years to gather force and rise to the surface. Along the way, she held her share of jobs in which she felt underemployed and often found herself frustrated and side-tracked in her career. If you share this problem, then it shouldn't surprise or discourage you to find that you're confused and unsure about whether or not starting a business is really right for you, or if you feel strongly that you want to be your own boss but aren't completely clear about exactly what you want to do. You also may be trying to decide whether to take the plunge now or wait—until the economy picks up, you save more money, or you can test the waters to see whether your idea has real market potential.

If you find yourself thinking seriously of turning your entire life upside down by making a move from corporation to cottage, then the number-one question you're probably struggling with right now is, How do I know when I'm ready to take the plunge? It's the kind of dilemma that keeps you up at night and compels you to pore through magazine stories about successful female business owners in search of the dreams and seeds of discontent that drove them to strike out on their own. If I'm right, then you'll probably find this chapter both comforting and sobering—and perhaps even a little frustrating. Why? Because there's no simple answer to the question of timing. I'd like to be able to tell you, Here are three symptoms to watch for. If you experience them, then you'll know you've caught the entrepreneurial bug and you're ready to turn in your corporate ID card and order your new business stationery. Or, Here's a psychic cost-benefit analysis you can do to help weigh the pros and cons of making a move. Or better still, Here's one of those "Test Your Entrepreneurial IQ" quizzes that I've designed with the help of experts especially for this book. If you score sixty points or above, then you've got what it takes to make the self-structured life work for you.

If only it were that easy! But it isn't. Timing, like life itself, is a very personal affair. Since knowing how to gauge your own emotional readiness for entrepreneurship is such a key issue, I'd like to be able to give you a cost-benefit analysis, a quiz, a silver bullet, or a magic formula. But I can't, because no such easy answers emerged in my interviews; the responses about timing that surfaced were too complex and individualistic to be reduced to a one-size-fits-all formula. I found different degrees of emotional energy, different thresholds of frustration, different family responsibilities and pressures, different financial situations, and, above all, different dreams and desires. But before you throw up your hands, read on: I also found a number of scenarios and emotional "pressure points" that should provide some helpful guidelines as you wrestle with that all-important question, To leave or not to leave?

As a way of clarifying your own situation, let's take a close look at the decision-making processes that impelled four women to give up the rewards and security of corporate life and start their own businesses. As we'll see, one of these women, Kathy Lloyd-Williams, exhibited strong entrepreneurial tendencies early in her career—she was already a principal in a small company when she began her current company, xoxo international. The other three women, Joyce McClure, Lorraine Gerstein, and Judith Grant Palma, all took more indirect paths to their new ventures.

Let's begin with Joyce's story. She's traveled the world in her corporate career, from London and Florence to South Africa and points in between. But it's the tiny community of Castine, Maine, that she calls home today. Here's how she got there.

JOYCE MCCLURE:
CONVERGING FORCES AND A NEST EGG

Joyce made a dramatic change in her work and life-style when she left a fast-track corporate career in New York City and relocated to Maine. Joyce still has strong ties to New York and hasn't quite abandoned all of the trappings of the high-powered life-style she once enjoyed there: her down-jacketed friends in Castine kid her about the fur coat she runs around in when winter hits the Maine coast, and she still has her long blond hair cut at the same salon in New York when she visits every couple of months. At the time she made the move from employee to entrepreneur, Joyce had been in public relations for more than twenty years and was earning a six-figure salary as an executive vice president with one of the largest independent public relations firms in the country. But things hadn't been going well for a while.

"I had actually been thinking about taking some other course in my life for a number of years," Joyce recalls, "but I was curious about how far I could actually get in my public relations career. I had been in my last position for less than a year when the situation there turned sour for political reasons over which I had no control. It was my last job that pushed me over the edge. I finally knew that that was it. I didn't want to put up with the garbage anymore. I had been in PR for a number of years and I knew it wouldn't be any different if I went to another firm. I didn't like what was happening in my industry and I had no more curiosity about it. I knew that the next step was taking charge of an agency myself, and I didn't want to do that.

"So I started the process of making a move. At the time, I was a high-powered businesswoman who had a career, but no personal life. I didn't understand what a personal life was. I had lots of friends in New York and we were all very involved in our career paths. If we caught up with each other every six months, we were lucky. I had been to Maine several years before on an infrequent vacation and fell in love with Castine quite by accident. I would go back there whenever possible, which wasn't very often. During those years, I might have visited three or four times. I finally ended up with a picture of the Castine harbor on my desk at work and found myself focusing on the calmness it conveyed when the hard times started at work. Actually, I had been to Castine five or six years before, and I remember sitting on my bed there asking myself, Okay, is it time? I analyzed my situation and I said to myself, No, not yet. I'm still curious about the public relations business. I've got to go back to New York and see what more is going to happen. But once that was over, it was time to go."

When her job situation began deteriorating, Joyce found herself feeling depressed and trapped. "I sat myself down one evening in the middle of my bedroom and looked at the four walls and said, You got yourself into this, now you have to get yourself out. I was very fortunate because I had no one else relying on me. And I realized I could do anything I wanted to do. And I finally said, Okay, the time is now. That's it."

After making the professional decision to leave her company, Joyce made a tough personal choice as well: she decided to put her home up for sale and move away from New York. Joyce had purchased her house back in 1979 and had painstakingly renovated it. "I loved that house," she recalls, "but at the time I sold it in the late 1980s, it was the peak of the market and I decided to take advantage of it. It was pretty scary. I didn't actually know what I was going to be doing, but I knew that the money from my house was going to be my financial stake. The closing took place at the end of March 1989, and by April 1, I was in a car heading for Castine."

When she put her house on the market, Joyce took an apartment in Castine, sight unseen. The trip to Maine was exciting, Joyce recalls. "I was thrilled. I had a big check in my pocket from the house. I decided to do a lot of things that had been on the back burner for a number of years. I canoed around Penobscot Bay for the summer and read a lot and met people and got involved with various activities in the village. At this point, I had money in the bank and didn't have to worry about my finances. I had a wonderful time that spring and summer. When fall arrived, I worked for a while in a little shop called the Waterwitch. I also received a call from a woman about doing a marketing plan for her. It never panned out, but I began thinking about how to use my business background."

Joyce was forty-one when she made the move from New York to Castine, and, looking back, she sees that her age was a factor in her decision. As she points out, "I knew that I had a certain window of opportunity and that after a certain age, probably forty-five or forty-six, I would not have the same opportunities to reenter my field in New York if I chose to. I wanted to go to Castine while I was still young enough to take advantage of my situation. Today I still have people calling me about jobs in New York, so I haven't closed the door."

In looking at Joyce McClure's move, it's clear that a complex set of factors were at work: She had been thinking for a while about leaving New York and found herself fantasizing about moving to Maine. She had finished fixing up a house and knew she could get top dollar for it because the real estate market at the time was going through the roof. Her job situation was less than ideal, she didn't like the direction top management was taking, and her position made her very vulnerable. She was also past forty and began to feel that if she didn't make a move soon, she'd miss the moment. Yet, even with all of these factors pressuring her, Joyce *still* wasn't sure that she was ready to take the plunge. At one point in her decision-making process, she actually went into counseling to try to get an objective opinion on why she wanted to make a move like this and whether she was making it "for the right reasons." "It was a little frightening emotionally," she recalls. Her whole situation seemed to be "like a big black hole, a void. Not knowing what was coming up, at the time, I couldn't tell whether it was the right move or not." Only later did she come to realize that that "black hole was also a clean slate and I could do anything I wanted with it. . . . And I'm still here. I'm still very curious about what's going to happen; I'm excited and charged by it."

LORRAINE GERSTEIN: AN EMERGING SENSE OF STRENGTH AND A TICKING CLOCK

Lorraine Gerstein's road to entrepreneurship was a long and rocky one. In many ways, as she recalls, the early choices she made were very traditional. For instance, she married a doctor rather than becoming one herself, even though she definitely had the ability to attend medical school. For the first forty years of her life, she found herself struggling with some difficult emotional barriers: "I was brought up to feel that I would be married and taken care of—that was the background I came from. I accepted the view that I didn't really have to have a profession or that if I did, I would just be a dilettante. That I didn't have to work hard. And that if I ever did decide to commit myself to a career, I couldn't possibly be successful because I was somehow genetically deficient. I think that's why what's most meaningful to me about starting my own business is the sense of confidence it's given me in my own ability."

After her marriage and several short-term jobs, Lorraine pursued a master's degree in education and taught both public and private school for about five years. Next she went back to school and obtained a second master's degree in counseling and eventually entered the field of private rehabilitation. She worked for a large national company and then joined a smaller firm and was promoted to management. After a short time, she left to join the staff of a hospital in New Hampshire and found that she "hated bureaucracy—and there was nothing more bureaucratic than a hospital." It was at this point, in 1987, that she decided to reenter the private rehabilitation field on her own. She started out as a sole practitioner and operated that way for a period of six to eight months. When she found herself with more referrals and more business than she could handle alone, Lorraine hired her first employee. She operated her business, Rehab Inc., out of her home for the first two years, even after hiring more employees. When the business became so encompassing that it overflowed into every part of her home life, she finally set up a separate office.

"In terms of going out on my own," says Lorraine, "I think the hospital job, which I held for about sixteen months, was the straw that broke the camel's back. Not only was it very bureaucratic, but there were people in upper management who knew less about running a program than I did, and yet I was accountable to them for how I spent my time. It just wasn't a productive atmosphere; it seemed like people were wasting time and not getting the job done—or letting me do my job. So my move was the culmination of a lot of years of feeling that I could be successful as an entrepreneur and realizing that I wanted to call the shots myself without having to answer to anyone else. I needed to be in a position where I was the ultimate designer of what my business life would look like—to know that I was taking the pen and drawing the picture instead of fitting into someone else's vision.

"I think there was also another factor: the clock was running. I was getting older and felt that if I was going to establish myself in business, I needed to do it now; later on I might not have the energy. Actually, I had entertained the thought of doing this two years before I actually made my move. At that time, I had spoken with a nurse about working together and began planning in that direction. Then she pulled out and I didn't feel capable of doing it on my own. Now I regret that I didn't launch the business two or three years earlier, when I originally wanted to, and that I thought I needed someone to share the responsibility. As things turned out, I was able to handle it on my own. But I think you need to have a sense of your own strength to move in this direction, and it took me a few years to feel that."

Because the hospital was having a very difficult time replacing her, Lorraine continued to work there part-time for about three months while she started her business. By the end of three months, she was up and running. Even though the transition proved to be fairly smooth, she had her moments of doubt: "I remember waking up one night at three in the morning," Lorraine recalls, "and thinking to myself, I'm giving up a substantial salary, a wonderful benefits package, and job security, with no idea of what the future will hold and whether this venture will be a success or a flop. There was no way of ensuring that it would go in either direction. It was really a gamble, and I was concerned about not making it and having to admit to myself that I had tried and failed. . . . At the same time, apart from my anxiety, I felt very excited and positive. And I didn't miss my job at all."

Today, seven years later, Lorraine's company is growing at a steady pace, despite the recession that has rocked the New England economy over the past few years. Her business has increased tenfold and she has expanded from her home base of Bedford, New Hampshire, into Rhode Island and Massachusetts. She has built a team of eleven employees who work for her on a full-time or contract basis, and her company works closely with insurance firms, helping them to resolve outstanding worker compensation cases by getting people into successful rehabilitation programs while containing medical costs. About three years after she went into business for herself, her husband joined her company and began handling its financial operations. While working with her husband hasn't always been easy, Lorraine feels that his business perspective has been very valuable. The rest of her family hasn't been so supportive. "They still think I'm nuts," says Lorraine. "They know that I work many more hours a day being self-employed than I would if I were working for someone else. They still believe that a female should be married and be supported by her husband. So they don't quite understand why I'm doing what I do. My friends, on the other hand, have a certain amount of admiration for what I've done and for the fact that, as one of them put it, I've 'pulled it off.' "

KATHY LLOYD-WILLIAMS: COMBINING MOTHERHOOD AND CORPORATE EXPERIENCE

For Kathy Lloyd-Williams, launching her own company was part of a consciously designed career strategy aimed at combining motherhood and her business skills. When she and her husband married in 1987, they knew they wanted to start a family and that Kathy's shift from corporation to cottage would offer her the opportunity to integrate her family's needs and corporate training in the role of a working home-based mother. As Kathy puts it, "In our case, my husband and I really wanted our children to be raised at home. In many ways, it was actually an ideal time to think about starting a company. It was a very calculated move. We knew that this was what we wanted to do in terms of our family."

Today, as the founder of xoxo international, a company that develops and manufactures innovative children's products, Kathy serves as her company's president, chief executive officer, and chief financial officer and employs about ten people. The Stanford-educated banker-turned-mother-turned-entrepreneur began her corporate career in 1980 while still an undergraduate, when she began a stint with IBM in systems development and marketing. After three years, she joined American Express International Banking Corporation, where she was involved in systems development, operations, and strategic planning. She then moved on to a high-powered job with Rothschild Ventures Inc., where she administered venture capital funds and developed new investments.

After her marriage in 1987, Kathy made her first foray into small business by becoming a principal with Equity Communications, a firm specializing in public relations and financial communications. By 1989, when she was pregnant with her second daughter, Kathy had relocated to the West Coast and found herself "really wanting to do something on my own that combined being a mother with what I'd done in the past." Says Kathy, "I spent about six months looking at a variety of business opportunities and talked to a number of people. While the possibilities I was exploring had some bearing on my previous work, they were all heavily focused on problems related to either mothers or children or a combination of the two. Over that six months, I looked at corporate day-care centers, recruiting services for women at high professional levels who wanted to work out of their homes, and any number of different ideas. In the process, talking to people helped me clarify three problems I had as a mother going out and buying products for my children: I often felt I was making a compromise, and as a result, although I'm not very artistic, I began making things. I also saw a wide disparity in the relative value of products. And then, finally, there are the problems associated with shopping when you have children. In my single heyday in New York, I had a black belt in shopping—that's what my friends and I did for recreation. But with two children, the task has become very difficult. Then there's the informational issue—what, when, and where you should buy products. In this period of research, the most important thing I came away with was a real focus on these problems. By this time, I was looking at different product ideas.

"Then, in the fall of 1989, about six months into the thinking process, my daughter Christina and I were making Halloween cards. We had a super time cutting up pumpkins and ghosts—and got a great reaction from the friends and family we sent them to. They said they would much rather receive a handmade card from Christina than a store-bought one. This gave me the idea to make crafts kits for kids, and I began doing more research. In February of 1990, I put together some prototypes and went to the New York Toy Fair and basically walked the show to see if there was anything out there like my kits. I also talked to some important retailers. I came back and reworked the prototypes and then, lo and behold, I arranged to see the number-one buyer at Nordstrom with a second set of prototypes and walked away with a large purchase order! Oh, great, I said to myself, now I have to figure out how to make the kits!"

The company Kathy created, xoxo international, was officially incorporated in February 1991. At that point, Kathy was working out of her garage in San Mateo, California, with an outside designer developing the concept. She started shipping her first kits in November of 1991. In 1992 Kathy introduced xoxo's new BIG BIZ product line for kids three and up. She also expanded her business by negotiating a joint venture with a major company to design some products for the mass market that would be sold under a different label. This was a very exciting year for xoxo international: it became a multiple-product company and developed multiple distribution channels.

By mid-1993, Kathy's company was absolutely bursting at the seams and she relocated both her home and business to Huntington Beach, California, where her company's corporate office now operates from not one but two garages! She has a number of exciting joint ventures in the works and continues to pursue creative approaches to both marketing and manufacturing. "For what is a fairly low-tech product," notes Kathy, "we've taken a very high-tech approach to design. We're working with extremely sophisticated computer-generated design equipment that allows us to reach the market and produce new products much more quickly. We've really tried to think smart and operate efficiently. Great people and the use of high-tech design are part of our strategy, and we believe these two assets help differentiate our company in its field."

JUDITH GRANT PALMA: SURVIVING AN UNEXPECTED LAYOFF

Faced with fierce international competition and crushing debt loads, some of the country's largest blue-chip companies—AT&T, IBM, Kodak, Citicorp, and Xerox among them—have responded by merging and consolidating, restructuring and downsizing. The impact on employment has been staggering: Over the past decade, the Fortune 500 laid off an average of 400,000 workers a year. Since the mid-1980s alone, some 2 million middle-management jobs have been eliminated. During the recent recession, cutbacks accelerated dramatically; overall, 25 million women and men—one in five of all American workers—were unemployed at some point during 1991, according to the Conference Board. From mid-1990, when the recession began, through early 1992, 1.9 million jobs disappeared. In 1992, employers continued to cut jobs at the incredible rate of almost 2,600 every working day. And still the ax grinds on—many economic experts believe that corporations will continue to reduce their workforce, at every level, throughout the 1990s. Dan Lacey, editor of a newsletter called *Workplace Trends*, predicts that Fortune 500 companies will lay off at least 4 million more employees before the decade ends. Other experts warn that annually through the year 2000, close to 10 percent of the country's work force will face the loss of their jobs.

JUDITH GRANT PALMA is one of the people behind these cold, hard statistics. Dark-haired and soft-spoken, she radiates a quiet confidence about her transformation from financial services executive to aesthetician. The demands of her new skin-care business are very different from those she faced in the banking career she painstakingly built for herself in the 1980s. Starting in an entry-level position with a large New Jersey bank, by 1988 she had worked her way up to the job of financial services representative, a very prestigious and visible position involving new business development with preferred customers. Then she learned of an opening for a sales manager at one of her employer's sister banks. She applied and was hired to take charge of the bank's marketing and sales training. It was a big change, and Judith felt the strain.

Things went well for about ten months. As one of her most demanding projects, Judith managed the opening of a second branch. "Everything went beautifully that Saturday," She recalls. "At my suggestion, the bank was doing radio commercials, and both the vice president and president were involved. We even had the local radio station on hand at our opening. It all went perfectly. I was on a natural high. Monday morning, with all the hard work on the opening behind me, I was back at my office planning my next project. That same morning, I was called in and told that my job was being eliminated. It was so strange! The bank managers had this ashen look on their faces. They told me that I'd receive outplacement counseling and severance because I was an officer. I asked, 'When is this effective? Do you mean you want me to leave today?' They said yes. So I emptied out my desk and left."

When Judith went home and told her family, they were in shock. How could this happen, they asked, after all she'd accomplished? Judith didn't have an answer. She entered outplacement in January, was terminated in February, and started looking for another corporate job. As she tells it, "I went to business card exchanges and to several career days at some of the local hotels in my area. I talked to a lot of people. It was good to find out about different companies, but I couldn't see how I was going to fit into a corporate setting anymore. This wasn't what I wanted to do. It wasn't me. I was burned out."

After a year of searching, Judith was still floundering. At the same time, her husband was experiencing his own problems as a corporate vice president and decided to leave his job. After making this decision, he encouraged her to take another look at a skin-care business she had expressed interest in some months before. "It wasn't something I needed his approval for," she recalled. "But I needed his support." She took a four-week training course, used some of her severance pay to purchase supplies, and slowly began developing a local clientele. In Judith's case, her firing forced her to think long and hard about what she wanted to do. At one point, she chose the word *rejuvenation* to describe the services she offers her clients. It also seems to capture the feelings of renewal she's experienced in starting her own business. Ultimately, all of the marketing and sales training Judith gained in her banking career has helped her in her new venture. "My marketing experience, knowing how to sell myself, and how to advertise and work with the newspapers have all been very valuable. But even more important, I love what I'm doing."

OF the four women profiled here, Kathy Lloyd-Williams probably had the clearest sense of vision about launching her venture. Even in Kathy's case, however, finding the right start-up vehicle was a process. It took her six months of sitting in her garage and doing intensive research to hit on the idea that she ultimately turned into xoxo international. Likewise, the decision to shift from corporation to cottage didn't hit Joyce McClure or Lorraine Gerstein or Judith Grant Palma like a thunderbolt. Yet, for a variety of reasons, each of these women found themselves at a point where they had to make a commitment to an idea and take the plunge into entrepreneurship. Their decisions were the result of a cumulative, almost unconscious process that finally forced them to make a decision. While a single, clear-cut event or situation finally triggered the move and became the "straw that broke the camel's back," the decision was often years in the making. For Joyce McClure and Judith Grant Palma, it was a career crisis—a corporate shake-up and a layoff—that proved to be the decisive factor. In Lorraine Gerstein's case, it was a smoldering sense of job dissatisfaction. For each of these three women, however, it was a convergence of factors that actually pushed them over the edge into entrepreneurship.

Taking the Plunge:
Ten Telltale Signs to Watch For

How do you know when it's time to leave the corporate world behind? How do you pick one idea out of the dozens you may have? What signs should you be looking for when it comes to your own personal situation? How do you measure your readiness? How can you prepare yourself professionally? Again, there are no easy answers to these questions. But there are some specific emotional "pressure points" or "triggers" that seem to impel many women to choose the entrepreneurial route at critical points in their corporate careers. Before identifying these warning signals, some general advice from Jackie Farley may prove helpful. As a business owner, wellness consultant, and founder of CenterPoint in Aspen, Colorado, Jackie has talked with many entrepreneurs and worked with many women struggling to make the move from corporation to cottage.

"When is it the right time to start your own business?" she asks. "This question is sort of like asking, When is it the right time to get pregnant? My way of answering is to ask you to listen to yourself. In your reflective moments, as you contemplate your continued association with a corporation, how do you feel? If it seems like a burden to you or it doesn't excite you or it seems to be draining away your energy, then perhaps it's time to think about a move. At the same time, when you look at starting a business, how do you feel? Are you energized by the idea, even though you have some anxieties about it? Is the desire to learn something new and to be challenged in a new way driving you to make the transition? When you run out of things you can learn in a corporate setting and you can't find another corporation to go to that will allow you to continue to grow, then that's the time when you can no longer not do it. But when it comes to timing, it's very important to decide whether you're simply feeling burned out and drained or whether something more is happening to you. That's why it's vital that you listen to your own inner voice and take some time out to renew yourself or go on a retreat of some kind, even if it's only for fifteen minutes a day. The transition from corporation to cottage is too serious a move for anyone to make when they are negatively motivated. It's something that you have to have a positive pull toward."

As Jackie Farley points out, making the decision to start a business purely on the basis of negative feelings about your existing work situation can be a dangerous, and even self-defeating, proposition. While distressing and frustrating factors in the corporate environment may initially push you out the company door, some positive idea or drive must ultimately pull you through the cottage gate. Yes, the pressures you are feeling right now make starting a business of your own seem like a tantalizing idea. But the real question—and it's one only *you* can answer—is whether or not launching your own venture will relieve those pressures. If you are not emotionally and professionally equipped to handle the demands of a business start-up, then taking this route can create more problems for you than it solves. With this in mind, let's explore ten "trigger" situations that may have some relevance to your personal decision about timing. Think of them as signposts alerting you to pay closer attention to your inner voice. Their message: Warning! You Are Entering the Land of Entrepreneurial Longing. Proceed at Your Own Risk! If one or more of the signals described here seem to be exerting a powerful influence or inward pressure on you, then you probably should give serious thought to making the transition from corporate life to a more independent work style.

One: Your Values and Those of the Corporate World
Seem to Be Mismatched

As you contemplate the kind of radical career change that the shift from employee to entrepreneur requires, it is essential that you look closely and honestly at your current attitude toward your future within the corporate environment. How do you see that future unfolding? Where will it lead? Are your personal values at odds or in harmony with the demands and rewards of corporate life? One way to begin answering these questions, according to Jackie Farley, is to "look at the values and the mission of the organization you are with and then create your own 'personal mission statement' and see how they align. Your sense of personal effectiveness is absolutely going to be related to the 'fit' between these statements."

Later we'll discuss developing a "personal mission statement" as a kind of verbal umbrella that captures your life and work goals in broad terms. If you were to create such a brief statement of your own personal values and beliefs today, would it be in synch with the objectives of the company you work for? If the answer seems to be no, then perhaps it's time to reexamine not only your current job, but your commitment to corporate life in general. How satisfying is this life for you right now? How fulfilling will it be five to ten years from now? Would moving to another company, or even another industry, really make a difference, or would you just find more of the same? What are your expectations about the corporate world and the kind of success it offers? Are you asking too much—or too little?

Edward Hallowell, psychiatrist and coauthor of *What Are You Worth?* has worked and talked with "many people who work for corporations, schools, hospitals, law firms, and a wide range of institutions. And what I've found is a constant sense of unfulfilled promise, a sense of being underappreciated, and of disappointment because people are not having their needs met." In Dr. Hallowell's view, much of this dissatisfaction has to do with the fact that "the agreement people have with companies is unrealistic, but it's also very real. It's based on the belief in the corporation as the beneficent mother, feeding me, taking care of me, clothing me, giving me my paycheck even when I am sick, giving me health insurance, giving me security, giving me attention, giving me a network of people, giving me a support group, giving me a shoulder to cry on, giving me colleagues, giving me advice, giving me a family.

"But you have to realize that all this is not true. The corporation is giving you nothing. In fact, in many ways it is just taking advantage of your desire to be taken care of. Corporations will get rid of you the minute you become nonproductive. They are heartless and merciless, and not the warm, loving family you want them to be. The cottage can become that. Yes, you will have to face realities that you have been avoiding by banking on the corporation as the beneficent mother. And you will have to provide your own health insurance, your own pension fund, your own set of colleagues, your own office, and your own paycheck. You will have to set the whole thing up. But it will be yours and it can truly be what you want it to be. You can, in fact, create a warm, caring, stable institution—if that is what you want."

The hard, but honest, message here may be one that you already have confronted and understand all too well: most corporations and institutions are not places where people are nurtured and where personal growth is rewarded. And all too often, their environments offer both men and women little in the way of emotional and psychological fulfillment. What kind of "agreements" have you made with the corporations you've worked for? How satisfying and fulfilling have they been? Are the rewards you've looked for from corporate life as much emotional as they are professional? Have you fallen into the trap of viewing the corporation as the "beneficent mother"? As you begin to redefine your ideas of success and satisfaction at this stage in your life and your career, you may find yourself peering through the cottage gate more and more often. You also may begin to wonder whether starting your own business can be the means to creating a work environment in which your personal values can be expressed fully and freely.

Two: Your Curiosity Wanes and Your "Learning Curve" Flattens

One of the first signs of deep-seated discontent that Joyce McClure saw in herself was that her enthusiasm and desire to learn more and absorb more about her job began to disappear. At one point, she was thinking about leaving but decided that the time wasn't right because "I was still curious. I still had things to learn." When she passed that point, she knew it was time to think long and hard about what she wanted her next steps to be. Joyce also found that she was disenchanted, not only with her own company, but with her industry as well. She was disturbed and disheartened by the changes she saw taking place in the public relations field. A similar feeling came over Ann Hull. After ten years in a high-pressure position, she found that her work as a conference planner for the Modern Language Association (MLA) had become very repetitive; as a result, she wasn't growing, either personally or professionally, through her career.

When this happened, Ann realized that the nature of her job wasn't going to change, so unless she changed her attitude toward it, she would continue to feel unchallenged. When she found that she was unable to "reenergize" her feelings about her job, Ann came to the conclusion that she needed to think about changing her situation. Ultimately she left the MLA and began working for the Junior League and other clients as an independent consultant.

Three: You Find Yourself Stressed Beyond Burnout

Anyone who works at a demanding job for a while begins to experience some of the symptoms of career burnout. You probably recognize the signs: you feel unchallenged and bored because you've mastered the most complex elements of your job, your responsibilities seem static, recognition for your work isn't as satisfying as it once was, or you feel tired and unable to summon up any enthusiasm for the projects you have to tackle. In many cases, the solution may simply be to restructure your job. Or more radical steps may be called for—changing companies, for example, or changing industries, or even changing your career.

But for some people, and you may be among them, none of these approaches proves adequate, because they all require working within a corporate or institutional environment. The kind of dissatisfaction that both Joyce McClure and Ann Hull experienced, for example, goes beyond burnout. It was the result of a deep and long-standing feeling that their opportunities for personal growth were severely and probably permanently limited by the corporate structure itself.

If you find yourself in this no-win situation, then it's likely that you'll experience some degree of emotional and physical stress. What are some of the signs that you may have moved beyond the burnout stage and need to reassess your future as a corporate employee? According to wellness consultant Myrna Ruskin, everyone reacts differently to this kind of emotional upheaval. "Some people have trouble sleeping at night. Others find themselves suffering from backaches, dizziness, headaches, shoulder pains—all of which should be checked out by a doctor. But be aware that any of these symptoms can be stress-related. Then there are other signs: emotional outbursts, lack of concentration, memory slides, slight depression—all of which can affect your work and productivity. You may also find yourself suffering from more colds than you would normally have, since stress definitely lowers your system's resistance.

"We all know when we feel balanced and happy and when we feel frustrated and out of control. So it's important to be aware of yourself, your feelings, and your perception of the stress you may be experiencing. Are you overreacting to your job situation? Are you seeing it through other people's eyes or are you really attuned to how it is affecting you? What really makes you happy? Do you like a more peaceful life? Is the corporate world, with all its demands, really grating on your nerves? Or does that kind of high-powered life energize you? Will the isolation of working as an entrepreneur be too limiting? Or is the idea of having more control over your life enormously appealing? Are you ready to take the risks involved in starting your own business? Or are you extremely fearful about risk taking because of messages you received as a child? Start to learn what works for you and what doesn't."

Four: You See the Handwriting on the Wall and Realize It's Time to Take Charge

Jan Berg is a former executive with many years of experience in the corporate world. When she found herself on the receiving end of a senior corporate management shuffle at her last job, it quickly became clear that business as usual wasn't the order of the day. As soon as the new management settled in, an unspoken, but unmistakable, message went out: This isn't a place where women or older workers will be welcome. So powerful was this message that some employees eventually brought a class action suit against the company. For Jan, the writing was on the wall. She could either leave on her own terms or find herself working in an environment that she felt was "joyless, dreadful, and without meaning." So she decided to make a change and began restructuring her work life dramatically.

Debra Oppenheim found herself facing a different, but equally compelling, situation. A seasoned executive recruiter, Debra radiates a warmth and sense of humor that make you want to spend more time with her. It's easy to see why people have often sought her support and counsel during a major career crisis or turning point. As one of the few female partners in Nordeman Grimm, an international executive search firm, Debra found herself facing a career crossroad of her own in 1990. At the time, her firm was facing a tough economy, and she was under pressure to concentrate on high-paying financial services companies. As a result, Debra was forced to turn away business from nonprofit organizations, the very clients she was most interested in serving. After more than seven years with her firm, she found her salary and bonus being cut and the client base she'd worked hard to build being eroded. Taking stock of her situation, she quickly realized two things: first, there was little support in her firm for the kind of searches she wanted to do, and second, she had an opportunity to carve out a rewarding niche for herself in the search field if she launched her own business. And so, in the spring of 1990, she joined forces with Jane Phillips, who was already working on her own in the private foundation field, to form The Phillips Oppenheim Group.

"Aside from economic necessity," recalls Debra, "I think what really pushed me into making this decision was the fact that I had two clients in hand, which allowed me to start the firm with a financial base of about forty thousand in billings. My partner was actually more financially secure than I was when we began working together because she had been working on her own for several years. Her client base is also more steady than mine. So I had business coming in and my partner had business coming in and that made it viable. Otherwise I think I would have been really frightened to do this. Because it's one thing to be pushed out the door and forced to make it on your own and it's another when you make the decision to leave. I wasn't pushed out. I left by choice. But I felt I needed the security of a client base to make the move."

Five: You've Been Fired or Laid Off, or Your Job Is at Risk and You're Fed Up

Without question, the massive layoffs triggered by the recent recession have helped fuel the surge of talented women and men into small business ownership. In fact, one out of every three managers who lost their jobs in the early 1990s started their own businesses— up from a mere 3 percent in 1980. Lonah Birch, an administrator who's been with the Small Business Administration (SBA) for more than twenty years, has witnessed this growing interest in business ownership firsthand. A former small business owner herself, Birch is energetic, innovative, and dedicated, and she conveys an optimism that's as refreshing as it is rare. For sixteen years, she was the regional women's business ownership coordinator in the Midwest, a position through which she helped thousands of women and won national recognition for her successful programs. In her current role as assistant regional administrator for Public Affairs and Communications, Birch has oversight responsibility for SBA outreach programs in four states: Missouri, Kansas, Iowa, and Nebraska. She definitely has seen an upsurge in the number of women seeking SBA assistance in recent years.

"Management layoffs are one of the major reasons" that more and more women are choosing the option of working for themselves over seeking another corporate job, notes Birch. "Nothing is sacred anymore. Women who worked at AT&T, for example, and thought they had a job for life are finding out that they were wrong." Many of the people that Lonah Birch sees coming through SBA programs have been unemployed for a while. "In order to keep themselves going," says Birch, "they may have business cards printed and go into consulting as a stopgap measure. As a result, they are often ill prepared to be out on their own, because they haven't developed a strong business plan and don't really know what it takes to handle inventory, market, and make a profit. They just start testing the waters, try it for a while, and if it works, they continue." According to Birch, however, women who really are committed to new ventures are "better equipped than ever before to go out and start that business. Women traditionally have a high success rate when it comes to running small businesses because they are very service oriented."

*Six: The Glass Ceiling and "Lack of a Level Playing Field"
Are Limiting Your Growth*

After twenty years of so-called progress for working women, 97 percent of all top executives are still male. Will women crack the glass ceiling anytime soon? According to Harvard Business School professor Regina Herlinger, it takes an average of thirty-five years for a college graduate to advance to CEO. Based on the number of female MBAs graduating in the mid-1970s, she predicts that we could see from twenty-five to thirty female CEOs in corporate suites across America by the year 2000. In the meantime, more women continue to leave corporate jobs than men, often because they find the barriers to their advancement simply too high and too frustrating.

Jayne Tear, an expert in gender dynamics, has seen this scenario play itself out many times since she began consulting in the 1970s. Says Jayne: "It is women more than men who don't necessarily leave the corporate world because they have an unfulfilled dream, but because they clearly recognize that they have reached a point where there is no longer a level playing field—they are not competing on an equal footing with their male counterparts. If these women could look ahead at the potential career path in their own corporation or another corporation and say, Look, I have as good a shot at the top as any man or woman, given my talents and abilities, and I'm going to go for it, then they might stay. It is not necessarily their lifelong dream to be an entrepreneur, but they can see that the odds are stacked against them. So many women leave by default and not to follow a dream. Sometimes you reach a point where you realize that there is no one to blame, it's not due to a lack on your part, and you can't shake your finger at your industry or your corporation. This is simply the way it is in companies throughout the United States—even though we're further along than any other place on the globe in terms of treating women equally in business. Given the planet we're on, this is as good as it's going to get."

You may find yourself increasingly dissatisfied with the opportunities for professional growth available to you within the corporate structure. The limits corporate life places on your earning power also may be a major issue for you. As Lonah Birch of the SBA points out, "Research has shown that people who own their own businesses are probably going to develop a more sizable net worth more quickly than someone who just works for a company. So if you are looking for bottom-line results, then opening a business is probably where the opportunity is."

Seven: You Find Yourself "Fantasizing" More and More About Starting Your Own Business

Now and again, many of us think about leaving the corporate world behind and striking out on our own. For some of us, the idea of "living the simple life" has the most appeal—giving up our jobs and going off to bake bread or start a small press in Vermont. For others, this fantasy revolves around "doing well by doing good"—producing products that are environmentally friendly or becoming successful enough so that we can make a difference in our communities. Sometimes our dreams have dollar signs attached to them; our vision of entrepreneurship revolves around having enough money and the economic freedom to be totally independent. Whatever form our fantasy takes, for most of us, it remains in the realm of make-believe—a daydream we feel free to indulge in from time to time precisely because we know, in our heart of hearts, that it will never be more than a flight of fancy. Daydreams like these are a means of releasing tension, a no-risk way to play in the fields of the free for a while. But sometimes our fantasies take firmer root in our minds and hearts than even we expected—or wanted. We find ourselves spending more time than we should imagining another way of working and the emotional and financial rewards it would bring us. If you find that your daydreams are becoming more powerful than your will to work at the job you have, then it's a sure sign that you should be listening to yourself more closely and taking those dreams more seriously.

Eight: You Find Yourself Moonlighting Compulsively in
Response to an Inner Drive

Moonlighting for fun and profit is something many of us have done from time to time in our careers—nothing unusual here. But when you reach a point where you derive far more psychic and emotional satisfaction from moonlighting than from the work you do to earn a paycheck, it may be time to reexamine your job situation. As we'll see later in the case of Sara Harrell, sometimes moonlighting can be so much more lucrative and challenging than a nine-to-five position that it becomes the basis for striking out on your own. Making this decision when you have only one or two clients can be a risky business, however, since their demand for your services could be short-lived. If you are tempted to chuck your day job and pour all of your energy into a moonlighting venture, be forewarned that there's a big difference between moonlighting with the security of a regular paycheck and trying to transform a part-time avocation into a full-time business. You may be far better off both emotionally and economically if you keep your job and build your business slowly and steadily during your free time until it can provide adequate financial support on a consistent basis. This is especially important if your income is essential to your family's survival and well-being. As Barbara Brabec suggests, "When someone is the family breadwinner and currently employed full-time, I advise them to keep their job while they're launching their business. It's very hard to do this, but few home-based businesses will generate a living wage in the early years of existence. It's especially important to hang on to any medical insurance packages that come with one's job, first, because it's more expensive to buy insurance as a self-employed individual; and second, because some individuals simply can't get private insurance because of preexisting health conditions."

Nine: Your Career and Family Priorities Are Undergoing a
Major, Life-Changing Shift

There are any number of reasons why you may be reassessing your career plans and their impact on your family. You may, for instance, have found yourself on the "daughter track," assuming more and more responsibility for taking care of your parents as they grow older. Or perhaps you have found yourself suddenly thrust into a step-parenting situation, where the pressures of blending two families together become almost overwhelming and come to overshadow and redefine your career needs. Probably the biggest single factor influencing the career-family balance is—you guessed it—motherhood. As any new mother will tell you, once your child arrives, nothing will ever be the same. Or as one friend told me half-jokingly, "We talk about our lives together in terms of B.B. and A.B.—before the baby and after the baby." If you are in the process of adjusting to the joys and upheaval of starting or building a family, then it's more than likely that at some point, you may reevaluate your work situation and think seriously about starting a business of your own.

Given tensions that arise from the often-conflicting pressures of career and family, it's understandable that many women are making a decision to step off the fast track, either temporarily or on a long-term basis. Once this decision was a lonely and isolating one, but in the 1990s, there is far more support than ever before for professional women who make this choice. One encouraging example is *ConneXions*, a newsletter and networking vehicle for "connecting home-based mothers in business." According to its founder, Caroline Hull, the *ConneXions* reader has "traded her briefcase for a diaper bag, business lunches for peanut butter and jelly, and power meetings for car pools, yet the home-based working mother still works from fifteen to forty hours or more on her business each week, patched in around nap times, school time, *Sesame Street*, and Little League." These "entrepreneurial mothers," Hull adds, "are customizing their work schedules and defining a family-work blend that gives them the *flexibility* and *control* still lacking in the formal workplace." As the mother of four who left a fast-track corporate career, Hull knows firsthand the special challenges that home-based working mothers face: Many women who choose this route find themselves woefully unprepared for the stress it can create on the home front. They also have unrealistic expectations about replacing lost income from the corporate jobs they've left behind and about the difficulty of meeting their child-care needs while working at home. For those women who are deeply committed to making this option work, however, it can be a very rewarding, if slow, route to entrepreneurship.

Ten: You've Begun to Realize That You Would Rather Lead Than Manage

Are leaders born or made? An entire industry has cropped up around this intriguing question, giving rise to seminars, surveys, books, and enough articles to circle the globe and back again. Lots of ink has also been spilled about the difference between managers and leaders. For women who've pursued demanding corporate careers, these issues aren't to be taken lightly; being pegged as a competent manager or singled out as a potential leader can make a big difference in the way your company views your contributions and career path. As we approach the mid-1990s, it is clear that developing leadership skills within corporations will continue to be extremely challenging, especially for women. One of the central reasons for this, which Sally Helgesen explores in her pioneering book *The Female Advantage: Women's Ways of Leadership*, is that women tend to lead differently from men. In her research, Helgesen found five key characteristics that defined the leadership styles of the women she interviewed: (1) they focused on relationships and on nurturing and empowering those around them; (2) they were comfortable playing multiple roles and didn't feel compelled to totally compartmentalize their lives; (3) they welcomed and encouraged diversity; (4) they preferred to communicate directly at all levels; and (5) they structured their organizations as "webs of inclusion" rather than as hierarchies.

Given these qualities, it's not surprising that women with strong leadership potential may find themselves out in left field in most corporations. After all, building relationships, nurturing, empowering others, diversity, direct communication, and nontraditional operating structures are not generally high priorities on the agendas of most companies and other institutions. Is it any wonder, then, that many women feel driven to take control of their lives and shape their work environments to meet their needs and talents? Warren Bennis, a management expert and popular author, describes successful leadership as "fully becoming yourself." As you look at your own future within the corporate world, how likely—or unlikely—is it that you will receive the encouragement and training needed to test and strengthen your leadership skills? Equally important, do you feel a powerful drive at this stage in your career to make the leap from manager to leader, from employee to entrepreneur?

TIMING: MAKE IT EASY ON YOURSELF

Taking your emotional temperature and deciding whether or not you've caught the entrepreneurial bug isn't easy. And trying to separate your feelings of dissatisfaction and frustration about your work from the circumstances and events that may have created them is no picnic either. Then there's the push-pull dilemma: Yes, factors within the corporate environment may be pushing you out the door, but how strong is the pull you're feeling from the entrepreneurial cottage? Is your current disenchantment with corporate life causing you to paint too rosy a picture of life outside what one woman called "the corporate nest"? Why are you thinking about this option now? What's happened in your life to make it seem attractive? What are the biggest barriers you see to making the move? How much emotional and financial support can you really count on from your family, friends, and business contacts? How big an emotional investment are you prepared to make in reshaping your business identity? Are you prepared to handle the tensions that working for yourself may create in your personal life? As you think through these questions, here are some pointers to keep in mind:

Listen to Your Own Internal Clock

As you think through your concerns about timing, it's very important to try to screen out as many external distractions as you can and separate your feelings from the circumstances surrounding you. As strange as it may sound, what's happening with your job, your company, or even the economy as a whole may have little or no bearing on whether or not you should strike out on your own at a given point in time. The real issue you have to be concerned with is figuring out your own internal timetable. Debra Oppenheim, for example, left the security of a partnership in an executive search firm at the height of the last recession to form her own firm with a partner. Yet, when she decided to make her move, she never really gave any thought to the economic downturn—or to the impact it might have on her success or failure. She was driven by her own frustration with her company and by the fact that she was being forced to turn away the very nonprofit clients she wanted to work with. "It never even occurred to me to ask myself how I could try to start a business in the economy we were in," says Debra. "That thought surfaced only when we had been in business for a couple of months and other people started saying, 'How could you give up a good job now and start your own firm?' Then, eureka! I found myself asking the same question: How could I have been insane enough to take such a risk? But believe me, that idea hit me *after* I'd already taken the plunge."

Karen Fried's situation, too, demonstrates just how important intuition and a strong inner sense of timing are when it comes to launching an entrepreneurial venture. In her case, emotional readiness combined with a great idea to give her the surge of energy she needed to create her word game, Think-It Link-It. "Prior to the game," she recalls, "my father became sick and died. This was a miserable period for me. I was also in a really bad relationship and that took all my time. But when I was finally freed up emotionally from these dramatic events, there was a vacuum. So timingwise, when the idea for my game came along, I was ready emotionally. People always think that to make an idea work, you have to have the right timing in a business sense, but that wasn't true for me. In terms of business, for me, the timing couldn't have been worse—I was in the middle of closing some of the biggest deals of my real estate career. But emotionally, I was ready to commit myself."

Look Before You Leap

"Go for it—but know what you're getting into." That's one of the first pieces of advice Barbara Brabec gives to would-be entrepreneurs in the *National Home Business Report*. "Do research—read everything you can on entrepreneurship, finance, marketing, and home business," suggests Caroline Hull, the publisher of *ConneXions*. In the chapters that follow, you'll hear this same message time and again in many forms: Do your homework. Research your market. Talk to people. Ask questions. Don't be afraid to say you don't know something or to make mistakes. In short, when it comes to starting a business, the more information you have, the better your chances of success—and the more confident you'll be about timing your move. In many ways, there's more help available to you than ever before. Women's networks, training seminars, and mentoring programs are growing both in numbers and sophistication. Successful female business owners are using a wide range of forums to inspire and inform other women about the rewards and challenges of entrepreneurship. Women are reaching out to women in new and exciting ways— through videos, special awards, conferences, and mentoring programs that offer one-on-one counseling (for more specifics, see Appendix 3: Helpful Publications and Organizations). Take advantage of these resources to give yourself a firm footing before you take the plunge and you'll be far more likely to land safely.

This information-gathering process offers many benefits: it can help you minimize the risks you'll face, manage your fears, and zero in on a winning start-up idea. To find the clarity you'll need to make your move, you need to keep thinking, communicating, talking about ideas, and taking them to the next step. Eventually one idea makes enough sense so that the others fall by the wayside. It picks you. But you have to open yourself up to new possibilities and not be afraid to admit you don't know something. To find the one good idea that sparks your imagination and fuels your energy, you may have to work through your share of bad ones. Unless you're willing to go through that process and make some mistakes, you're not going to recognize the right idea when it comes your way.

Ease on Down the Road

Most people are scared about going out on their own, and with good reason. Being totally responsible for yourself, professionally and financially, can be a frightening proposition. But you can make the process much easier and less nerve-racking by taking it in stages and creating a transition that gives you some breathing space. Working for yourself doesn't have to be an either-or situation. You don't have to quit your job in order to start your business; you can orchestrate your work flow in a way that allows you to juggle both for a while and keep your options open. Moonlighting is the most obvious transitional route. Although it's physically and mentally demanding, it can enable you to bypass, at least for a time, the financial worries that giving up your paycheck will trigger. In addition to moonlighting, there are other steps you can take to ease yourself into entrepreneurship. You can establish a "freedom fund," for instance, and set aside part of every paycheck to build a nest egg to finance your venture. If you've been laid off, you can use the outplacement services your firm may offer to explore opportunities for starting your own venture or even buying a franchise. You can concentrate on attracting one or more "anchor" clients as a way of underwriting your start-up. You can take the partnership route and team up with a business owner who already has an established operating structure and a track record. With some thoughtful planning, you can even use the time and talents you contribute as a volunteer to create a bridge to your entrepreneurial dream.

So, as you ponder your move from corporation to cottage, remember that there are many roads to your future. Yes, the time will come when you have to take the leap, when the pressure to make a break becomes so strong that, as Jackie Farley puts it, "you can't not do it." But you can prepare for that moment now, today, by taking steps to arm yourself with the information you'll need, by creating a scenario for yourself that makes your transition as smooth and positive as possible, and, above all, by listening to yourself and paying attention to your own internal sense of timing.

3

ARE YOU READY EMOTIONALLY?

Emotionally speaking, I've found that many women don't visualize themselves as business owners. Often this is because women in industry haven't been given key leadership roles and so they may lack the business skills required. As a result, some women have a hard time validating themselves and saying, "I can do this. I have the confidence. I will make this happen."

—*Kathryn Frazier*

Being an armchair entrepreneur is a comfortable proposition. After all, thinking about making the move from corporation to cottage is easy enough. And so is talking about it. But putting rubber to the road and actually *doing* it is a risky, sometimes nerve-racking, business. You may have the greatest idea since gourmet popcorn and a drive strong enough to move mountains and win markets from Texas to Tokyo. But be prepared— once you leave the corporate environment and launch your new venture, you can quickly find yourself on an emotional roller coaster that's hard to hang on to and even harder to let go of. Without a doubt, you're going to face some tough obstacles, both within yourself and outside your control. The challenges you'll face along the way will test your staying power, make you question the value of what you're doing, and wonder what crazy impulse possessed you to trade in your corporate ID for a walk on the wild side.

"Readiness is all"—that's how Hamlet described his recipe for success. It may not have helped him much in the end, but still, he had a point. Readiness—*emotional readiness*, that is—separates the winners and the losers pretty quickly when it comes to starting a business. As you gear up to take the plunge—or stay up nights *thinking* about taking the plunge—just how emotionally prepared are you? Are you really willing to make the sacrifices this life-style demands? Can you cope with the disappointments it will bring you? Do you have the stamina and resilience you'll need to weather the emotional highs and lows you'll face, especially during the start-up phase of your business?

Regardless of the kind of work you want to do or the skills and experience you have to offer, there are five emotional "tools" you'll need to succeed: vision, passion, independence, courage, and fantasy. These are the building blocks that will form the foundation for shaping your new professional identity. If you construct that identity on a solid emotional base, then you have a good chance of surviving the critical start-up stage and developing an exciting, rewarding, and profitable business. On the other hand, if the emotional reserves underpinning your sense of professionalism are easily exhausted, then you'll quickly find yourself on shaky ground. While image is certainly important, it can take you only so far. If your mental attitude and your image aren't in synch or you find yourself overwhelmed by the demands your business is making, then it will be hard not to convey these messages to the people with whom you're working. Since the emotional tenor of your business life is so important, let's take a closer look at the inner resources you will need to tap when making the move from employee to entrepreneur.

VISION: A GOAL THAT EXCITES AND COMPELS YOU

Talk to a true entrepreneur for any length of time and you'll find yourself talking to a dreamer as well as a doer—in short, someone with a *vision*. Visions come in all shapes and sizes. They can involve a sense of mission and purpose. A goal you're impelled to achieve. A strong sense of personal ethics and integrity. A burning desire to put your values into action in the workplace. A "dream" that absorbs and energizes you. An idea for a product or service that you're driven to make a marketplace reality. Any of these objectives can excite and motivate you. While the specific goal you're reaching for is certainly important, it's *having* a goal that really counts.

EMOTIONAL READINESS:

FIVE INNER RESOURCES

YOU'LL NEED TO SUCCEED

VISION

A goal or mission that excites and compels you. Your vision should embody a strong personal desire and be in harmony with your values. Your vision can be clear-cut and easily described or it can evolve gradually. But its pull must be strong enough to trigger decisive action and forward motion.

PASSION

Intense emotional excitement. The drive to do what you love and what you're good at. Passion is the fuel that feeds your vision. Your venture must be absorbing and intrinsically satisfying to sustain passionate commitment. It has to challenge you to stretch and grow and create enough tension and discomfort to keep you moving toward your goal.

INDEPENDENCE

The desire for freedom and autonomy. The drive to take control of your work and your life. A strong belief in your own judgment and the desire to exercise that judgment on your own terms. A willingness to take responsibility for both the success and failure that may result from your decisions. An inner core of security and confidence in your abilities and experience.

COURAGE

The ability to manage your fears and learn from them. Recognition that fear is a healthy response to the risks you're assuming. Acceptance of fear as a creative force and a powerful incentive to succeed. Realizing that courage is often a matter of endurance and finding the staying power to handle the ups and downs you'll face.

FANTASY

Daydreaming with intent and purpose. Staying in touch with the deep desires that can inspire you to make your business vision a reality. Fantasizing isn't the same as having a vision or visualizing; it's an open-ended voyage of discovery.

The desire to achieve a personal vision—often in a public arena—emerged as one of the strongest emotional drivers compelling the women I interviewed to leave the corporate fold and strike out on their own. Everyone, without exception, found herself grappling with the need to build a new life around a defining principle, a product or service idea, or a notion of either the kind of work she wanted to do or how she wanted to work. In many cases, the original target that triggered a move into entrepreneurship quickly faded and was replaced by a new, sometimes more realistic, objective. But the sense of forward motion provided by having a vision and reaching for a goal was absolutely critical in helping these women get off the mark and on with the job of shaping the lives they wanted to live. A vision is more than just an idealized, pie-in-the-sky dream about having it all and doing it all. It's a touchstone, an emotional yardstick that helps you measure how far you've come, where you want to go, and whether you're headed in the right direction. It also can be a lifeline when things get tough. As Jordana Simpson puts it, "There are weeks when you don't make any sales. And you don't get a check on Friday, because no one is paying you a salary anymore. You don't even have any clients. When you're not getting paid and you're not working, then who the hell are you? Who you are is what you stand for and what your vision is. That vision is going to have to keep you company on some very cold nights and during the long weeks when there are no results to point to for all the time and work you've invested."

Identifying the true nature of the personal vision that lies at the heart of your business venture can be a major challenge. This is especially true because at some point, as we'll see, it will be important to translate your vision into a strategic road map by getting it down on paper in some sort of business plan. But we all have to start somewhere. And the sooner you take steps to think through and identify your vision, the farther along on the entrepreneurial curve you'll be. As you begin this process, here are some guidelines that should prove helpful:

A Strong Personal Goal or Desire

Your vision should embody a strong personal goal or desire. Some visions, it's true, are grand and far-reaching—building the Brooklyn Bridge or the Taj Mahal, for example. But even accomplishments as sweeping as these began as personal quests. To have any chance for success, a vision must be personal; it must express a heartfelt desire. Your vision also must be in harmony with your values—it must be something you really want, not something you *think* you want because you feel bored or burned out, underpaid, or under-valued in your job. To sustain you emotionally, a vision has to be a positive rather than a negative emotional driver. It has to be firmly grounded in who you are and the kind of life and work that excites and absorbs you. As Jordana Simpson said so well, a vision is what you take to bed with you after you turn out the lights and you're alone with yourself. It has to keep you warm on those cold nights when you're worried about making it, and inspire you to work on those long days when nothing seems to be happening.

Your vision also may take some hard knocks in the real world; unless you're deeply committed to it on a personal level, it may not stand you in good stead when the going gets tough. No one knows this better than Alison Cross. An award-winning screenwriter, Alison began her career as a television journalist and anchor. She started writing screenplays at night and during her off-camera breaks, sold the first script she penned, and left her broadcasting job to pursue a career as a screenwriter. Alison sees the vision she is reaching for as a message that runs throughout her work: "I've always had the same theme, ever since I was a reporter. In the case of the assigned stories that I take, even though they don't seem to serve the theme, by the time I've finished, there it is again. It's not terribly compli-cated. The message I try to get across is just, Fight the good fight. Don't take the easy road. Be a hero."

Or heroine. The drive to make this message come alive in her work helped sustain Alison through nineteen difficult drafts of *Roe v. Wade*, a controversial docudrama aired on NBC in 1989. At one point, Alison's personal vision had been altered to the extent that she was prepared to remove her name from the screenplay she'd written and rewritten, over and over. Ultimately, however, the TV movie that emerged after three years of work and frustration remained true to the message that Alison wanted to convey. It also won an Emmy for actress Holly Hunter, another Emmy for Alison as coproducer, a Golden Globe for actress Amy Madigan, and numerous awards from constitutional rights organizations and women's groups across the country. Keeping one's personal vision intact in the real world of deadlines and dollars isn't easy, but it can be done, even in a medium as public and collaborative as television. Reinterpreting her vision each time she writes, in the face of outside pressure to compromise or abandon it, is a constant challenge for Alison Cross. At the same time, the drive to keep that theme alive is what fuels her writing.

How You Want to Work

Your vision can focus on how you want to work as well as what you do. It's extremely comforting when your vision involves a specific product or service. In these cases, it's fairly easy to develop some form of business plan and to identify your markets and competition. But you may find that the vision or goal that excites you most doesn't involve the kind of work you want to do so much as *how* you want to work. In other words, having the opportunity and the means to express your personal values in the workplace may be as important to you as the actual work you plan to do. As the old saying goes, it's the journey rather than the destination that fires your imagination.

The vision that prompted Jordana Simpson to start a graphic design firm, for example, revolved around "creating a standard of integrity in working with people," both the clients she designed for and the staff she hired. When she first began working, Jordana quickly found that graphic design was a highly competitive field with little sense of teamwork or camaraderie. "The way people were treated on the job was terrible. There was no sense that we were human beings. We were simply job descriptions. I didn't want to be a job description and I didn't want to treat other people like one." During a three-year apprenticeship with Tomas Gonda, an internationally recognized designer with a powerful vision of his own,

Jordana began to "gain a sense of who I was and what I stood for. I worked very hard to develop client relationships. And I began to think that maybe telling the truth, treating people well, and bringing values I learned from my family and Tom Gonda to my business could actually work, even in a competitive field like graphic design."

While visions like Jordana's may be harder to pin down, they can be every bit as compelling as more concrete goals like starting a small press or manufacturing computer software. In situations like these, your key motivator may be providing a level of service that far exceeds that of your competitors, offering a work environment that nurtures employees, creating a new market niche, or experiencing personal growth through your work. The real challenge here, as Jordana learned, lies in recognizing that your vision really stems as much from a concern with *process*—how you want to work—as it does with the product or service your work produces.

Clarifying Your Vision

Your vision doesn't have to be crystal clear at the onset of your business. Some business visions are straightforward and easily described—publishing a community newspaper for downtown Los Angeles is the goal that motivated Sue Laris-Eastin, for example. Debra Oppenheim's mission involves finding high-quality managerial talent for nonprofit organizations, which she feels have been poorly served by traditional executive search firms. Clearly, Sue and Debra have definite business goals to aim for. Not everyone is this focused and directed. Some women who pursue the entrepreneurial route find that clarifying their vision—identifying exactly what they want to do and what they have to offer—proves to be a gradual process.

This was certainly the case for Caroline Hull. It took her several years of soul-searching and trial and error to find her entrepreneurial niche. Caroline's last corporate position was operations manager for the New York office of a Canadian computer company. Her job was a very satisfying and fulfilling one that involved, among other benefits, the chance to travel all over the country and a ground-floor opportunity to help develop an exciting new software product. Just as she was entering a peak period of career growth, however, Caroline found herself coping with a problem pregnancy. Her first baby arrived, she returned to her firm as a part-time consultant, and then she soon found herself expecting twins. Ultimately she left the work force and had another child. A mother of four children, Caroline had put an exciting and satisfying career on hold and now faced a dual challenge: meeting her family's needs while satisfying her own need for personal growth. This situation provided the inspiration for the business venture she eventually launched, a newsletter called *ConneXions*, aimed at home-based entrepreneurial mothers.

The idea for *ConneXions* took almost three years to emerge. Says Caroline, "I knew that flexibility and control were paramount for me as a mother in terms of my working career. I couldn't work full time and I couldn't afford to spend the next eighteen years at home without working. I wanted to work . . . [and] I wanted to do it on my own terms. That was the genesis of *ConneXions* and my whole involvement in this area. I spent many a day and many nights trying to come up with ways of bridging the gap between home and work. My husband and a friend of ours who used to come over would tease me about all my research into what I wanted to do. 'What's this week's grand plan?' they'd ask."

During the three years she found herself searching for a niche, Caroline made a few false starts, but she persisted in seeing them as learning experiences rather than as failures. At one point, she decided to write a book about having twins and actually found an agent. Then she moved from New York to Virginia and took a part-time job, so the book idea fell by the wayside. Next she started looking for other women in her new community of Manassas, Virginia, who'd had professional careers and felt ambivalent about being at home full time. Eventually she cofounded a chapter of a national organization for professional women who had left the work force to raise their children, but she soon realized that the group didn't meet her need to combine work and family and create a balanced life for herself. At this point, Caroline found her vision emerging more clearly: "I wanted to come up with a practical vehicle for women in my situation—women who wanted to stay home but needed to work. I had a computer and some software, and eventually I decided that my contribution would take the form of a newsletter which I could write while the kids were in school. I began slowly, working about ten hours a week. My game plan was always to start something that could provide a springboard for interesting work that could become more profitable as time went on. Initially my goal was to provide a local resource for women who wanted to stay home and a vehicle for them to feel connected to each other. As time went on, it quickly became apparent to me that my interest was in realistically portraying ways for women to earn money from home. The second issue of *ConneXions* focused specifically on home-based entrepreneurship for women. I interviewed a number of women with home-based careers and it really inspired me that these women were combining their careers and families in what I regarded as a pioneering way. It was at this point that *ConneXions* became something that was firmly looking at this option."

Caroline Hull's staying power in shaping a vision in tune with her personal values is a perfect example of how intention creates opportunity. As she says, it took her three years and many long nights to get a handle on what she really wanted to do, and to find the right vehicle to do it. She also made several false starts along the way. Because of her experience, Caroline is quick to point out that "the first idea you have may not be the 'big' idea, the one that really works, but it's important to get started on something. Get out there. Start networking. Start making contacts and begin to feel like you're getting someplace. And remember, priorities and schedules change as time goes on—especially for working mothers. It's only natural that your business may change too. What interested you when your children were babies is going to be very different from what you want to do when they're six or seven."

This has certainly proven true for Caroline. In addition to her newsletter, she also has started consulting with small businesses in need of marketing expertise. When Caroline Hull began *ConneXions*, she had no background in publishing or journalism. Nothing in her career up to that point had any direct relation to the venture that eventually emerged from her researching and soul-searching. Instead it was deciding to take the plunge into a business of her own that mobilized her energies and helped clarify her vision. This often proves to be true for female entrepreneurs. Just the act of making the decision to work for yourself seems to provide focus and direction.

So if your vision is strong and clear, then you have a powerful asset at your command—one you should make the most of. On the other hand, if you're one of the many women whose vision seems to be a "work in progress," then accept that reality and don't waste your time second-guessing yourself and agonizing because you're not exactly sure what you want to do. Instead take Caroline Hull's approach: Rely on forward motion. Take action. Chart a general direction for yourself and start researching and talking to people. If you're strongly committed enough to creating a new work life for yourself, then that intention will help create the opportunities you need—and at some point, all of the pieces will fall into place, just as they did for Caroline.

PASSION: INTENSE EMOTIONAL COMMITMENT TO YOUR VENTURE

If having a vision or goal to reach for is the first emotional building block of a self-structured life, then passionate involvement in the work you've chosen is a close second. When we hear the word *passion*, most of us think of love, not work. It's the stuff of *Peyton Place*, not the workplace. Yet passion—intense emotional excitement—is the fuel that feeds your vision. Without its spark, your vision will never really catch fire. With it you can overcome almost any obstacle. If there's one piece of advice everyone who runs a successful business can agree on, it's this: do what you love and what you're good at.

"If I were counseling someone just starting out about working on her own," says writer Sara Harrell, "I would say that whatever you decide to do, give it your deepest, heartfelt intensity. Sometimes at first you have to go at it with everything you've got before you can find the joy or happiness in it all. All too often, as women, we feel that we have to prove ourselves. And sometimes, in trying to prove we can succeed, the joy of what we're doing is lost. I wish we were taught from our earliest days that doing what we want to do and enjoying it is just as important as the goals we set for ourselves. We have to set goals to get where we want to go, but the path we take is also important. In terms of my own work, I wish I had allowed myself to enjoy it more as I went along."

Finding something that you can do with "heartfelt intensity" and allowing yourself to enjoy it is also the advice Caroline Hull gives women who ask for her help. "One of the first things that I recommend to women who want to start their own business," she says, "is that they do something they truly feel passionate about. If you are going to work at home doing something you don't really care about, then it is probably not going to be self-sustaining. In my own case, I probably couldn't have picked something better, because I just get so high talking to women and knowing that perhaps I'm making a difference to them. It's especially rewarding when I get calls from people who say, 'Reading your newsletter has been so helpful and so inspiring to me.' That's a great feeling! Now that I have established a far-reaching network of contacts, I'm asked to make presentations to different groups and educate them about this huge segment of talented women who are really trying to do something that benefits their families as well as their careers—which I think is helping society in the long run. . . . I've also moved into offering consulting services to corporations interested in helping their employees find a better work-family balance. This satisfies my sense of missionary fervor about making things easier for women."

"Missionary fervor" is what passion is all about. Your new venture may involve writing a newsletter, selling books, designing gift baskets, manufacturing baby food, advising small businesses, or planning special events. Any of these business vehicles has the same basic potential for success or failure. What really makes the difference in whether they thrive or wither on the vine is your emotional investment—how you feel about what you're doing, day in and day out, and how skilled you are in translating your passion into outstanding performance. Does the business you want to start excite you and energize you? Will building that business and watching it grow satisfy a deep inner need or longing? Is your conviction powerful enough to persuade other people—especially clients, suppliers, and your family—that you can make the transition from paid employee to business owner? To help you answer some of these questions, let's explore more fully the link between passion and work.

"Flow"

Your venture should totally absorb you and be intrinsically satis-fying. In sports, when track stars or swimmers talk about moments of peak performance, they describe these experiences as "entering the zone." During these moments, their concentration is so intense that time seems to stand still and they are in absolute harmony with their goal—the archer feels at one with her bow and the swimmer at one with the water. Psychologists have a different name for this kind of total involvement; they call it "flow." We experience flow most intensely when we concentrate so deeply and are so absorbed in something outside ourselves that we forget about who we are. Doing and being become one and the same. Here's how screenwriter Alison Cross describes this kind of experience: "If it isn't hard, then I'm not challenging myself. In my field, the only thing you have control over is the work, especially the first draft. And that's where the pleasure is. You work for the moment when you don't know what you are going to be doing and you sit there and suddenly you forget that it's you and it becomes something else. And it writes itself. And suddenly, it's three hours later and you have this perfect little gem that emerges almost unconsciously. To me, happiness is forgetting yourself. That's why people are happiest when they're doing something that engages them thoroughly, whether it's work or sports or family life. Turning outward and away from your own problems is the real key—and that's what you have to do with this kind of work. To abandon yourself and reach something else. To be-come the characters you're writing about and hopefully have a fusion of all your life experience, everything you believe, everything you have ever heard. To feel it come together and make something new."

Most of us have experienced this feeling to one degree or another when working on a project or hobby that's personally rewarding. But making a business out of doing work that we love and creating a work environment that nurtures our enthusiasms remains a major challenge. Even though women, more than men, consistently rank job satisfaction as their top priority, finding fulfilling work continues to be an elusive goal for many of us. Often it's easier to settle for less than what we want and try to meet our needs for growth and fulfillment outside the workplace. After all, these moments of total involvement tend to be few and far between; that's why they're called peak experiences. As anyone who works for herself will be the first to admit, there are plenty of valleys in between the peaks. Or, as a John Denver song puts it, "Some Days Are Diamonds, Some Days Are Stone."

To pursue a self-structured livelihood, you have to value those moments of "flow"—of feeling right about who you are and what you're doing—highly enough to be able to handle the valley experiences that are a fact of life when you're working for yourself. You also have to be able to get through those "days of stone," when things seem to be falling apart or it seems as if there's no movement and you're getting nowhere. Of course, you can just as easily experience these ups and downs when you're working nine to five, but they tend to be far more intense when you work for yourself—the lows are lower and the highs are higher. It takes tremendous emotional resilience to handle this pattern of activity. Unless you have the commitment and ability to cope with this rugged emotional terrain, you'll find that being in business for yourself will be more mentally and physically draining than it will be satisfying.

Challenge Creates Intensity

Your work has to create tension and force you to "put yourself on the line." To sustain the emotional intensity you'll need to succeed in a self-structured life, your work has to do more than satisfy and absorb you; it has to challenge you to stretch and grow, professionally as well as emotionally. It also has to create a certain amount of discomfort in order to keep you moving toward your goal. Sara Harrell has worked as a free-lance advertising marketing writer for ten years; she's a seasoned pro when it comes to making creative tension work for her. Before striking out on her own, she worked as a senior executive at a number of ad agencies and eventually advanced to a job as creative director at a marketing promotions firm. While free-lancing certainly has its ups and downs, Sara has always enjoyed a passionate involvement in her work and felt that she was "doing what I was meant to do." As she describes it, "Sometimes

I haven't one more minute to spare in meeting my deadlines. But as soon as I turn on the computer, something switches on in me, too. My interest is focused. There's something in me that wants to make everything I do the best that I can make it. And there's an intensity that comes out of that. Whatever it is I'm working on, I'm driven to make it different, creative, and worth something. Once I sit down and get going, I have to make whatever I'm doing new and exciting."

For self-starters like Sara, the self-imposed pressure she feels when she tackles a new piece of work can be very seductive. And satisfying the inner drive she has to make each project better than the last is a powerful incentive. But this kind of intensity and edgy creativity isn't for everyone. As Dr. Brian Schwartz, a psychologist and career management consultant, points out, "It's a question of how people want to live their lives. People who go out on their own, for whatever reasons, certainly find that their life is more intense, for the most part, than it would be if they were working in a corporation. Of course that's not always true; there are jobs in corporations that can be quite intense and quite exciting—jobs in which one invests a great deal. But there is still a difference. When you are getting a paycheck, you're still being 'fed' by the corporation. There's an exchange, of course; you're not entirely an infant. But there is a dependent relationship with this larger entity. Whereas when you're on your own, it's almost like working the streets—being alive, seeing where the opportunities are, and saying to yourself, If nobody buys what I'm selling or retains my services, I may not eat. I may not be able to feed my family or pay my rent or mortgage."

In order to succeed in running a business, as Dr. Schwartz describes it, you have to "stay hungry," putting yourself on the line, financially, emotionally, and professionally. Pressure to beat the odds and continually outperform yourself can be energizing, exhausting, or both at the same time. Think about whether you really can thrive under these conditions. Given your personality, work history, and the stage of life you've reached, is this kind of tension and discomfort really going to be productive? Is it going to bring out your best? All things considered, you may be better off settling for emotional equilibrium on the job and saving your "peak" experiences for your vacations to the Smoky Mountains. It may be more practical to meet your need for more fulfilling work by moonlighting, at least for a while. Keeping the day job that pays your bills and lets you sleep at night until you've built a strong base for your own business makes powerful sense.

Feeling Your Desire

To sustain your passionate involvement, your work has to spark desire. To feed the wellspring of emotional intensity you'll need to craft a self-structured life, your work not only has to satisfy some of your deepest inner needs, it also has to create new needs and desires. In other words, if passion fuels your vision, then desire fuels your passion. Melinda Pancoast and her husband, Malachi, have been working with small and emerging companies for seven years to help increase their sales, profitability, and product quality by focusing on both employer and employee productivity and satisfaction. They also have worked with married business owners. As a specialist in organizational dynamics, Melinda is an expert on motivation. Through her work with entrepreneurs in a range of industries, Melinda has come to recognize the vital role that desire—or "appetite," as she calls it—plays in running a business:

"Without appetite, there is no production. In business, if you don't have something you really want, something to go for, then your work becomes stale. It becomes production for the sake of production. Our society is really production-oriented: we value production and we dismiss appetite. We don't even acknowledge it. In this sense, business is still a man's world. Because men equate satisfaction with production, not desire. If they want something, it's generally tools—things—that will help them make and produce. Women, on the other hand, understand appetite as well as production. Wanting and desiring are the motivators behind their drive to produce. In our consulting practice, we have people write up 'want' lists—what they want for their company, for their families, and for themselves. I worked with one woman, for instance, who found she was making a lot of money but was very unhappy. She was so involved in producing that she wasn't taking time to think about why she was producing and what she really wanted. She had given up that whole side of her life. Our work was all about helping her focus on what she wanted to be happy. Because what you want, your desires, are a big part of what your business is all about."

As Melinda Pancoast has learned firsthand from her experience in advising other business owners, desire must be renewed constantly if it is going to remain strong enough to motivate you to take action, keep moving, put your passion to work, and transform your vision into reality. Equally important, your business venture must be expansive enough and challenging enough to continually generate new desires and new goals. If it is too limited in scope or too inflexible, you'll quickly outgrow it and find yourself without the inner motivation to continue. This often happens to business owners who have struggled to survive the first few years of operation and have slowly built an organization. Once their initial longing and hunger to "make it" and prove themselves have been satisfied, they find themselves immersed in production, yet dissatisfied, because they've lost sight of the importance of desire.

INDEPENDENCE: SELF-RELIANCE AND A STRONG DRIVE FOR CONTROL

Are you ready to take charge of your life and your work? Do you really believe that the success or failure of your business venture depends on you, and you alone? Do you have confidence that the problems you'll face will be within your personal control and influence? Are you willing to take responsibility for your mistakes as well as your accomplishments? If the answer to these questions is yes, then you already possess one of the most powerful emotional tools you'll need to succeed as an entrepreneur: A strong belief in your own judgment and the desire to exercise that judgment freely and on your own terms. Independence. Self-reliance. Confidence. Whatever word you use to capture this quality, you have an invaluable emotional driver at your command. Remember "The Avon Report" (page 18)? Well, according to the successful female entrepreneurs surveyed, the "desire for career control" (and the flexibility it offered) was the single most important force motivating them to take action and start their own businesses. The need to exercise more control

over their work was also one of the main incentives cited in the
NAFE survey results from women business owners (see page 19).

Often when we think of the word *control*, we think of it in terms
of power—of dominating or influencing someone or something. But
the kind of control these women are talking about is very different.
It really involves independence and the need to feel that they are
the cause of events in their lives. In making the decision to start
their own businesses, "what people are looking for," says Dr.
Schwartz, "is autonomy, the ability to control their work life—the
way in which they work, when they work, how they work. Autonomy
doesn't mean control in the classic sense. Autonomy means that you
have a greater ability to dictate how you are going to spend your
time and with whom. It's freedom."

The desire for greater freedom was a recurring theme in my
interviews. At some point in their careers, all the women I spoke
with experienced the need to declare their own personal independence from the companies or organizations they worked for. In some
cases, the price these women paid in trading their time and talent
for a salary and some form of job security, however illusory, simply
became too high. They were not learning enough or earning enough.
For others, the shock of being axed or downsized triggered a need
to take charge of their situations. When faced with the decision to
look for another job or start their own business, these women opted
to give up the dependence on corporate stability that had put them
at risk and turned them into corporate casualties. And for a handful
of the women I interviewed, the positive work experiences they'd
enjoyed in the corporate world actually whetted their appetites for
greater freedom to reshape their work lives as their goals and needs
changed. Let's take a closer look at what exercising this kind of
freedom really involves.

Personal Empowerment

Having control over your work means taking control and empow-
ering yourself. In describing her shift from employee to employer,
Lorraine Gerstein says, "For me, the move was a matter of control.
I needed and wanted to be in a position where I was the ultimate

designer of what my business life would look like—to feel that I was taking the paint and drawing the picture myself instead of fitting into someone else's picture. I felt that I had better insight and judgment than the people I had been working for. It was really that I wanted to be empowered. I wanted to empower myself with the ability to make decisions about how I did my work, independent of anyone else's thoughts on the subject."

For Debra Oppenheim, like Lorraine Gerstein, personal empowerment was also a big issue in her decision to make the move from corporation to cottage. For Debra, one of the most exciting aspects of the new work life she's created for herself is "the sense of freedom and independence." Says Debra, "I haven't gotten over feeling guilty if I take three hours off or if I come in at ten o'clock on Monday instead of eight-thirty or nine. Sometimes I have to stop and think to myself that I'm my own boss. I can set my hours as long as I make my clients happy, get my work done, and have time to develop new projects. . . . I've managed people before, but in this case, there's more involved than just managing people. I have to manage a business. And I really didn't think I had it in me. I may not be at my best when it comes to finances and long-term planning, but it's working. We've just taken a new office and hired an administrative assistant. While my partner and I made these decisions together, for me, it's just a wonderful feeling to be the boss. It's triggered a big change in me. And it has nothing to do with control. It has to do with how I feel about myself.

"It's wonderful not to be at the mercy of someone else who has a say over what and how you do things. Just one example: Every time I wrote a proposal, I would have to go to the managing partner for approval, simply because he wanted to have his hand in it. And something would be changed and I would have to go back to him for approval again, about a fee structure or a piece of work I was doing. The fact that the buck now stops with me and that I can decide how a proposal goes out and set a fee structure that I think is fair really makes a difference to me. Often I was in situations where I felt that my clients' needs were being addressed unjustly, but I didn't have control over what happened.

"Sure, there are lots of sleepless nights where you say to yourself, What am I doing? But underneath it all there is that wonderful feeling of exhilaration. The kind of work I was doing with nonprofits didn't attract much attention in my firm. And this was terribly destructive to my self-image. Although my colleagues were absolutely wonderful, I didn't get the support I needed from my firm's managing partner. I found that I was beaten down inside myself. I knew that I could do the work, so it wasn't a question of ability. It was more an issue of, Why aren't I appreciated more?''

Strong Self-Image

Exercising control over your work life requires strong self-confidence. To take charge of your life in this way, you need to have a strong image of yourself as a professional and an almost infectious confidence in your skills and experience. Without this core of inner security, it will be exceptionally hard to handle the day-to-day demands of building a self-structured work style. According to one seasoned Fortune 500 female executive who specializes in corporate training, it takes many women at least ten years longer than men to recognize exactly how skilled and experienced they are and how marketable their talents can be. Whether or not this is true, large reserves of self-confidence don't well up overnight for most women. Like developing a vision, feeling secure about their skills and capabilities is a gradual process. And all too often, lack of confidence about their skills is the major emotional hurdle many women face in starting a small business, according to former SBA advisor and small-business owner Kathryn Frazier.

"Instead of believing in themselves and saying, 'I can do this,' I often hear women saying, 'I just can't seem to make it. I can't seem to make this happen. I don't understand why.' Emotionally I think the questions women need to ask themselves here are, What is motivating me to move ahead? Do I *have* to make it work? Am I going to give myself permission to be successful? Many of the women I've worked with just haven't allowed themselves to think in those terms. Sometimes it's as simple as making affirmations about your business success and saying to yourself, I can do this."

As Kathryn Frazier suggests here, self-confidence is rooted in an inner belief in your capabilities and a positive mental attitude—you have to be willing to give yourself permission to succeed. Self-confidence is also the result of research and planning. "In some cases," says Kathryn, "women tend to work in a vacuum. They think they are doing the right thing, but they haven't really checked it out. Knowledge is power and having it can give you confidence. Research can give you a solid base from which to move forward. Going into something without adequate preparation undermines your chances of success. It either puts you in a win-lose situation, where someone else wins and you lose, or in a lose-lose situation, where everyone misses out. To make a small business work, you have to take responsibility for preparing yourself."

ACQUIRING leadership training, basic business skills, and a solid foundation based on previous work experience are also key confidence builders. Often it takes women some time to develop these tools. As Jordana Simpson points out, "I think a lot of people begin asking themselves that question, What would it be like to have my own business? at the age of thirty or forty, after they've been working for ten or twenty years and developed a certain level of competence. At this point, they've set some parameters, and they have the discipline and the framework to go out and create something on their own."

Acquiring the self-confidence she needed certainly proved to be a gradual process for Lorraine Gerstein, who launched her own business as a rehabilitation consultant. As she said earlier about timing, "You have to have a sense of your own strength to move in this direction. It took me a few years to feel that." In thinking back · on her decision, Lorraine believes that "the smartest thing I did was to rely on the ability as a case manager that I had developed. I had the ability and I knew I had it, and this is what allowed me to move forward. I knew that I was a better case manager than just about anyone around."

This belief in her own strength and ability gave Lorraine the inner resources she needed to make the move from employee to employer and to capitalize on relationships that she had already established in order to start her own business. Lorraine also has found that her success in building a small company has increased her sense of personal power. "My confidence in my ability has grown. I know now that I can be a successful, financially independent person—and that I never have to rely on another person in the way I was brought up to believe I had to. There is a sense of freedom in this new image of myself that goes beyond anything you can imagine."

Managing Choices

Having control over your work life means managing choices. For Susan O'Hara-Brill, feeling that she has some measure of control over her work means that she is constantly making choices about how to manage her time and her life. A former banking executive, Susan is a native of England. She lived in India for a while and has traveled extensively. When she and her husband, Adam, were married, they finally began thinking about putting down roots. As a freelance illustrator, Adam was a seasoned veteran at coping with the demands of an independent work style. In 1990, after researching a number of communities around the country, Susan and Adam decided to relocate from New York City to Chapel Hill, North Carolina. Soon after making their move, Susan became pregnant with their daughter Rachel. After taking on some part-time work, Susan decided to begin a typing and desktop publishing service out of her home. Building a new life in a community where she didn't know a soul, having a new baby, and trying to start a new business hasn't been easy. Susan talks about how she has approached her new life with a feisty resourcefulness that has won her both new friends and new work:

"I hadn't taken fully into account just what working for a large corporation actually meant when I left my job. They own you for forty hours a week, and in return they give you A, B, C, and D. I was very concerned about giving all of this up. At the same time, this move to North Carolina has really brought home to me what the trade-off is and what you give up when you work for someone else. As far as I'm concerned, it just isn't worth it. I am gaining tremendous satisfaction from being my own resource and making the choices I need to make. When I was at the bank, most of what I complained about were things I didn't have control over. Now I have control, and even more important, I am it. If I screw up, I suffer. If I make a mistake, it's not the bank that suffers, or some department in the bank. It's me—I immediately suffer the consequences of a bad move or the rewards of a good one. And I've discovered that I'm not built the way I thought I was."

In Susan's case, having control means taking responsibility for her actions and making choices—choosing at any moment to do things in a way that works in terms of the life that she and her husband are trying to build together. At one point, her newfound sense of independence "really changed something for me," recalls Susan. "One day I was organizing some of my papers, and I suddenly realized, This is my own filing cabinet. I can set it up any way I want. I can organize my home and my office any way I want. This gave me a tremendous feeling of freedom. If I did something one way and it didn't work, it didn't really matter, because I could do it some other way. There is a freedom about this structure that really works for me. My preference would be to have a lot of paid work over the weekend so I can do other things during the week, when everyone else is working. Ultimately the daytime may be my time off and nighttime and weekends may be my work time."

To make this open-ended approach work actually takes careful planning and resourcefulness. Without discipline it's easy to let the choices you have about management overwhelm you. When this happens, it's easy to squander the time you have and let it slip through your fingers instead of using it most productively. As Susan points out, "You're continually laying tracks and you always have to have the next move or possible moves you want to make identified. And you need lists and agendas of things you want to have happen. But you also have flexibility; when I find that I am not getting something done or that I don't want to do it, then I stop. So I am always doing what I'm doing by choice."

COURAGE: MANAGING YOUR FEARS

"Courage is doing what you're afraid to do. There can be no courage unless you're scared." That's how Eddie Rickenbacker, an ace aviator in World War I, described his own ability to face danger and overcome obstacles. General George Patton expressed the same idea in eight brief, powerful words: "Courage," he said, "is fear holding on a minute longer." If courage is doing what you're afraid to do and holding on just when you feel like letting go, then that's also a pretty accurate recipe for success when it comes to running a business. We tend to think of entrepreneurs as consummate risk takers who boldly put everything on the line and carve out market niches where the rest of us fear to tread. While there's some truth to this image, it's also true that fear is the flip side of courage. As Eddie Rickenbacker said, you can't have one without the other. You may find this surprising. I know I did.

In looking at people who took the plunge into entrepreneurship and those who wanted to but couldn't, I always thought that the key difference between the two groups was the ability to conquer their fears. Those who actually started their own businesses had somehow overcome their fears about failure (or success), while the people who held back just couldn't take this step. Through my interviews, I learned that successful business owners don't overcome their fears, they learn to manage them. In talking to women of all ages and backgrounds, I found that everyone, without exception, had strong fears when they started. I also learned that the fears you experience in starting your own venture may change, but they never really go away. They are always with you. In fact, learning to live with fear and discomfort are a big part of what being an entrepreneur is all about. "To go into business for yourself," graphic designer Jordana Simpson points out, "you have to be willing to seize the moment. Sometimes people wait, either to be comfortable or not to be frightened. And you can forget about not being frightened. Anything that's big is going to frighten you. If you wait not to be frightened and if you wait until you're comfortable with the idea, then you can forget about it. Going into business for yourself is not about being comfortable and not about not being afraid. It's about doing what you want to do and following your dreams."

The Biggest Fear You'll Face

The single biggest obstacle anyone faces in starting their own business isn't lack of money, or lack of time, or lack of management skills. It's an emotional barrier, not a professional one: fear of the unknown. It's this fear that keeps most women—and men as well—from "going for it" and seizing the brass ring by taking control of their work lives. And it's this same fear that scares people most even after they've launched their businesses and begun to succeed.

Barbara Brabec, the author of *Homemade Money* and the small-business counselor we met earlier, has seen firsthand just how widespread this fear is, among both entrepreneurs and would-be business owners. In a survey conducted in twelve of her workshops, she asked people to write down the one thing that scared them most about starting their own business. She found that people with different backgrounds, different ages, and in different parts of the country all gave the same set of answers. Some said they were afraid of failing. Others said they were afraid of success and the changes it would bring. Still others were afraid of looking foolish and letting themselves and their families down. In Barbara's view, "what all these answers boil down to is that people are afraid of the unknown—especially unknown elements within themselves. When you start a business, you don't know whether you are capable of doing what you are telling yourself to do. And even if you've been successful in the past, you're still afraid, because you're on new ground. So you have a lot of personal fears about letting yourself down. . . . There are many emotional stumbling blocks to becoming an entrepreneur, but fear is probably the biggest. Many people don't tell anyone about these fears. A lot of women have confided to me about them in letters because they have no one else to talk to."

In making the move from corporation to cottage, fear of the unknown can be especially powerful and often paralyzing, precisely because the characteristics of a successful entrepreneur are so different from those required for advancement in the corporate world. How do you begin to get a handle on this fear so you can make it work for you, instead of against you? If you do decide to take the plunge and start your own business, the first step in the process is to acknowledge that fear of the unknown is going to be a powerful force in your life. Be honest with yourself about the depth of your fear and don't let your ego get in the way of getting the support you need to handle it; build a network of fellow entrepreneurs who understand what you're going through and talk about it with them. Instead of keeping your fears to yourself, force yourself to talk about them with a few friends and members of your family who you know have confidence in your ability to beat the odds.

Giving your fear a name also can help. If, as Barbara Brabec suggests, fear of the unknown really means fear of "unknown elements within yourself," then it's important that you pinpoint the inner lack or weakness that you believe might keep you from taking the plunge or succeeding in your chosen endeavor. Are you afraid you're not skilled enough or experienced enough, or that you're too old to start something new, or that you aren't enough of a risk taker, or that you don't have the perseverance to keep going when things get tough? What, exactly, is holding you back? Once you've pinpointed the root of your fear, you can begin to find ways to master it. On the other hand, if your fear remains vague and diffuse, it can undermine your confidence in your abilities to the point where it becomes a real stumbling block instead of an opportunity to strengthen your inner resources.

Another step you can take to master your fear is to transform the unknown into the known by taking the "knowledge is power" approach (see page 56) in order to boost your confidence. The more information you can gather and the more research you do about the business you want to enter, the stronger and more secure you'll feel about your abilities—and the more imaginary dragons you'll slay. So read books, send for brochures, look into training courses, attend seminars, and join an association of female business owners. Learn the basics of putting together a business plan and begin thinking about building a nest egg to finance your venture. At some point in this process, if you're serious about it, you'll cross an imaginary line and realize that you know more than you think you do. When this happens, you'll find that your drive to get out there and try it will be stronger than your fear of getting started. As Ann Hull puts it, "I think you should do a lot of research in the field you want to enter, but at some point, you should just do it. That's the most important step. No matter how long you think about it or fantasize about it, or idealize it or plan for it, at some point, you just have to go forward. I don't think there is anyone I know who's been successful who hasn't been willing and able to take that risk."

Healthy Fear

Remember that feeling fearful about the step you're taking is a healthy response. Reminding yourself that you're not alone and that everyone who ever started a business had fears of their own can help you manage your anxieties. When Ann Hull left her high-paying, comfortable job at the Modern Language Association, her biggest fears had to do with "insecurity, both financial and in terms of my professional identity." Ann felt she could be seriously damaging her earning power and that she was giving up a professional identity that she'd worked many years to build. After eighteen months of working on her own as a consultant for the Junior League, Ann's original fear had receded and was replaced by a new one: that she would lose the one big client around which she had built her new business and would have to start all over. When Jordana Simpson started her own graphics design firm, she faced a very different fear: that she wasn't experienced enough and that in the process of learning on the job, she would "damage a client" and lose a lot of money she couldn't afford to lose. In Lorraine Gerstein's case, the biggest fear she had to deal with was the fear of failure. Even though she had a great deal of confidence in her ability, she admits, "it was such a gamble. I guess I was most concerned about not making it. My biggest fear was the fear of failure—that my business wouldn't work, that I would think less of myself, and that I would suffer financially."

All of these fears—the fear of losing hard-won professional status, of losing a client, of suffering financially, of not knowing everything you need to know, of failing and damaging your sense of self-esteem—are not only natural, they're also rational. But perhaps even more important, you have to recognize that fear is a healthy response to the stressful situation you are voluntarily thrusting yourself into.

Everyone experiences some or all of these fears when starting a new business; it comes with the territory. As long as you keep reminding yourself of this and resist the temptation to isolate yourself and feel that you're all alone, you'll be taking a big step toward managing the anxieties that are par for the course when you start something new.

Creative Fear

Recognize that fear can be a creative force and a powerful incentive to succeed. Once you learn to accept your fear, according to the entrepreneurs I interviewed, you'll find that it actually can be a positive emotional tool—and a powerful motivator. It can energize and enliven you and give you the edge you need to succeed—*if, and only if,* you learn how to control and channel it. The better able you are to handle your fears by mastering your responses to them, the more focused you'll stay and the more open you'll be to new opportunities. On the other hand, if you let your fears and feelings overwhelm you, they can sabotage your efforts and sap your strength. In short, fear can be a building block or a stumbling block. It can teach you just how strong you are and push you to go forward and make things happen—or it can knock you flat emotionally. It all depends on whether you manage it or you let it manage you.

When Susan O'Hara-Brill and her husband relocated to Chapel Hill, North Carolina, neither of them had jobs. Soon after they moved, Susan became pregnant. They didn't really have any business contacts or know where their next dollar was coming from. It was a frightening time but also an exciting one. "A lot of my worst fears, especially the financial ones, haven't been realized," says Susan. "We are still here. We've continued breathing, and we still have a roof over our heads. We've developed a support network. Yes, a lot of what's happened to us has been scary and unpleasant, but I've found that we can take a lot more than we think we can."

Fear can be a powerful teacher if you don't let it overwhelm your sense of discovery. At some point, you have to be willing to live with your fear and say, OK, I'll see where this takes me. Maybe there's something more valuable down the road. If you let fear stop you, then you'll never make it as an entrepreneur. "When my friend Jordana went off on her own," Susan recalls, "she would tell me, 'I wake up every morning afraid.' And I remember thinking to myself, She's out on her own and she's having a good time; what's wrong with her? Now I understand what she was saying, because Adam and I wake up every morning feeling fear ourselves. And I've learned that what keeps you moving a lot of the time is fear. It's really a kind of baptism by fire. Because you can do great work and still be afraid. It never goes away. At the same time, many people say that when they're most afraid, they're most alive. I've felt that myself. When things are terrible and you're doing everything by the seat of your pants, you really get moving. You do what you have to do. Fear can be enlivening."

As Susan has found from experience, fear can be a creative force or it can immobilize you. It can keep you in bed with the covers pulled over your head or it can drive you to get up, get out, and do what you have to do to survive. It can impel you to use your ingenuity, make the most of your resources, and stretch yourself in ways that you wouldn't have to if you felt comfortable and secure. When she first started her business, Lorraine Gerstein's biggest fear was that she would try and fail. Once she'd been in business for more than five years and built a successful small company, she became afraid that "business would dry up" and that her referrals would stop, mainly because New Hampshire, where she works and lives, has been in a recessionary tailspin. Far from hampering her, this new fear has energized her. "Every time I get a new referral now," she says, "it really recharges my batteries." Lorraine's fear that she might not be able to keep her business afloat has renewed her determination to beat the odds and succeed, in spite of a tough economic climate. She also has found that managing her fear isn't just a personal issue, it's a business necessity. Now that her husband has joined her company and she has other employees depending on her, she can't afford to let her fear stop her from doing what she needs to do.

FANTASY: DAYDREAMING WITH INTENT AND PURPOSE

Daydreaming—setting yourself adrift in a sea of desire with no real goal in sight—may not seem like an especially useful activity to you right now, but it is. In fact, when it comes to launching a business, giving free rein to the playful, wishful side of your imagination can be one of the keys to success. Why? Because fantasizing and day-dreaming can put you in touch with the heartfelt desires that can inspire you to make your business a reality. And once you've actually taken the plunge and activated your desire, the emotional release that daydreaming offers can be a lifesaver. It can lift you above the pressures and problems you'll face on a daily basis and renew your will and passion to succeed. It can move you out of a "production mode," as Melinda Pancoast calls it, and reawaken your feelings about why you're in business and what you really want for yourself. Since it's so important, let's explore the power of fantasy in creating a self-structured life.

A Fantasy Is Not a Vision

Having a fantasy isn't the same as having a vision or visualizing. As we discussed earlier, having a business vision means having a goal, a mission, a sense of direction. But fantasizing about what you want is very different. When you fantasize and daydream about the business you want to start, you're engaging in a far more open-ended voyage of discovery. You have no goal to confine you, no limits to your imagined success, no shore to head for, no signposts to follow. Instead you are setting yourself free to go where your imagination takes you, and you are expanding your horizons. Yes, you are doing this with intent and purpose—to energize yourself and tap your creative powers. But you are doing it without a specific goal or direction in mind to inhibit you.

Fantasizing also is different from visualizing what you want. When you visualize, you are trying to impress an image on your mind of how something will happen and the steps you will take to make it happen. You are watching a drama unfold in your mind's eye in which you are center stage. You see yourself in a business meeting, for example, making a presentation. You see everything that happens in sharp detail—the way you are dressed, the poise and force with which you speak, the pleased reactions of the people you are trying to persuade to give you the work you want. You are preprogramming events so they will unfold in a way that fulfills a predetermined goal—to win an account, make a successful speech, and so on. In short, visualization is an effort to control events; it's also very goal-oriented. Fantasizing is the exact opposite. It's a tool designed to free you from trying to control events or reaching for a goal.

One of the questions I asked female entrepreneurs across the country was, "What was your fantasy when you started your business?" Everyone I spoke with understood exactly what I was talking about. Melinda Pancoast's fantasy was that she and her husband would move to Vermont, start their organizational consulting business, and be wildly successful instantly. They'd be meeting with clients left and right, making speeches, writing articles, and spreading the word about the power of their approach to productivity and profitability. Jordana Simpson's fantasy was that her management style and ability to nurture and empower her employees would have a tremendous impact on the workplace and allow her to become so successful that other business owners would embrace her approach. Debra Oppenheim's fantasy is that she and her partner will build a business that will be successful enough to attract young, talented executives who share their management philosophy and will take it over and continue to make it grow, once Debra and her partner have decided to move on.

For Melinda and Debra, the fantasies they created for themselves are on the way to becoming realities. Both of their businesses are growing and moving into a new, more mature phase of development. They are past the survival stage and moving forward. Jordana's fantasy has had a different fate. Somewhere along the line, she realized that it was beyond her power to realize and that while her way of doing business might change her own life, it wouldn't change the world. And so the fantasy that helped spark her entrepreneurial drive has been replaced by a new one: to explore a different facet of her creative talents by moving away from commercial graphic design and into product design, with the goal of designing beautiful, carefully crafted objects for the home. Some fantasies can come true and are meant to come true. Others are meant simply to inspire and energize. Yet, however fanciful and pie-in-the-sky it is, a fantasy can be a powerful emotional incentive for purposeful, successful action.

Using Fantasy

Make fantasy your friend, but don't get too carried away! If you are just beginning to think about starting a business of your own, then you're in a perfect position to take a blue-sky approach to your venture. Daydream about it with abandon. Brainstorm about it with friends. Set aside your concerns about the "production" aspect of the venture you're considering and focus intently on desire. What's your wildest fantasy about how successful you can be? About how you'll be spending your time, who you'll be working with, and how much money you'll be making? What kind of physical space do you see yourself working in? Is it a bright, sun-filled loft, with your computer station at one end and your living area at the other? Is it an old Victorian house that's been transformed into a quaint but professional space, one that speaks volumes about your sense of style and success? Or do you see yourself on the move, bustling happily from one client to another in a sporty roadster with mobile fax tossed on the backseat and cellular phone in hand? Do you see yourself working day and night feverishly on tight deadlines but with long periods of downtime in between, when you can indulge a hobby or even travel? Do you see yourself working from a geographic location that's dramatically different from the place you're living in today? Whatever your fantasy, it may be light-years away from the small closet that houses your computer today, or the corner of the basement that's your only safe haven right now from the rest of your family's living space. Forget about today, just kick back and enjoy imagining the most beautiful, luxurious, state-of-the-art work space possible. Who knows, some day soon you might just find yourself right in the middle of it!

If you've already taken the plunge and are feeling all of the slings and arrows that a struggling entrepreneur is heir to, then fantasizing is even more important. It's an emotional release that can help you handle the stress and daily pressures that you are bound to be feeling. So give yourself a break! Create your own private "fantasy island" by taking time each day, or at least once or twice a week, to indulge in a mental minivacation. Give yourself permission to be wildly successful—and to see yourself and your family reaping the rewards of that success. If you're feeling overwhelmed, force yourself to take some time to listen to an inspirational tape, to do a little window-shopping, or to leaf through a travel magazine and fantasize about taking a long, leisurely trip to some exotic locale with your hard-earned profits. In short, do whatever you need to do to remind yourself why you're working and what you really want from it all—and rekindle the desire that fuels your production. So let yourself go and give wings to your wildest dreams! After all, who's stopping you? What you fantasize about is up to you and solely for your own enjoyment. It's between you and your brain cells.

A word of caution here: it's important to remember that most fantasies should remain exactly that—fantasies. Trying to turn them into realities can be very costly, or even fatal. Just one example: A successful marketing executive in New York who decided to go into publishing fantasized zealously about the type of environment she wanted to work in. She saw herself in a small but beautifully appointed office on Park Avenue with a small but dedicated staff working contentedly by her side. She saw herself power dressing, lunching casually but intently with editors, and making deals. And Park Avenue is exactly where she located her company and hired her staff. Things perked along nicely for about eight months, until she began to realize that her pricey office and dedicated staff were eating up all of her profits and threatening to put her out of business. In order to survive, she had to make a decision to give up the costly fantasy she'd indulged in for almost a year and make the sacrifices required to keep her business afloat. That meant closing her Park Avenue office, letting her staff go, and moving back home to work out of her basement with cast-off furniture from her teenage son's room. And that's exactly what she did. The moral of the story? Think wild but don't *go* wild—unless you're already wildly successful.

4

Reshaping Your Business Identity

We all have different aspects of ourselves we want to develop. But you have to get out there and make it happen. Don't wait for opportunities to come to you—you've got to go to them. And create some new ones for yourself as well.

—*Joyce McClure*

At this stage in your career, you already may have invested considerable time, talent, and energy in acquiring the skills, nurturing the relationships, and mastering—or at least surviving—the cultural politics that have contributed to your corporate identity. In thinking about reshaping your business image, you may, understandably, have very mixed emotions. You may be tired of corporate game playing, the glass ceiling, and not being paid what you're worth. And you may feel disenchanted with the way in which your hard work and creativity have been undervalued or, worse still, dismissed with a quick fall of the corporate ax. At the same time, it's only natural that you should feel extremely attached, both emotionally and professionally, to the professional image you've created. In choosing to make the move from corporation to cottage, you may feel that you're "copping out" by making a choice to step off the corporate ladder in mid-career, instead of going the distance and advancing or fighting your way to the top.

If these concerns strike a chord, then I have some good news— and some bad news. The good news is that no matter how dramatic a change you make in your work style, *there's no need to totally abandon the professional identity you've developed in pursuing your corporate career.* Your old professional persona isn't something you take on and off like a coat. To move from employee to entrepreneur, you don't have to say, This or that is a part of my old life and I'm starting a new one now. I have to let go of everything I've done and start again from whole cloth. Instead of this drastic approach, your goal will be to take key aspects of your corporate identity and weave them into a new pattern. Yes, you are refashioning your image as a business-person, but the new identity you're creating is firmly rooted in your past experience and success. At its core, this process involves integrating the old and new rather than breaking away from and rejecting the past.

So the good news is that you don't have to start over from scratch; you can take advantage of all you've learned working for someone else in order to create a new, more satisfying, self-structured life for yourself. And the bad news? Crafting a new business identity will demand a serious commitment of time and energy. If you handle this challenge skillfully, you should enjoy a sense of continuity and make the transition from employee to business owner with relative ease. If you find yourself struggling through this transition, you run the risk of plunging yourself into a full-blown career crisis. The key to success lies in sorting out what facets of your old identity to retain and build on and what you need to redefine. Making these decisions can be confusing. So before we explore the tools you'll need to create your new business image, let's talk about what you'll have to surrender.

WHAT YOU WILL GIVE UP

Your Corporate Mind-set

If there's any employee-turned-entrepreneur who's qualified to talk about changing your corporate identity and status, it's Jan Berg. A seasoned strategic planner and turnaround specialist for more than thirty years, Jan pursued a highly successful corporate career. So successful, in fact, that in 1983 she was chosen by *Savvy* magazine as one of the top twenty corporate women in America. At the time, she was working for General Electric. During her long sojourn in the corporate world (interrupted several times by her own business ventures), Jan worked for an impressive list of blue-chip companies, including IBM, AT&T, Ernst & Young, Westinghouse of Canada, and U.S. West. At Ernst & Young, for example, she was a management consultant involved in large-scale systems studies. During a stint as vice president of the Vancouver Stock Exchange, she managed a massive reorganization and turnaround. At MacMillan Blodel she made a career shift, moving away from computers and entering the field of strategic planning. After MacMillan she joined Heublein as its first female vice president. She later joined General Electric as a strategic planner and eventually was recruited by U.S. West, where she was appointed chief financial officer of its cellular phone company. In five years, she built the business from a $10 million to a $110 million operation. Then, as the result of a corporate shake-up at U.S. West, she found herself "stretched out and burned out." That's when she left the corporate world.

Today Jan works out of her home in a small town of five thousand people about two hours outside Seattle as a strategic planning consultant and prosperity counselor. She's traded her business lunches for long walks on the beach with her dogs and an entirely new work life. Here's how she describes the move from employee to entrepreneur: "There's a whole different mind-set you need to play the corporate game. When you're raised and groomed for success in the corporate world, a lot of what you do is based on style—what you say and the clothes you wear. You also have tons of support: you have secretaries running around and as you go up the corporate ladder, you can always find someone to do the things you don't want to do. When you become an entrepreneur and start your own business, I think the biggest shock comes when you find out that you have to do everything. You can spend a whole day stuffing envelopes. Then there's the mindset it takes to be an entrepreneur: you're living on the edge.

"There are also twinges of ego. Today I no longer need to buy $500 shoes and spend $500 or $1,000 on business suits and all the trappings. But when I go into Seattle, there's still a part of me that says, Wouldn't it be nice to buy this or that? But it's not really the prestige I miss so much as the excitement of working with senior people on very complex, creative situations or deals. There's a kind of synergy, a level of energy and interaction that's very appealing—the buzz you get occasionally when there's a crisis, but especially when you're working on something complex. Sometimes the whole is greater than the sum of its parts. It's exciting when everyone is working together and you're pushing each other to create something that is more than the original concept you began with. This is one aspect of the corporate life that I miss. Right now, while it's not impossible, I'm finding that it's hard to find people I can interact with at the same level of creativity.

"Remember, too, that the corporate world looks down on the little Joe, the innovator and entrepreneur who works alone. There is a whole I'm-better-than-you-are attitude that people in companies have because they've taken on the identities of the organizations they work for. And when you make the transition to the cottage world, all of that is stripped away. You are not just standing out there alone—you're naked."

Camaraderie

For Sara Harrell, the sense of aloneness Jan Berg describes is the toughest obstacle she's faced in building her free-lance writing career in Phoenix. "I didn't expect the loneliness of being on my own to be so great," she recalls. "I had to get used to being separated from working in a group of people and not being able to depend on them or enjoy their camaraderie on a daily basis." Even today, after more than ten years of working for herself, Sara still finds herself struggling with these feelings. "The biggest problem I face now is that I've gotten so used to solitude. Because I'm not married and I haven't had a long-term relationship, I've found that it's really easy to get caught up in your own world. And to have the four walls of your house become that world. The uneven cash flow you experience just adds to this feeling. You find yourself asking, What should I do? I have to force myself to get out—I literally have to make myself leave my house from time to time. I am on the board of an advertising organization in Phoenix, which helps. And there's a farmer's market

I go to each week. I'm also one of the movie industry's biggest profit centers."

Your Power Base

For Ann Hull, surrendering the power base as well as the perks that she enjoyed as convention director of the Modern Language Association (MLA), the largest academic conference in the world, is the biggest sacrifice her new work style has demanded. She and a small staff ran the MLA's annual meetings—multimillion-dollar, four-day marathon events that involved up to 15,000 attendees, 200 exhibit booths, 900 meetings, and as many as 2,500 presenters. Since she was the key person selecting meeting sites and handling all of their logistics, she and her family enjoyed some very attractive travel benefits as part of her job. In 1989 Ann decided that ten years with the MLA was enough, and at fifty-two she decided to start her own business. The changes she experienced when she left her full-time job to become an independent contractor have been dramatic. Ann recalls, "My biggest fears had to do with insecurity, with financial concerns, and with giving up my identity. In my field, I had status and I found it hard to watch someone else move into my corporate identity. As I saw someone else using my title, I found myself saying, That's me. There was a certain twinge and a feeling of loss. I had a lot of power within the MLA's organization structure. Since the convention was its biggest activity and I headed that, I was considered an important person by the MLA membership. When I told individual members I was leaving, they were even more shocked than the people inside my office. They said things like, 'How can you leave? You *are* the MLA!' "

As a consultant to the Junior League, now about 80 percent of her business, Ann views her role as that of "a professional advisor and implementer." She helps League members define their goals and then she does the best she can "to set up a structure to meet those goals and make things happen. But I am one step removed . . . I am not part of the power structure at all. I'm plugged in, but I'm not part of the hierarchy. The disadvantage is that sometimes employees are confused. They don't see where I fit into the organization, and that can cause problems. . . . This is one of the negatives of my situation today: as a consultant, you do not have an unquestioned power base. So you have to negotiate much more. You have to persuade people within the organization to cooperate with you. Having to work this way can be a drawback, although I find that it is compensated for by the fact that you have independence and an identity that's your own. You also don't get the same kind of feedback on performance when you're a consultant. Sometimes I also miss having a staff and the perks I had at the MLA. I did a lot of traveling and I had major concessions with airlines and hotels. They were terrific; I never traveled anywhere in the back of the plane. Now I do. But that's one of the trade-offs."

Financial Security

In Chapter 1, Debra Oppenheim talked about the feeling of exhilaration that starting her own business has given her. At the same time, during the start-up stage of her business, she found herself coping with some major financial anxieties. "When someone starts a business, especially a service business, there is a certain amount of naivete involved. You have the feeling that God will take care of all little children and me, too, if I behave myself. When I look back on it now, I realize how really gutsy it was for me to do this after fifteen years of experience with large firms. The biggest problems I've faced have centered around money and time allocation. When you have no regular salary, you are at the mercy of your clients when it comes to getting paid, and you really have to watch your cash flow very carefully. . . . I've had many sleepless nights over all this. Sometimes you lie awake and ask yourself, 'OK, I'm using up all the revenue that's coming in, so what will I do for an encore? Can I keep the pipeline supplied?' The money is there. There is enough to take me into next year. So I know that some of my anxiety is excessive and that the insecurities I feel are sometimes unfounded."

As Jan, Sara, Ann, and Debra know firsthand, leaving a prestigious, well-paying corporate job isn't easy; it involves some serious professional sacrifices on your part. When you surrender your corporate status, or find it taken from you, you also lose the "buzz," the emotional high you can get from working as part of a talented team on creative projects that you care about. There's also the loneliness that Sara Harrell talked about, the feeling, as Ann Hull described it, that you're suddenly an outsider looking in. Then there's the issue of money. The security of a paycheck is probably the most important professional asset that you're surrendering. The kind of anxiety that Debra Oppenheim voiced about making it financially is all too familiar.

At the same time, reshaping your business identity can be an exciting, challenging, and extremely rewarding process. It can enhance your confidence in your abilities, give you flexibility and freedom over your time and work, and encourage you to fine-tune your networking skills and expand your personal support system. And, while starting a business certainly involves serious financial risks, it also offers the potential for greater financial rewards. But reaping these benefits isn't an overnight process. You'll have to be prepared to stretch yourself constantly and to make some tough decisions about what aspects of your current image will contribute to your success as an entrepreneur—and what you'll need to jettison. (See also appendix 1, The Trade-offs—What You'll Give Up if You Leave Your Job and What You'll Gain as an Entrepreneur). At this stage, let's take a closer look at the tools you'll need to reshape your business identity:

LEADERSHIP: BUILDING AN ''INTERNAL'' POWER BASE

Your success in making the move from employee to entrepreneur will depend on creating a strong internal power base for yourself, one that's grounded in a deep sense of personal self-worth and professional ability. Building this inner core of strength and security will require you to make some fundamental changes, both in the way you do business and in your mind-set—how you think of yourself as a businessperson. During your career as a corporate executive, you managed projects, handled budgets, solved problems, and trained and worked with staff members, colleagues, and vendors. As an entrepreneur, you'll still be performing many of these same roles, but with one very big difference: *you are running the show*. At a stroke, you've transformed your professional identity from that of a follower-manager to a leader-entrepreneur. Making this transition demands that you reinvent yourself professionally, both in your own eyes and in the eyes of those who've worked with you in the past. Doing this isn't just a matter of printing new stationery and setting up shop. It takes some fundamental changes in the way you perceive and handle your role as a businessperson.

As a manager, for example, you were part of a highly structured, finely tuned hierarchy, with a history, culture, resources, and identity that you shared and drew power from. As an entrepreneur, you are an organization of one, or two, or a handful of people. You have no history, except for your personal accomplishments. You also have no culture to draw sustenance from; you're creating it as you go. Your resources are personal, not institutional. As a corporate manager, consensus, compromise, and team playing were among your key tools for success. As a leader-entrepreneur, you have to make things happen largely through personal initiative and drive; you have to convey your vision, take a stand, and take charge. As a manager, you often played the role of catalyst and facilitator. As a leader-entrepreneur, your primary responsibility is that of creator and new-business generator. You don't just react to goals or projects imposed on you by others, you shape those goals and projects and must inspire those you work with to believe in their value and add their energy to yours. As a manager, coordinating activities and balancing competing demands were key functions. As a leader-entrepreneur, coming up with new ideas and fresh approaches will be vital to your survival. At times you'll have to throw things off balance, force action, and pressure yourself and others. As a manager, imposing order and keeping things under control were key facets of your job. As an entrepreneur, you'll have to learn to live with a degree of chaos and develop a tolerance for ambiguity and uncertainty about your security and work-related events. You'll have to handle unforeseen crises, cash flow problems, and a feast-or-famine work pattern that can strain your resources.

In short, as a corporate employee, your authority and status flowed from an external power base outside yourself; it was conferred by and "borrowed" from the organization you worked for. As an entrepreneur just starting a new business, your power is internal. It flows from your personal ability to build on past experience, to innovate, and to inspire confidence in your talent and drive. Any influence you exert is not the result of your title or corporate identity. Rather, it is the result of your success in persuading others to believe in you and share your point of view and in negotiating for the work and resources you need to build your fledgling enterprise.

FLEXIBILITY: EXPANDING YOUR SELF-IMAGE

Building an inner core of security and strength will depend largely on your capacity to move beyond your existing ideas about who you are, what you've done, and how you've done it. To succeed as an entrepreneur, you're going to have to push past the boundaries of your current self-image by adopting a more expansive, more fluid view of yourself and what you have to offer. You will need to rescope your skills and experience, take on different kinds of work, and think creatively about new ways to "package" yourself. Challenging long-held and even cherished ideas that you have about yourself as a professional may turn out to be an extremely difficult, even painful, process. And doing things that make you uncomfortable is never the easiest way to acquire a new skill. At the same time, this process can be enormously energizing and freeing. It can force you to confront and overcome limitations you may have imposed upon yourself or had imposed on you by people you worked with, or even your own family and friends.

Remember Joyce McClure? When she moved to Maine, Joyce had a nest egg large enough to allow her to explore her new community, and that's exactly what she spent a few months doing. Eventually she opened a small office on Main Street, which she closed a year or so later after finding that "it was very tough to make a living, particularly by yourself. Maine is the land of entrepreneurs, but none of them have any money to spend. So I sort of struggled along, but I could see that my funds were starting to run out."

At this point, Joyce made contact, through a friend, with a man in town who had a lot of business connections. Impressed with her business background and staying power, he became a sort of informal mentor. As a result of this contact, Joyce began teaching marketing and business planning—something she had never done in New York. She also began running seminars for the University of Maine on marketing, new business, and public relations. This work led her to realize that there was a real need across the state for basic business information. Eventually she came up with the idea of doing a weekly radio program aimed at small business owners and persuaded a community radio station to give her air time for the show. This exposure, in turn, put her in touch with many businesspeople, she became well known around the state as an expert on marketing, and she became very active in professional and trade associations.

Over the next year, Joyce found herself reassessing her self-image. As she puts it, "I have a much broader identity here in Castine than I ever had in New York. I found that I was adding on, I was subtracting, and I was deciding what I wanted to do when I grew up all over again. At the same time, I've found that part of this process has involved a strengthening of my conviction that I know what I know. . . . In New York, when you work for a large agency, you can feel beaten down because you always have to justify your existence. You are only as good as the next placement you make. I was exhausted by this process—that was one reason I had to make the break. And because of it, I had never really understood how much knowledge I had. In fact, during my move, a very good friend of mine said to me, 'You've never had the confidence in yourself and your abilities that all of us have.' So I created a new sense of myself in knowing what I know and in knowing that what I have to offer is valuable to a lot of people. I'm still learning how to make a buck off it. Even so, it has been very empowering to know what I know. It has given me great strength."

"Adding on" and "subtracting" and "deciding what I wanted to do when I grew up all over again"—what Joyce is describing here is the ongoing process of reshaping her business identity in response to her new environment and evolving work style. During this stage of her new business start-up, Joyce began to gain fresh insight into her experience and skills and found herself deriving great strength from "knowing what I know." Joyce was beginning to build an internal power base. As this inner core of confidence began to grow, Joyce was free to explore different dimensions of the public relations and marketing skills she'd acquired over twenty years in corporate life. It was at this point that she came up with the idea of a radio show. Eventually the new business image Joyce was creating for herself allowed her to take another important step: she applied for and won a position as dean of enrollment management of Thomas College, a small one-hundred-year-old business school in Waterville, Maine. Today, she handles all aspects of the college's marketing program. This arrangement has given her the stability she needs to continue developing her skills as a small business advisor and marketing specialist.

RESHAPING your business image also requires that you let go of self-imposed limitations that can prevent you from doing what you need to do to succeed. When you are it—when everything starts or stops with you, as it does in a small business—you learn very quickly that you can and will do things you never thought yourself capable of in order to survive. If you don't know how to do something and if you need it badly enough, then you'll figure out how to get it done. The results may surprise even you. You may discover skills and talents you never knew you had and inner resources you never would have tapped if you remained captive to your old image of yourself. You also may find that what you thought you wanted to do when you first started your business is very different from what you actually enjoy doing, once you get going.

"The thing that really shocked me was that what I went into business for is not what I ended up loving most," says Jordana Simpson. "My fantasy was that I was going to transform the workplace—I wanted to create a certain working environment for myself and the people working with me by using my graphic design skills. But I discovered that I loved interacting and being with people far more than I liked being locked in my little office and designing. I found that my creativity happened not at the drawing board, but in my dialogues with clients. At one point, I suddenly realized that my business wasn't going to be about graphic design; it was going to be about something else very different. I discovered new skills and found I loved working with them more than doing what I originally set out to do. I think a lot of people go into business for themselves the way I did—by doing what they did when they worked for someone else. You have to be prepared for some big shocks about yourself."

Once on her own, Jordana not only discovered some untapped skills, she also found herself in the middle of a far more difficult career change than she had bargained for. Jordana started out thinking she wanted to do one thing and quickly learned that she didn't like it as much as she thought she would. But in order to help her business survive, she had to take responsibility for everything—even the aspects of her work that she didn't really like doing or was afraid of. As an entrepreneur, she quickly found that the buck stopped with her. "You can't say, I wasn't good at math when I was five years old or twelve, and therefore I don't have to be responsible for it now," warns Jordana. "If you do, you're in big trouble. These things come back to haunt you when you're working for yourself. So you have to push yourself to get over the initial fear and to gain a certain degree of understanding, if not mastery, before you can responsibly give the job to someone else. But at first, there is nothing you can give away. You have to do it all—what you like to do and what you don't."

EMPOWERMENT: TAKING RESPONSIBILITY FOR YOUR GROWTH

When Jan Berg embarked on a journey of self-discovery and surrendered the self-imposed barriers she'd erected during thirty years of corporate life, she found herself in the midst of a major emotional upheaval. As mentioned earlier, Jan is a seasoned strategic planner who worked for a raft of blue-chip companies. In the late 1980s, she decided to take a sabbatical from corporate life that turned into a spiritual quest and led her to a far more satisfying, but radically different, work and life style. Today the cottage industry she created is based on three or four interrelated activities. She still does management consulting and strategic planning, but she now focuses on helping nonprofit organizations and individuals as well as corporations. She's involved in fund-raising and grant writing. She also developed what she calls a "New Age prosperity product," gives workshops on prosperity, and is involved in holistic healing.

The foundation for the new work that Jan does today actually evolved from a series of major career changes she made during which she forced herself to learn new skills and to challenge her corporate image. "I was on a track where I was continually pushing the frontier," says Jan. "I've made three or four major career switches and entered whole new fields. When I went into cellular phones, for instance—an industry I didn't know anything about—I went from being a strategic planner to a chief financial officer."

As Jan sees it, charting a new direction for her life and work has been "a process of my own empowerment, based on the revelation that I was giving a lot of power away to the corporations I worked for." But even the major career changes Jan had made didn't fully prepare her for the anxiety and fear she experienced when she left the corporate world at this stage in her working life. Making the transition from corporation to cottage took far more time and emotional energy than she had ever expected. "I thought it would take three months, but it's taken me almost three years," she notes. In Jan's case, there was a great deal of anger and pain involved in this process. She had found herself feeling unappreciated and even abused by the corporations she worked for; this was true especially of her last job, where she was virtually forced out as the result of a takeover.

As part of her severance arrangement, Jan received outplacement counseling, which lasted three or four months. The placement people she worked with challenged her to ask herself some tough questions about what her next move should be. During this period, Jan felt so emotionally drained that she couldn't really focus on her career. "I knew I needed to do something different and that I was going to make a big transition, but I didn't know what it would be." Initially Jan planned to take a year-long break and write a book. Eventually she found that she loved the freedom that a cottage work style offered. Slowly she began crafting a new, more independent identity for herself. Her focus shifted radically, from externally driven corporate goal setting to "inner work on the spiritual path." In pursuing this work, she has found that her "creativity has gone up exponentially. My whole intuitive and expressive side is coming out in all different forms in my life—something that never happened when I was only paying attention to the logic-based male-behavior business model. I never wrote poetry. Now I sit down and write poetry. I never sang. Now I sit and write songs. Management always depends heavily on planning and controls. I've thrown out a lot of detail planning and I've found that the more control I throw out, the better my work is. Because I'm internally motivated, my work flows without pressure. I don't have to worry about deadlines or create false crises to keep myself productive.

"I have gone through times when I didn't know where the money I needed was going to come from. But I discovered that it was really just my own fear that I was responding to. And I've learned that this process is all about letting go of my fear and getting down to the things that are really important. I've also found that if I really needed something, it was always there, if I went inside and asked. The resources were always there. It was tough for me to learn to ask; I had to let go of my old image. There were times when I sat and cried—my world had fallen apart. But then I realized that it *had* to fall apart, because I had to let go of my old world in order to create a new life for myself. The rewards of the new life I've been able to build for myself are spiritual and inner-driven; they've taken me from anger to calm, from fear to safety. Now that I've discovered a new way of working and living, there's no going back to the old way, because the benefits of my new life are beyond belief: peace of mind, creativity, and knowingness."

In Jan Berg's case, reinventing a new, more satisfying work style involved abandoning the traditional business model that she'd embraced during her corporate career and creating a new model based on the creative, intuitive, even spiritual aspects of her personality. Surrendering her old image of herself and rebuilding her world proved to be a long and difficult process; it took her years instead of months. It was also far more intense than she had anticipated. Jan's experience underscores just how important it is to realize that your corporate identity springs from a powerful emotional undercurrent. Reshaping your business image is bound to be an emotionally demanding and disruptive experience. Just like Jan, you may find that it takes far more time than you think to let go, pull yourself together, and redirect your energies. As we'll see later, it's a mistake to underestimate the emotionality involved in giving up a corporate identity in which you've invested great energy and creativity. It's essential that your transition from corporation to cottage includes time to decompress, reorient yourself, and deal with the emotional fallout of your move.

Objectivity: Transforming Passion into Performance

As Jan Berg's experience proves, it's important to recognize that your corporate identity doesn't just reflect your business expertise; it also mirrors your emotional makeup. It's based not only on your skills, experience, and sense of competence, but also on your mental attitude—how you think about yourself as a person, your sense of self-esteem, and your beliefs and value system. Reshaping your business identity requires that you master your emotions, just as you master other aspects of your business life. Translating your passion into performance and channeling your emotional energies into sound, objective business decisions is one of the biggest challenges you'll face. Emotionalism can be both an asset and a liability in a business context. Conveying the passion, enthusiasm, and intensity that you bring to your new venture will be vital to your success. But letting your emotions overwhelm your objectivity or cloud your business decisions and relationships can prove to be dangerous and counterproductive.

In the view of Jayne Tear, a specialist in gender dynamics, female entrepreneurs face a special challenge in managing their emotions in the business arena. "Business is a game," she says. "And whatever image suits you, you have to take your field, your personality, and your style into account and reach some kind of compromise. You are no longer representing the corporation you once worked for; you're representing yourself. Don't do anything by chance. Whether you are choosing your letterhead or your clothing, choose it by design. You are creating an identity that might sell you to fame and fortune. And at the very least, it might pay your rent for the rest of your life. And that's no small thing. So choose it. Design it. Think it out. Don't let a detail just happen. Think strategically. I've found again and again that men are more intuitive about thinking strategically in business, while women spend more time thinking about the emotions involved.

"In my experience, women, more than men, tend to bring a model based on personal dynamics into their business interactions. By this I mean they tend to use a model based on how they feel about another person and to make assumptions about how that person feels about them. But your feelings, your opinions, the degree to which you like someone else and are liked by them, and your judgments about their character are all issues of personal dynamics. While they are crucial in social life, it's important to remember that the business world is not a social world. The business world is an agenda-based world. It is a world based on achieving desired results and not necessarily on having a pleasant experience. Women tend to react to people in terms of how they feel about their personalities and character, rather than assessing them in terms of the lack or presence of skills needed to further their agendas as businesswomen. This tendency becomes more treacherous for women who start their own businesses, because they are often working alone and representing themselves; there may be no one to remind them to focus on results and agendas rather than on personalities. So when you are out there networking and making contacts, it's easy to slide into a social dynamic and ask yourself, Do I like this man or woman? How do I feel about them? Is it a pleasant experience to be with them? These are fine questions to ask if you want to make a social friend, but they are secondary questions to ask as a business owner."

Translating your passion into performance requires that you think strategically about your business and avoid letting your personal feelings dictate your business relationships. It also requires that you master the way you respond emotionally to business situations on a day-to-day basis. You may find yourself facing bigger crises and more pressing problems than you ever bargained for. How you choose to react to those circumstances will be critical to your survival and to your ability to take charge of your business and make it succeed. Spending too much time taking your emotional temperature and talking about how you feel about your immediate business problems can make you seem less than professional and not in full control of your time and resources. Of course, it's important to share your fears and concerns, but not with everyone you talk to and not all the time.

As Jayne Tear puts it: "Reactive emotions are like ticker tape. The tape is running whether you are standing there reading it or letting it fall on the floor. Men tend to know this and they don't spend a lot of time processing the feelings they're having. Everyone works. Everyone has many different feelings when they get up in the morning. There's no way to predict what emotional state you'll be in on a given day. And whatever your internal state is, there is no way you can change it. But you can create your behavior. You can separate how you feel from how you're going to act. And learning how to do this by training yourself internally is an invaluable business skill. Our feelings and our external behavior are two separate domains. For the most part, we do not have a lot of control over how we feel, but we can develop the skills to be not only in control, but extraordinarily creative when it comes to our behavior. This isn't being phony, it's really high-level, skillful living."

Without a doubt, it's important to respect our feelings and to realize just how important they are to our business identity. And getting in touch with one's emotions and finding a business outlet to express them is largely what a self-structured life is all about. But remember that your feelings and your actions may have to be separate but equal when it comes to running your business. It's one thing to acknowledge your inner emotional state and another to let that inner state prevent you from doing what you need to do to build relationships, sell business, and inspire confidence in the people who work for you. Keeping your emotions under control doesn't mean you have to check them at the door of your office. It just means that there's a time to focus on them and a time to concentrate on the business at hand, regardless of how you're feeling at the moment.

GOAL SETTING: DEVELOPING A BUSINESS ROAD MAP

Whatever product or service you intend to offer, writing a business plan is an essential step in reshaping your business identity. In fact, a plan that accurately captures your vision is one of the most powerful tools you have to help you make the leap from employee to entrepreneur. There are numerous books and seminars available to help you master the fundamentals of developing a business plan. The SBA, for example, runs intensive prebusiness workshops that can help you map out your strategic vision, prepare a budget, plot cash flow projections, and pinpoint potential markets. Since you can easily seek out detailed guidelines about the mechanics of plan design, we're not going to cover that here. What we are going to look at is how and why crafting a plan of action for your venture can help you think and act like an entrepreneur.

"If you were going to take a cross-country tour on your summer vacation," says Lonah Birch of the SBA, "then you would take a road map with you and use it to chart your route. That's exactly what a business plan is—it's a road map. It's also your lifeline to the outside world. Your business plan should be a living document. It should be flexible and change; you may not meet every business goal that you set for yourself. But if you don't have goals in your business life, then you can't establish benchmarks so you'll know where you're going and be able to measure how far along you are."

Many people find that writing a business plan is difficult; they see it as a roadblock rather than a road map. Putting pen to paper and trying to capture our dreams and goals in words can be intimidating; it forces us to confront the risks our business involves, as well as its potential for growth and profit. It also can bring to light the weaknesses we have to overcome as well as the strengths we have to offer. It's not surprising, then, that most of the women I interviewed didn't put together a business plan before they launched their businesses; instead they started more or less by the seat of their pants. If this describes your situation, then you probably have plenty of reasons for not having developed a written road map for your business. For one thing, you may be financing your venture on your own or with the help of family and friends, and you may feel that writing a plan isn't necessary because you aren't looking for invest-ment dollars from a bank or venture capital fund. Or you may be working as a sole proprietor or partnership and feel that because you're basically doing the same work independently that you once did for someone else, you don't need a plan. But whatever your situation, some formal goal setting is essential for many reasons.

Putting Yourself in the Driver's Seat

The very act of developing a business plan, even a loose one, can help you take charge of the new phase of your working life you're entering. Why? First, because it signals, both to yourself and to others, that your commitment to your new venture is real—you're prepared to move beyond thinking and talking about it to making it happen. Even if you're planning to approach only your family and friends for financial help, a business plan can reassure them that you intend to take an objective, professional attitude toward their investment dollars. Second, the very act of putting your goals, re-sources, and financial outlook down on paper can help you clarify your vision and pinpoint your assets and liabilities while your venture is still on the drawing board. Having some form of plan also helps you keep your eye on your long-term goal at a time when the day-to-day struggles of managing a start-up can threaten to overwhelm you. It also can help you get a realistic handle on your financial situation; even more important, it encourages you to look at your venture from an investor's perspective. And finally, a business plan is also a powerful communications tool; it can provide you with valuable insights into how, when, and where to market your product or service. For all of these reasons, it's very important that you take primary responsibility for developing your business plan. Even if you turn to accountants, lawyers, or a consultant for help in working out the details or writing a draft, be sure that when it's finished, it's *your* plan, not theirs.

Using Your Business Plan As a Marketing Tool

A business plan is really about vision; it's also a valuable marketing tool. "Your family, your husband, and your friends—these are the people who are really committed to your life turning out the way you want it to," says Jordana Simpson. "These are the ones who are going to lift you up and hold on to your vision for you, even when you're not up to it yourself. So ask them for help." Though it sounds deceptively simple, there's much to be said for this approach as a starting point. In a nutshell, having a vision of your business means knowing who you are, what you are planning to do, why you are doing it, whom you are going to help, how you are going to reach those people, and how much it is going to cost. So while we tend to think of a business plan as a formal document, it's really a tool for capturing your vision on paper and convincing people that you have the management skills and resources to translate that vision into a viable, potentially profitable enterprise.

That's why a clear, well-crafted statement describing your business vision should be the focal point of your plan. In a few sentences or paragraphs, it should communicate your primary business goals and how you propose to achieve them. While investors, by definition, have their eye on the bottom line, even they attach a great deal of importance to this statement. They want to know how your vision relates to your personal goals and what you want for yourself from the venture you're proposing. They also want to know whether your goals are in synch with industry trends and consistent with their objectives.

When Melinda and Malachi Pancoast launched their business together, they spent a great deal of time thinking about what their mission was and how they would describe it to prospective clients and other members of the business community. Eventually they were able to communicate the essential aspects of their business in a brief statement:

Milestone Management Consulting Services, a full-service management consulting resource headquartered in Burlington, Vermont, has been providing consulting services to small and emerging businesses in the United States and Canada since 1986. Our educational programs are designed to increase employee productivity and satisfaction in the workplace, resulting in significant increases in profitability, sales, and product quality.

Unique to Milestone Management Consulting Services is our proprietary technology in managerial effectiveness and organizational transformation. Our approach puts life into the hopes, dreams, and visions of people at work and translates their intentions into effective action.

In a few short sentences, Melinda and Malachi have described the work they do, who their market is, what benefits their approach offers, and the unique edge that their "proprietary" training techniques can give their clients. While the statement is succinct, it provides a wealth of information. It also communicates a clear sense of direction and purpose. That's what a mission statement is all about. Writing it may take you considerable time, but it is well worth the effort, since it can help you clarify your goals and get to the heart of your venture.

As Barbara Brabec points out, "Writing out a description of your business forces you to figure out what that business is really all about. To write it, you have to answer some important questions: If you are going to create a product, then who is going to do the actual work? Once you have created the product, who is going to package and distribute it? How are you going to advertise? Who is going to design all the materials you need to sell it? You may suddenly realize, To make this work, I'm going to need some help! Then you have to ask yourself, Where am I going to get the money to pay for it? A business plan forces you to make decisions that you would otherwise wait until the last moment to make. It also uncovers problems you are going to encounter down the line that you might not have thought about without it. It gives you a chance to prepare before they are dumped into your lap."

According to Barbara, there's an added benefit as well: a strong mission statement also can be a powerful marketing tool. "Once you have a working plan," she points out, "then you know something very important in terms of your marketing approach and your advertising copy and brochures. I used to tell people that I was a writer. When they asked me about my business, I'd say, 'I write books, a newsletter, and magazine columns, hold workshops, and do consulting on the side.' That was until I read a book by Herman Holtz, one of my favorite marketing writers. He said everyone needs a brief positioning statement that describes what they do. I thought about that and came up with the concept that 'I help people succeed in home-based businesses.' That's what I do. I am not a writer. I don't sell books. I help people succeed. Getting a handle on what I was really doing made a big difference in how I began to market. If you never write anything out, then you just don't have this perspective."

A Business Plan Should Be a Living Document

One of the reasons entrepreneurs may resist the whole idea of writing a business plan is that they think of it as a complicated formal document filled with pages of marketing statistics and financial data. While the typical plan submitted to a bank or investors' group tends to be detailed and ranges in length anywhere from twenty to fifty pages or more, your plan doesn't have to take this form. As Lonah Birch of the SBA noted earlier, it should be a "living document" that is dynamic and flexible enough to adapt to your changing goals and circumstances. It's not just a sheaf of paper that you put together and then leave on a shelf or in a desk drawer and forget about. Put it on your computer or find someone who can do this for you, so you can play with it and update it. Once you have something in print, keep a working copy in a looseleaf notebook, so you'll feel free to add to it as new ideas and new data come your way. Most people who take this approach to structuring a plan find that it changes from year to year—their experience grows, and they tap a new market and find that they have opened the door to a whole new audience for their product or service.

You can get still more mileage out of your plan by using it as a tool to direct and motivate you. Use it to set daily, weekly, and monthly goals for yourself and then check your progress against those goals. Take it to your banker or other business advisor and have them review it periodically, even if you are not looking for money at the moment, just to get feedback from an objective source. When you start thinking of your plan in this way, writing it will become a much more exciting and rewarding experience. A plan that's created using this approach also will help the people around you to better understand and contribute to the business vision you are working to realize. And when you find yourself in need of a major proposal or marketing brochure, you'll already have the information on tap.

Marketing: Getting the Word Out

Finding or creating a marketing niche and assessing the market potential of your product or service are vital steps in launching your new venture. They also are critical to reshaping your business identity. Coming up with the right message at the right time and finding the right markets for it are all key to success, whether you're IBM or a pocket-size desktop printing venture. Getting the word out about the benefits your new business offers is absolutely essential. How? By developing a marketing approach that plays to your strength and puts you in the path of new opportunities to build and expand your business. That's why cultivating a marketing mentality is part of your entrepreneurial arsenal.

The Name of the Game Is Communications

Whether you call it marketing, promotion, or even packaging, the real issue we're talking about here is *communications*. Communicating with your potential customers or clients is one of the biggest challenges you'll face as an entrepreneur. Yes, you may not be IBM or Apple Computer, or even Mrs. Fields Cookies. You may not have their name recognition, budget, or sales force. But on the plus side, you don't have to deal with their bureaucracies, spend millions on image advertising, or fend off their competitors. Learn to communicate creatively and consistently and you can be every bit as successful in your chosen market niche as the corporate giants are in theirs. Using the tools you'll need to build awareness about your background and your business may be a big stretch for you; they may even make you feel uncomfortable. If you do, then you have plenty of company. Some newly minted entrepreneurs find that they have a real flair for promoting their businesses and enjoy it tremendously. But these star marketers are the exception rather than the rule. Most new business owners find themselves swimming upstream when it comes to marketing and can bring themselves to do it only in fits and starts, usually when business threatens to dry up and they find themselves in a crisis situation. Some entrepreneurs find themselves so emotionally stressed by this role that they ignore it, hoping their product or service will magically find its own market niche.

"One of the biggest problems I see," says Caroline Hull, "[is that] people don't realize that when they start a business, they are responsible for getting the word out about it. Customers aren't going to come knocking on your door just because you have decided to become So and So Incorporated. You have to market yourself. You have to discipline yourself to market your product or service as part of your business plan. This is one of the biggest causes of business failure for entrepreneurial mothers, who just don't understand how essential an ingredient this is. That's why I concentrate heavily on this area in my newsletter [*ConneXions*]." Marketing isn't a big problem just for home-based mothers starting a business. Even corporate executives with MBAs and high-powered jobs have a tough time handling this area, according to Barbara Brabec, who also devotes a great deal of space in her newsletter, the *National Home Business Report*, to this topic. In fact, virtually every small business expert and entrepreneur I spoke with stressed the importance of effective marketing and pinpointed it as a major challenge. Lonah Birch of the SBA, for example, sees lack of marketing experience as a key issue for many of the female entrepreneurs she'd worked with throughout the Midwest. So does Joyce McClure, who's counseled many small business owners in Maine.

Why do so many otherwise confident people—women and men alike—find marketing to be such a tough area? In a nutshell, it's probably because, like most of us, they equate marketing with selling, rather than communicating, and have a hard time seeing themselves in this role. In fact, the whole idea of having to sell or promote their product or service strikes fear into the hearts of many people. There's a very good reason for this: Even those of us who've worked for many years in traditional corporate environments have had to sell ourselves only a few times—such as in job interviews or when we've had to pitch a project to a client or boss. Marketing or sales was someone else's department. As a result, the communications tools we're most

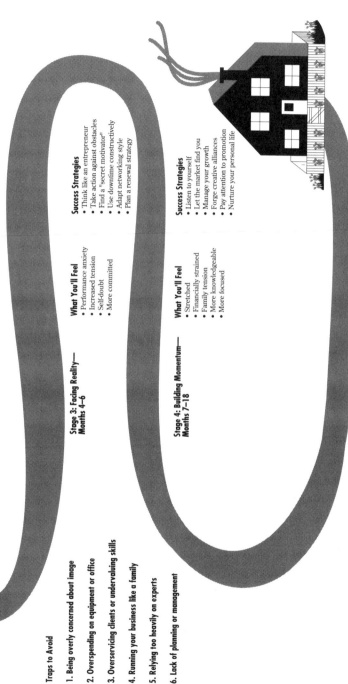

From Corporation to Cottage:
Your Emotional Road Map

Stage 1: Releasing the Past

What You'll Feel
• Grieving and loss
• Disoriented/uprooted
• Abandoned/fearful
• Hopeful

Success Strategies
• Accept your transition
• Be prepared for grieving
• Leave your corporate family
• Create a "ritual of release"
• Decompress and refocus energy
• Celebrate the new

**Stage 2: Launching Your Venture—
Months 1–3**

What You'll Feel
• Exhilarated and free
• Loneliness
• Image Anxiety
• Financially Fragile

Success Strategies
• Manage your stress
• Identify your mission
• Focus on your first 100 days
• Create a new structure
• Watch spending patterns
• Enlist family and friends

**Stage 3: Facing Reality—
Months 4–6**

What You'll Feel
• Performance anxiety
• Increased tension
• Self-doubt
• More committed

Success Strategies
• Think like an entrepreneur
• Take action against obstacles
• Find a "secret motivator"
• Use downtime constructively
• Adapt networking style
• Plan a renewal strategy

**Stage 4: Building Momentum—
Months 7–18**

What You'll Feel
• Stretched
• Financially strained
• Family tension
• More knowledgeable
• More focused

Success Strategies
• Listen to yourself
• Let the market find you
• Manage your growth
• Forge creative alliances
• Pay attention to promotion
• Nurture your personal life

Traps to Avoid

1. Being overly concerned about image

2. Overspending on equipment or office

3. Overservicing clients or undervaluing skills

4. Running your business like a family

5. Relying too heavily on experts

6. Lack of planning or management

familiar with are resumes, memos, reports, internal meetings, and trade conferences. The brochures, press releases, flyers, pitch letters, cold calls, and media contacts that are the stock and trade of the small business owner are all foreign territory to us. Given this reality, it's understandable that marketing in its many forms can seem mysterious and confusing. But it doesn't have to be. If you're willing to recognize the key role that marketing plays and to work at mastering some basic techniques, then you can develop and fine-tune your skills in this arena with impressive results and a minimum of anxiety.

PROFESSIONALISM: MORE IMPORTANT THAN EVER

In this chapter, we've explored many aspects of redefining your business image—making the transition from a follower to leader, building an internal power base, developing a strategic "road map," and cultivating a marketing mentality. Managing all of the changes required will demand tremendous concentration and commitment. At times you may find yourself slipping back into old patterns of behavior or struggling to master several new skills simultaneously. You also will find that your whole approach to relationship building and networking takes on new urgency and new sensitivities. During these moments, you may feel extremely vulnerable, even fragile. When this happens, it's vitally important that you devote both time and attention to constantly renewing and enriching your vision of what you want your business to accomplish and how you want to work. See yourself taking ownership of and enjoying the new professional persona that you are creating for yourself. Talk to other women who've moved beyond the start-up stage of their ventures and made the transition you're going through. Read inspiring success stories of entrepreneurs who've met and overcome the obstacles you find yourself facing. But most important, be sure that you are ready to accept responsibility for the demands that expanding and redefining your business image will make on your personal and emotional life.

You may be starting on a shoestring and working from your kitchen table or bedroom, but you must never let that affect your professionalism when it comes to dealing with clients and customers.

Your business may be small, but the quality and level of service you provide should match or even exceed that offered by bigger enterprises. If you commit to a deadline, be sure you can meet it. If you promise to get back with a quote or information, be sure you follow through quickly and efficiently. If you can't take on a project for lack of time or resources, then go the extra mile by helping the client find another supplier. Equally important, never misrepresent yourself by promising more than you can deliver, by trying to act larger than you are, or by fudging your track record. Play to your strengths, and don't try to disguise your limitations. When you hold yourself to a high standard of professionalism, you'll find that you stretch and grow to inhabit your new, expanded self-image comfortably and confidently.

FOUR STAGES OF SUCCESS

The next four chapters map out the four stages you can expect to pass through during the first eighteen months of your new business start-up. Their goal is to provide you with a rough map of the emotional terrain you'll encounter during the early days of your new venture's growth and evolution. The chart on page 114 captures the four stages for you visually and may help you pinpoint where you are and what to expect. Chapter 5 focuses on releasing the past and mastering the intense feelings you'll experience during the early days of your transition from employee to entrepreneur. Chapter 6 deals with setting the stage for success by making some smart strategic and personal decisions during the first one hundred days of your new enterprise. Chapter 7 identifies some challenges you'll face once the honeymoon is over and reality sets in. Chapter 8 offers advice on keeping your business on track and managing its growth.

5

STAGE ONE: RELEASING THE PAST

It's very important that you launch a new business with a proactive, not a reactive, agenda. One of the keys to doing this is finishing the emotional business of leaving. If you don't recognize the reasons you left and the feelings behind them, you can sabotage your chances for a successful start-up.

—Barbara Mackoff, Ph.D.

As anyone who's taken the plunge will tell you, starting a business is a life-changing event. No aspect of your personality will be untouched by your decision to take control of your work, earning power, and creativity. Your hopes, dreams, fears, anxieties, strengths, and weaknesses will all be exposed and tested, time and again. As a new business owner who's left the corporate world, one of the major challenges you'll face is the need to redefine yourself while planning and carrying out dozens of strategic and financial decisions: where to work, what equipment to buy, what to call your new venture, how and where to market, how to budget your time and money, whether to go solo or team up with someone else, and so on.

Preoccupation with the practical problems surrounding your start-up can easily distract you from paying adequate attention to your emotional ups and downs. But there's no avoiding the fact that your emotional well-being affects your business's health; to borrow an old metaphor, if your psyche has a cold, more often than not, your business will sneeze. Given this reality, how well you handle the emotional demands of your start-up can be just as critical to your success as how skillfully you manage your finances. The emotions you experience during this time will be intense. And although they may seem bewildering, many of these feelings are widely shared and predictable, especially during the peak period of your transition from corporation to cottage. The transition period is often the most difficult to navigate for many new entrepreneurs because of the many pressures and changes that must be confronted and handled. Dealing with the feelings that arise during this process can be extremely difficult because so much else is going on. This is doubly true if you've been fired or laid off and choose to start your own business on the rebound. But even if you make the decision on your own terms and while your job situation is still relatively secure, you still may find yourself struggling with many unexpected, strong feelings.

Saying Good-bye Takes Time

For most of us, the word *entrepreneur* conjures up images of the future, not the past; it calls to mind forward motion, not a trip down memory lane. Yet, releasing the past and letting go of old work patterns, structures, and expectations is a vital step on the road to entrepreneurial success. This process can be especially challenging if you have pursued a long and demanding corporate career prior to starting your business. During this initial stage, your goals will be to

- work through the feelings of sadness and loss you may experience;
- take time to "decompress" and gather your energies; and
- renew your commitment to the cottage work style you envision.

What You Can Expect to Feel

Whether or not you realize it consciously, there are many unresolved issues and lots of emotional baggage that you'll find yourself packing up along with your files and Rolodex when you leave your office and close the door for the last time. This is as it should be; for most of us, work—especially meaningful work—isn't just a matter of business, it's also personal and emotional. You've invested your time, talent, and energy in helping your corporate employer thrive. You've spent a good part of your life in that office building you're leaving. You've gained vital experience and confidence and, hopefully, enjoyed a sense of achievement. You've also experienced stress and deadline pressures and endured your share of disappointments and unfulfilled expectations. Now, for whatever reason, you've made the decision to move on and take more control of your time and your life. As you begin your journey toward a more independent work style, here are some of the emotions you may experience.

Grieving and a Sense of Loss

Given the web of associations and feelings you've woven around your work over the years, it's little wonder that releasing the past and letting it go often proves to be more painful and emotional than we expect it to be. And although it may sound strange, before you can rejoice and embrace the newfound freedom that the cottage life promises, it's very likely that you'll have to pass through a period of grieving for the old identity and work life you've left behind. During this time, you are likely to experience what seems to be a very confusing and distracting range of emotions. Although you and the people around you may not recognize the symptoms, they are both understandable and natural; you are entering a period of mourning that is a necessary step in releasing the past. Most of us think of grieving in terms of illness, losing a loved one, or an emotional crisis like divorce. Few people associate this idea with work. Yet, if you think about it, coping with job upheaval, making a major career switch, or forsaking corporate life to pursue an entrepreneurial dream are all stressful events. And each, in its own way, involves loss.

What are you mourning for as you leave the corporate nest? For the years spent with your company that can never be recaptured; for the friends you're leaving behind; for the promise your job once held but failed to deliver; for the familiarity and safe haven that your office environment provided; for the old, comfortable routines and rhythms of your workday; for the paycheck that enriched your life and gave it stability; for the prestige you enjoyed; and for the professional identity you must now reshape and redefine. It's only natural that your sense of loss may be very acute. You are, after all, giving up many valuable assets in order to pursue your dream.

As psychologist Dr. Brian Schwartz notes, "I think there is always a grieving process involved in major work decisions, whether someone loses a job or actually makes a transition out of one field or from one way of working to another. People grieve for the old self they are leaving behind. In fact, some people who are on the brink of making a major change go into a precipitous depression. When this happens, they are mourning an old way of being in the world that's often a very dependent one, or more dependent than the way of life they are choosing. Sometimes grieving takes place before someone actually makes a change—they've already completed the transitional work needed to reach the point where they are ready to take off on their own. But there is always grieving."

Does everyone making the shift from employee to entrepreneur really go through this transitional process? The answer to this question is yes, more or less. While a handful of fortunate souls never have a moment's regret or sadness about letting go of their old work life, they are the exception rather than the rule. Most people, to some degree, experience some form of mourning during the vital process of confronting major change and adjusting to radically different work patterns. As Dr. Schwartz mentioned, some people complete the grieving process before they actually leave their employers. Joyce McClure, for example, found her corporate job and working atmosphere so negatively affected by a takeover that she was virtually forced to let go of her old image of her position long before she walked out the door. Ann Hull gave her employer, the Modern Language Association, several months' notice before she left her job to become a consultant as a meetings planner. As a result, Ann was still on board when her replacement was recruited and began to assume her old responsibilities. By the time she received her last paycheck, Ann, too, had to come to terms with her feelings about letting go of the past and leaving her old work identity behind.

But for many women, the process of releasing the past and grieving occurs after we leave our corporate jobs and during the all-important start-up phase of our new venture. This kind of timing is the hardest to handle. Just when we're most in need of our drive and optimism, we're forced to devote some of our emotional energy to coping with the past, not planning for the future. How long does the period of mourning last? For some people, the grieving process proves to be intense but short; they feel sad and at loose ends for a few days, then find themselves swept up by the exhilaration and excitement of planning their new venture. But most people don't weather this type of radical transition that quickly or easily. This is especially true if your corporate career spans many years. If you're like most people, it may take you a period of weeks or even several months to accept your sense of loss, integrate fully the corporate assets you value most, and become totally focused on your new business.

Homeless and Disoriented

Like it or not, the corporate environment you're exiting may exert a powerful influence over you long after you leave. However ultimately unsatisfying and flawed that environment proved to be, your job made you not just part of a corporate hierarchy, but the member of a corporate family. In a sense, then, leaving your job, whether voluntarily or under pressure, is like leaving home. For Judith Grant Palma, who spent ten years working her way up the corporate ladder at a New Jersey bank, this feeling was very strong and positive, even after she was laid off without warning. Says Judith, "The company I worked for was a fantastic place. They promoted you, the training was wonderful, and they really cared about the people who worked there. It was a very positive atmosphere. I always had great managers and great staff situations. Leaving was very hard. It's like a family that you miss."

For Melinda Pancoast, the sense of family spirit and camaraderie her company created was integral to its culture. Melinda worked for a large, multimillion-dollar educational corporation that sponsored the Six Day Course, an organizational training program with a challenging, experience-based curriculum. After working briefly in administration, she became the first woman instructor to run the company's Ropes Course, a very demanding outdoor program in which she directed more than 175 staff volunteers and participants at a time. As a role model, she was given great visibility by the company she worked for: every week, Melinda, a petite dynamo with an infectious energy, found herself playing a "kind of female Indiana Jones" role in front of scores of people who valued and depended on her judgment and skill. In addition to the enormous attention and support her company gave her, she also met and became engaged to another trainer, Malachi, while she worked there.

After their marriage, Melinda decided, for a variety of reasons, that she wanted to leave her job. Although both she and Malachi agreed that it was time to move on, it wasn't easy. The organization they worked for fostered an atmosphere of intimacy and camaraderie that was very powerful. "I found there was a lot of pressure to stay with my company," she recalls. "It was very beneficial for management to have people working there who were highly trained, so they really wanted both myself and Mal to continue. I had already decided to give up my job when they started telling me all the new, exciting things I could do. It was very tempting; the family spirit was very strong. It was very hard to leave."

Even today, after seven years of creating a successful consulting business and enjoying a very flexible and independent life-style, Melinda recalls with some nostalgia the sense of family and support she received from the company she left. Now, she notes, "It's really Mal and I, standing on our own. We don't have that whole family behind us; it's just the two of us every day—and whatever client relationships we are able to build. This is definitely a different business experience."

"It's like a family that you miss"; "It was very hard to leave"— the strong attachment to their companies that both Judith and Melinda described isn't all that unusual. And certainly, the powerful sense of family and belonging that many people receive from their workplaces are very positive in many ways. A company where employees feel this way offers security and stability. It offers a forum for making lasting friendships and forging productive work teams. It makes one feel protected and connected. There is a downside to this form of attachment, however. Thinking about your place of business as a home away from home may seem natural, but it can make the transition from corporation to cottage more stressful and disorienting than it is for someone who has a more detached view about her business environment.

Anger and Abandonment

While the classic image of the entrepreneur is someone with a strong desire to bring a new product or service into the world, many people who choose to leave their corporate jobs and strike out on their own operate from a very different emotional framework. Dissatisfaction often plays a key role in their decision. In some cases, anger is a motivating factor. This feeling may be triggered by the way they are treated on the job, by unreasonable demands on their time and energy, and by the belief that they are undervalued and underpaid. At some point, employees who harbor these strong feelings realize that if they are going to invest heavily in their work, it makes more sense to do so as the owner of a company. If they have the drive and will to make a major change, then they can take that angry energy and use it positively and creatively.

People who decide to leave a job and go off on their own, notes Dr. Schwartz, "are probably operating on a certain kind of anger—and I don't mean that in a negative sense. They can make constructive use of it by taking that energy and molding it into some kind of opportunity for themselves. Sometimes it's a matter of feeling that, I'm not going to take this anymore. I'm not going to live like this. I'm not going to have my boss call me in on weekends. If I own the company or part of the company, then yes, maybe I'd be willing to work this hard. But not for someone else. People use a whole variety of scenarios. And of course, some of this is cheerleading one's self. Self-esteem is an issue here. People have to get themselves whipped up in order to go out and seize the time."

On the other hand, someone who chooses to start a business after being laid off or fired has a very different, and potentially dangerous, situation to deal with, he warns. "More often than not, they initially turn their anger against themselves by asking, 'What did I do?' 'How could I have avoided this?' 'Why didn't I see this coming?' Sometimes they are right in asking these questions. They may have done certain things that put them in jeopardy." People who react in this way, Dr. Schwartz points out, find that working through their anger and channeling it positively is a longer process; sometimes they are not able to mobilize their resources as quickly or as well as someone who has been more proactive about a decision to work for themselves. "A lot of people don't make the transition as a result," Dr. Schwartz believes, "because they are so busy beating themselves up that they end up working for someone else again."

It's also important, he cautions, to remember that a major change of any kind often triggers feelings of anger for another very powerful reason: it unlocks an emotional door that you may have closed many years ago. Why? Because making a dramatic change can open up a Pandora's box of feelings by forcing you to confront all of the compromises you've made from childhood on and to deal with all of the self-definitions and limitations that were imposed on you by teachers, parents, or other important people in your life. As Dr. Schwartz describes it, we all have "Ziploc bags of anger" that we all carry around inside us. "And when you begin to contemplate change," he says, "you unzip those bags. You are challenging those old reflections about who you are. So out comes the anger. This is what actually scares a lot of people away from making a change. It's such a painful process."

When emotional stress is triggered in this way, you may not even realize what is really happening. You may be perfectly reasonable in assuming that the anger and frustration you are feeling have to do with business-related anxiety about money or a problem confronting you at the moment. But in fact, something far more subtle, complex, and potentially disruptive is actually taking place: you are being forced to confront feelings that have a long history behind them and are deeply rooted in your childhood and in your family's expectations about your abilities and your future. By choosing to make a radical change in your work style, you may be unleashing pent-up emotions that have everything—and nothing—to do with the immediate pressures and problems you're encountering in building your new business. If, after some soul-searching, you seem to find yourself in this situation, how do you handle it? As we'll see a little later, there are some helpful tools you can use to regain your balance.

PLANNING YOUR SUCCESS STRATEGY

If you've read this far, then you know that releasing the past isn't for the fainthearted. It also probably isn't what you had in mind when you first began fantasizing about starting your own business. And I wouldn't be at all surprised if the intense emotions that cottage life may trigger make you think twice about it all. If some of the feelings described here strike a chord, then you may already know all too well from personal experience that managing your emotions while trying to manage a business start-up is a lot like dancing on the edge of a volcano. And if you're in the throes of making your decision, then all of this discussion about grieving and loss may have dampened your enthusiasm a bit. Well, wherever you are, take heart. There is plenty of advice available to help you cross your emotional Delaware safely.

Acknowledge That You're in a Major Transition

As we discussed earlier, in striking out on your own, you are coping with a life change of major proportions. Given what you're going through, who *wouldn't* feel vulnerable and overwhelmed? At the very moment that you're trying to put the pieces of your new professional identity together, your emotional life is going through a major up-heaval. At this stage, probably the worst thing you can do is to try to deny what you're feeling and underplay the importance of the step you've taken. Women who've been there will tell you that it's far more helpful to accept the way you're feeling and then figure out how to push past it so you can do what you have to do to make your business work. Take heart from the words of an old song and re-member that "the first days are the hardest days." Your feelings of loss and rootlessness are likely to be the strongest and most discouraging during the first days and weeks of your new working life. This is the period in which what you've given up by leaving the nine-to-five world first becomes painfully apparent, when the risks you're taking begin to sink in, and when you haven't yet created a new operating structure for yourself to replace the one you've lost. Knowing that the first days are the toughest can help you take a "this too shall pass" attitude toward your emotional ups and downs. The peak period of your vulnerability is just that: a peak period. At some point, if you tough it out, you're going to hit that peak and find yourself safely on the other side, feeling stronger about your chances for success.

Understand the Grieving Process and How It Unfolds

Understanding the cycle of emotions you can expect to feel during your own personal grieving stage can be extremely helpful. Even if those emotions hit you like a ton of bricks, you'll know what you're up against. You also can take comfort in the fact that the negative feelings you may struggle with early in the grieving cycle will ultimately give way to more positive, uplifting emotions. While no one— not even you—can predict the intensity of your feelings of loss during this transition, the emotions you can expect to pass through can be outlined with relative certainty. Sadness, nostalgia, and a sense of loss; abandonment and, in some cases, anger; acceptance; integration; and renewal—these are the classic phases of the grieving process.

It's also important to remember that you won't experience these feelings in isolation; one phase of your emotional life impinges on the next. That's why, for many people, stages one and two of their new business life—releasing the past and launching their venture— occur simultaneously. Your feelings of sadness or anger may roil around just below the surface, ebbing and flowing, even as you are ordering your new computer or working on your business plan. Like background music, the range of emotions encompassed in the grieving process may alternately catch your attention and then recede. When this occurs, it's sometimes far more difficult to recognize exactly what you are confronting than it would be if you found yourself coping with an intense but brief depression.

If and when these feelings subside and you come to terms with your situation, you are likely to experience a sense of acceptance—of your vulnerability, the pain and anxiety your move may be causing, and ultimately, of the decision you've made to forge a new life for yourself and those you love. With acceptance will come a sense of wholeness as you absorb and integrate your old skills and beliefs into the new work life you are creating for yourself.

You'll know that you've reached the final stage of grieving—renewal—when you begin to feel a resurgence of energy, a stronger sense of purpose, and a deepening commitment to the new path you've charted. This makes it all the more important to acknowledge and accept the grieving process as natural and even inevitable, and to remember that it is something that thousands of other successful entrepreneurs have endured and survived. Above all, you must guard against ignoring or denying these feelings and struggling to suppress them rather then accepting the important role they play in helping you release the past.

Let Go of Your Corporate Family

Ultimately a company or large institution, however caring and supportive it seems to be, is a business, not a family. Much of the atmosphere it may try to create is really smoke and mirrors, a sobering fact that employees learn all too well when the ax falls. When editorial and commercial employees of the *New York Daily News*, for example, faced massive layoffs after two years of turmoil, many of them were deeply emotional. "We're a family up there," said one employee, "and I felt as though my family were being invaded. Even people who worked here for twenty years were treated the same way—no good-bye, and no 'I'm sorry.' " A sad but familiar story.

The experience of one former corporate executive–turned–consultant offers a prime example. She spent ten years working for the same firm in a small office where people were extremely loyal, there was little employee turnover, and team spirit was strong. Her journey toward the cottage life began when the company merged her office with another. She quickly found herself in a highly political atmosphere and came to feel that her days were numbered. A transfer to one of her firm's Midwest offices seemed to offer a solution to her problems; she could stay with the firm and continue doing work she enjoyed. But this move posed some risks. The Midwest office was unstable and might be closing; the clientele she would be serving was very different. Pressured to make a decision about the position over a weekend, she decided to take a chance and relocate. When she arrived in the town she was transferred to—a city of strangers to her—she felt isolated and disoriented. Although the people in her new office were friendly and helpful, she found herself extremely depressed. Ultimately she found her job situation so intolerable that she resigned and returned home, where she began building her own small consulting business.

The woman involved had seriously underestimated the strength of her emotional ties to her corporate family, the people and atmosphere she had enjoyed for many years. She also had no time to "decompress" and grieve for the loss of her old job before she was plunged into a new and totally alien work and living situation. Only after she uprooted herself in a stressful move did she realize that her transfer was doomed to failure; it was a fruitless attempt to recapture the corporate family she had lost when her old office was dismantled. This cautionary tale captures many of the problems that can arise when your attachment is so strong that leaving your job makes you feel hopelessly lost and abandoned. It is vital that you make every effort to disengage yourself emotionally from the company you're leaving and remember that you are giving up a job, not your home and family.

Finish the Emotional Business of Leaving

As you make your transition to cottage life, it's important that you begin with a firm foundation for the future and a sense of forward motion—what management psychologist Barbara Mackoff describes as a "proactive, rather than a reactive," agenda. This means that you need to reflect on and sort out both the positive and negative feelings you had about your corporate job, and identify both the approaches you want to transfer to your own business and the patterns and styles you dislike and want to let go of. Dr. Mackoff, a consultant, seminar leader, and author of several books, including *The Art of Self-Renewal* and *Leaving the Office Behind*, works extensively with women's groups, corporations, and associations. One of the areas she specializes in is managing change. Here are some of her suggestions for releasing your past.

"The emotional business of leaving really involves the issue of boundaries. There are some very discrete reasons why you've left the corporate world in search of a new life. Perhaps you didn't have enough freedom. Your company didn't care if you had a family. You had a certain kind of boss, or whatever. But if you treat your corporate life and managing your business as a continuum—without separating them—you can run into problems. You will still be dealing with unresolved issues because you haven't recognized the feelings behind them, and you can really sabotage the implementation of your start-up. I would encourage anyone making this change to express a number of things—to fill in the psychological blanks. First, it's important to state what you feel you've lost—your regrets. What are you giving up in leaving your corporate job? Your sense of identity, beloved colleagues, a career path? You can express these feelings by saying things like, I loved it when I used to be able to . . . ; or, It was great to be part of a company that's the best there is in. . . . Then you need to acknowledge the hardest part of the change you're going through—its most painful aspects. Is it losing customers or long-standing friends? How are you expressing your feelings? Through anger, anxiety, overeating, humor? And finally, you need to identify your biggest worry in leaving. Is it that you aren't a strong manager or that you're afraid you won't be able to stay on top of things? Is it financial?

"Once you've expressed these concerns, you can use transitional rituals to help you acknowledge the ending you're experiencing. If you've already left your company, then sit down and write a formal good-bye letter, one you will never send, but which expresses some of the things you're feeling—what you're losing, a really great moment you'll always remember, what you've learned. You may even need to have a ceremony for yourself.

"Regardless of where you are on the path to your new life, recognizing feelings that you could block, expressing your regrets and loss, and creating some kind of ritual for completion should all be part of your start-up. Otherwise you may feel that you are running from something. Identifying your feelings helps stop them from becoming roadblocks. It helps keep you from repeating old patterns. If you don't know what you're leaving and why, you can end up repeating old scenarios in a new place. Your clients will treat you the way your boss did. What's the point of simply restructuring what you already had? If you find that old patterns have a very powerful influence over you, then I would recommend some short-term intervention. Well-directed conversation with a professional can help you prevent them from becoming part of your new business."

As Dr. Mackoff suggests, creating a ritual of release can be one of the most helpful ways to say good-bye to your corporate life. When college students graduate, they often flip the tassels of their caps from one side to the other to signify that they've successfully completed a rite of passage. At West Point, they toss their dress caps into the air. Well, why not create a little ceremony of closure for yourself? It can be as simple as taking all of those outdated personnel manuals from your old job and throwing them away—or better yet, tossing an old pile of files into a friend's fireplace while you and she make a toast to your new venture.

Think in Terms of Release Rather Than Loss

If you've made a major investment of time and emotional energy in building a corporate career, then you may face a major challenge in your transition: combating the idea that you are walking away from or destroying everything you've worked so hard to build by leaving your job. You may find yourself feeling guilty about "abandoning ship" and that you're "copping out" or taking the easy way out instead of fighting your way up the corporate ladder. Stress management consultant Myrna Ruskin finds this fear to be a major stumbling block for many of the professional women she works with. They want to make a major change and pursue a more independent work style but are afraid that by doing so they'll be throwing away everything they've worked so hard for.

"So many women pursuing the cottage life feel they are walking away from the ten or fifteen years they've invested in their corporate careers," says Ruskin. "Nothing is thrown out the day you leave the corporate world. All your work has not been in vain. You're simply using it in a new way. Fear that other people will perceive them as a failure is also common. I hear this again and again. Some women find it hard to believe that people around them will see their move as something that they want. They are afraid their friends and family will think that they aren't doing well or that they can't cope. That the strain is too much for them on the job. My advice to these women is that they should make their decision for any one of several reasons, but none of them should be what other people think. That should have nothing to do with how you choose to live your life."

Instead of thinking in terms of loss, says Ruskin, try to focus on "everything you've gained in terms of expertise and knowledge and your sense of self." She adds, "there are three things in life we have to work with: our personality, our genes, and our attitude. You can't change your personality or your genes, but you can change your attitude. It's really our most precious possession." Your attitude—how you perceive and think about what's happening to you—can make all the difference in working through the grieving process and moving from sadness to renewal. As you come to terms with the reality of leaving your corporate job, whatever the circumstances, try to take a fresh approach to your situation and "accentuate the positive" as an old popular tune puts it. One way to do this is to focus on the idea of release rather than loss.

The word *release* has a dual definition. On the one hand, it means "to give up, relinquish, or surrender." But to release also means "to free or liberate anything from that which fastens or confines it." By realizing that you are letting go of and freeing yourself from a situation that was limiting or confining you, you can begin to take a major step on your journey toward a more independent work life. So start thinking in terms of letting go rather than of losing, and of integrating your past into your future rather than of abandoning it. And remember, you're not giving up friends you made or the strengths and resources you've gained, you're simply building on them in new ways.

"Celebrate the New"

Just as it's helpful to symbolize ending a phase of your corporate experience, it's equally important to "celebrate the new," as Dr. Mackoff puts it—to acknowledge that you are beginning a fresh and exciting chapter in your work life. She suggests, for example, that you "sit down with crayons and make a coat of arms for your new business, in which you symbolize all the things that you want it to be. It can also include some symbols of accomplishments you've achieved already in your career."

There are many other satisfying and enjoyable ways to celebrate the adventure ahead. You can start a scrapbook, for instance, that's filled with colorful, appealing pictures of homes and offices and captures the kind of work space you envision for yourself. Sure, you may be working on your dining room table today, but who knows what tomorrow will bring? If you follow your star, then sometime in the future, you may be out pricing a beautiful loft space or weekending in the country and looking for the perfect barn to house your growing business. Or if you fantasize about having the latest desktop publishing equipment but don't have the budget for it right now, why not paste a photo of the model you want in your scrapbook to inspire you? Don't just think big, think beautiful. Give yourself a visual feast for the eyes and the soul. It will refresh and energize you. The idea behind these simple but powerful and uplifting exercises is to shift your focus from the past by celebrating the future, with all of its joys and potential.

Take Time to Decompress and Refocus Your Energies

Releasing the past while keeping your head above water in the present is a tough balancing act. During this transitional stage, it's not surprising that you may be feeling at odds with yourself, uprooted, off center, and, perhaps, angry. But you can give yourself a big push in the direction of your dream by taking time—*making* time—to release pent-up pressures from your old job and to refocus your energies. If releasing the past is proving to be a difficult, even painful, process for you, then it's doubly important that you treat yourself during this stage with compassion and caring, just as you would your best friend if she or he were going through what you're experiencing.

You may think that taking time to deal with your emotions is a luxury you can't afford right now, but you're wrong. It's a necessity you can't do without. It's one of the first and most important declarations of independence you can and must make. Taking the time during the early days of your venture to reflect on and accept the grieving process, absorb the intense changes your identity is undergoing, and reorient yourself will pay enormous dividends in the future. It will help you replenish your inner resources at a time when they may be running low, giving you a reservoir of emotional strength that you can tap into when you need it most.

Many of the women I interviewed recognized this need intuitively and took time out after they left their corporate jobs before plunging into their new cottage life-style. Joyce McClure spent several months relaxing and rediscovering herself after she relocated to Maine. Jan Berg spent time in a company-sponsored outplacement program to sort out her next steps. Melinda Pancoast and her husband spent about a year in Boston, regrouping. During that time, Melinda worked for her mother, who owned a mortgage brokerage firm, while she and her husband considered the kind of business they wanted to start together and where they wanted to be.

Judith Grant Palma already had been laid off from her banking job for more than six months when her husband voluntarily left his stressful executive position in a small technology business. Even though their funds were low, Judith and her husband resisted pushing the panic button. Instead they decided to accept a friend's invitation to "leave everything behind and come down to Tampa for a while." Their first reaction was to say, "How can we possibly do that?" On second thought, they said, "Why not?" They left their two grown kids back home in New Jersey and took their first extended vacation in years. "We were gone about eight weeks," recalls Judith, "and we had a wonderful time. We visited all around Florida, thought about moving there, and then came back. Neither one of us had a job. It was after we returned from our trip that my husband suggested I reconsider my idea of starting a skin-care business." Ultimately Judy did decide to pursue this route and used her severance money to take a four-week training program before launching her business.

After ten years in financial services, in 1989 Cheryl Williams's company downsized and she found herself restructured out of her job. At about this time, her father's sudden death left her family's Chicago-based clothing business without a financial manager and Cheryl was asked to fill in the gap. She agreed to consider filling in on a temporary basis as a consultant, but before saying yes, she took more than two months to think about what she wanted to do. "I call it 'shock'—that feeling you have the first morning you wake up and you don't have to be in the office," says Cheryl. "I remember spending this time doing a lot of writing. Writing has always been very therapeutic for me. So I wrote in my journal and began thinking and evaluating what had happened in the past—and looking at my situation as a real opportunity. I was fortunate to have a very generous severance package, so that going out and finding another job immediately wasn't an issue. So I took time to figure out what I really and truly wanted to do. This had become a driving force in my life in the two years before I left my job, because I wasn't feeling fulfilled. I started listening to another side of myself and asking a lot of questions: Do I really want to go out on my own? Do I have a talent worth selling?"

If taking a few months or even a few weeks off isn't an option for you, you can still find creative ways to give yourself the gift of time at this critical point in your life. Jackie Farley, the founder of CenterPoint in Aspen, began her unique retreat program with the clear understanding that what many women need most, but feel they can least afford, is to break away from their busy, fragmented lives to "regain a sense of direction and purpose." With this in mind, Jackie holds three- and four-day retreats in her mountain lodge in Aspen. The retreats, held from June through October, combine daily hikes in the Rockies with relaxation, meditation, gourmet meals, and guided discussions about juggling personal and professional demands, improving self-esteem, maintaining energy levels, and dealing with transition. Many of the female executives, business owners, and entrepreneurs-in-the-making who have the resources to attend a CenterPoint retreat find that the results are powerful and long lasting.

You can organize your own personal retreat by taking a few days, or even just a weekend, to unwind at a nearby inn or spa. The real idea here is a simple one: if at all possible, give yourself some time out to reflect and regroup emotionally before you plunge into the long days and nights that launching your new business will require. Taking the time to care for yourself is always important when you're going through a major change. But learning to pay attention to your needs on a regular basis is also one of the most important skills you can learn as an entrepreneur. When you do, you'll find that your inner work is just as important as your outer actions in moving you toward your goal.

Transform Your Anger Into Opportunity

Whole books have been devoted to the topic of anger, and with good reason, for it is the toughest negative emotion to deal with. While detailed techniques for handling any anger you may feel during this stage are beyond the scope of this book, some advice from my interviews may prove helpful. Probably the single most important thing to remember here is that you must somehow find the strength and inner resources to release your anger and to transform it into a positive rather than a negative force for change in your life. As Jackie Farley noted so well in her comments on timing, starting a business is simply too big and demanding a move to make only on the basis of negative motivation. To have any chance for success, you have to have a positive pull toward it. In the end, it has to be something you really feel good about and not a decision that's made largely on the basis of anger, frustration, or fear.

As mentioned earlier, no one is immune to feelings of anger when making the transition from corporation to cottage. Even executives whose jobs aren't in jeopardy when they opt for the entrepreneurial life often do so, in part, as a result of feeling frustrated and angry about their work situations. Anyone who has endured the trauma of being fired, laid off, or compelled to abandon a position is especially vulnerable on this front. Circumstances like these are likely to trigger a range of powerful feelings, from surprise, disbelief, and fear to a sense of betrayal and deep anger. Even when a firing or persistent dissatisfaction with a job isn't an issue, anger can be a problem. As Dr. Brian Schwartz noted, dramatic life changes can unleash powerful negative emotions. Trying to make a radical shift in one's work style can awaken feelings of anxiety, inadequacy, and fear of failure (or success) that are deeply rooted in childhood and family experiences. When this happens, anger is often a by-product of the change process.

If, for any of the reasons suggested here, you find yourself feeling angry during the first weeks or months of your new work life, what should you do? As a first step, it's important to remember that your anger can work for you or against you. It can be a tool for change or an obstacle to change. Pinpointing the source of your anger also can be very helpful. Taking time to think through the reasons for your anger is often half the battle in handling it; knowing why you feel as you do can help you put your anger in perspective and either ride it out or exploit the energy it releases in a positive way.

Do you feel misused, underemployed, underpaid, and overworked? Are you angry at your boss or your company for letting you go, perhaps without warning or any recognition of your years of service? Are you angry at yourself for not seeing the danger signals that led to your dismissal, and for putting yourself and your family at risk? Are you simply so burned out and frustrated that being your own boss has suddenly become appealing? Is the change you're asking yourself to make more than you can handle right now? In opening the cottage door, are you in danger of triggering old fears and anxieties that can sabotage your chances of success? Answering these kinds of questions honestly may not be easy, but asking them may prove key to your survival. If any of these concerns hits a nerve, at least you'll have a better idea of the roadblocks you're facing.

Perhaps most important, you must remember that attitude is everything. You are in charge. You are the captain of your fate; you may not have control over your anger, but you *do* have some control over your attitude toward it. How you respond to this powerful feeling when it hits you can make all the difference. Your reaction can either fuel the negative emotion you're experiencing, defuse it, or transform it. With the right attitude, anger can be used constructively to help you make the transition to a cottage work style. If you can channel the energy your anger releases into creating a new life for yourself, then you'll find that this powerful emotion can have a positive impact on your business. It can drive you to do more and be more. On the other hand, if your anger turns inward or becomes so overpowering that it handicaps you and sends out danger signals to other people, then your business can easily self-destruct. In the case of anger, talking about your feelings with someone else can actually be a positive move. It can help you cool down and even see the point of view of the person or institution that triggered your anger. Ultimately, however, the choice about whether anger creates obstacles or opportunities for you is yours alone. No one can make it for you.

Get Up and Out—Every Day!

If you've ever had a serious case of the blues or have seen a friend or family member go through a depression, then you probably know how frighteningly easy it is to give in to feelings of malaise and helplessness. If you find yourself retreating into yourself, letting the four walls of your "cottage" close in on you, getting up late, and letting yourself go physically, then it's imperative that you quickly and forcefully pull yourself together. As a first step, stay with a nine-to-five timetable, at least until you discover a new and more effective working rhythm for yourself.

In the corporate world, you don't go to work in your nightgown. Don't do it in your cottage, either. Get yourself dressed and ready for action in a way that makes you feel professional and focused. Taking a casual attitude toward clothing is fine—one of the joys of working at home is that you can feel looser and more relaxed. But don't let yourself go. "I think this is a pitfall for a lot of women," warns Myrna Ruskin. "I've fallen into it myself. It's very easy to say, Oh, well, I'm not seeing a client, so what difference does it make if I'm dressed and my makeup is on? Then suddenly the phone rings and it's the head of human resources of a major company, and you feel off balance. It's all psychological. When you feel well put together, you simply function more effectively, whatever your environment."

It's also important not to continually isolate yourself at home, especially if you're working alone. Yes, you may become totally absorbed in some project you're working on and find yourself happily pecking away at your computer from dawn until dusk. When those times of total immersion come your way, count yourself lucky and see them as a sign that you're on the road to doing the work you were meant to do. But it's still important to try to get yourself up and out, and to do it *every day*. Have breakfast at a favorite diner, get the latest trade journal or copy of *The Wall Street Journal* at your newsstand, keep a calendar of seminars and meetings that relate to your business, take a lunch break at home or with a friend, become active in a professional association. While you shouldn't use these activities as time wasters or time fillers, they can be very helpful in making you feel that you're still part of the outside world. So make it a point each day to expand your horizons, whether you go for a walk or make a special trip to check out some new computer software at a local store. It will help you feel connected.

Reevaluate Your Attraction to the Cottage Life

Remember that the cottage life is a work in progress—a journey, not just a destination. Now is the time to ask yourself, Is this the road I really want to travel? Will this path take me where I want to go? If your answers are yes, then you've passed a major milestone on your journey—you've decided to begin pursuing a more independent life for yourself and your family. Or, as Jackie Farley says, you've "traded comfort for freedom." And in doing so, you've begun letting go of your old way of working in order to make way for the new. So pat yourself on the back and acknowledge the courage you've shown in reaching this decision. Then listen for a moment as those three gentle muses—acceptance, integration, and renewal—find the cottage you're in, tap you quietly on the shoulder, and whisper in your ear, "You can do this. You can create a new, exciting life for yourself!" What a wonderful sense of relief, happiness, and power you'll feel when this day comes. Enjoy it!

6

STAGE TWO: LAUNCHING YOUR VENTURE— MONTHS ONE TO THREE

> *When we first started our training company, I was excited, happy, and scared. To take what I'd learned as a manager and use it in a business was a big step. Everything I've done has been new to me. A lot of it is testing the waters to see how far you can go. And I've learned you can really go far.*
>
> *—Melinda Pancoast*

You've made the decision to release the past and embrace your future, and you've been rewarded with a renewed sense of purpose that you may find energizing and even purifying. It also can be a powerful motivator. At this stage, your real adventure is beginning. In releasing the past, you opened the cottage gate. Now you're finally ready to open the cottage door. You've cut the cord, broken the tie that binds, and left the corporate fold. To the best of your knowledge, you're committed to forgoing the security that a corporate job offers and embracing the risks and rewards of the entrepreneurial life. Congratulations are in order! You're making a bold move to take control of your time, talent, and earning power.

During this start-up phase, you are setting the stage for your new business and laying the groundwork for the future. You must nurture both your budding enterprise and yourself with care, wisdom, discipline, and compassion. The decisions you make—or fail to make—throughout this period will greatly influence the ultimate health of your venture. They also will send important signals to both your clients and the people closest to you about exactly how focused and committed you are to succeeding.

It would be comforting to know that the feelings you may have experienced during stage one are firmly behind you. But life is never that neat and tidy, is it? It's far more likely that releasing the past will be an ongoing process that still may take you some time to complete. Even so, it's time to put your back to the wind, set some goals, and move ahead with your plans. If those plans are straight-forward and the steps you need to take are sharply defined, then count your blessings. If, on the other hand, you're committed to the cottage life as a work style but find that your path isn't a straight and narrow one and your plans are in the formative stage, take courage! Think back for a moment to the discussion about vision (page 64). As your journey begins, your vision may just be taking shape. Like Caroline Hull, you may make several false starts as you struggle to clarify your goals and transform your desire to take charge of your life into a practical, manageable business venture. Or you may find that your vision involves *how* you want to work more than the actual work you plan to do. At this moment, having the freedom to express your personal values through your work may be more important to you than the specific product or service you plan to offer. Remember, your vision doesn't have to be crystal clear right now, but it must be compelling enough to keep you motivated and to drive you forward into a future that you want to define on your own terms. During this stage, your major goals should be to

- deal as calmly as you can with your emotional ups and downs;
- begin establishing boundaries and a new operating structure;
- make your first one hundred days as productive as possible; and
- enlist your family and friends for support.

What You Can Expect to Feel

This promises to be a busy and emotionally demanding three months. On the one hand, you may find yourself breathing a sigh of relief and pleasure as you put behind you the trappings of your corporate job—the office, the daily grind, the politics—and begin creating a new work environment. On the other hand, you may soon feel you've jumped out of the proverbial frying pan and into the fire as you cope with a new set of anxieties about your image, your finances, and the support you will or will not receive from those around you. To help you anticipate what lies ahead, let's explore the feelings you're likely to be dealing with during the all-important first days of your new venture.

Exhilaration

Free at last! Free at last! Many women, especially those who choose to leave their corporate positions of their own accord and on their own terms, describe their feelings as they enter this stage in positive, even glowing, terms. They feel upbeat about their future, excited by their newfound freedom, and empowered by their decision to take control of their professional destinies. Debra Oppenheim remembers feeling elated and even breathless, as if she were tumbling downhill. Melinda Pancoast felt happy and energized; she and her husband plunged into action, setting up a home office, calling people, making appointments. Joyce McClure experienced a tremendous "release of pressure" when she finally decided to leave her corporate job.

During this heady phase, you, too, may feel more hopeful than worried, more relieved about taking the plunge than concerned about surviving your fall from corporate life. In fact, leaving may seem much easier than you expected. You may wonder why you waited so long and didn't escape from the corporate cocoon months, or even years, earlier. In a best-case scenario, you'll feel reasonably secure about what lies ahead. You may have laid the groundwork for your move while you were still employed, created a financial cushion to give yourself some breathing room, and lined up a couple of anchor clients to ease your transition from employee to entrepreneur. You may even have invested time and energy in developing a full-scale business plan and found enough investment dollars to put it into action.

On the personal front, you may feel pretty comfortable that

you've covered all your bases. The feedback from your friends has been terrific; they're all telling you to go for it and giving you lots of advice. They just know you can make it. Support from your family may be equally strong; your husband or boyfriend, sisters and brothers, mother and father may all be rooting for you at this stage and cheering you on. They may express lots of confidence in your creativity, ingenuity, and staying power, and assure you that they'll back you up, whatever it takes. With all of this enthusiasm bubbling up around you, it's easy to find your fantasy taking flight—now that you're free to be yourself and make your mark, the sky's the limit. Anything can happen. You're filled with energy, ready to take on whatever comes your way. In fact, you may be so entranced with your new situation that you radiate a sense of confidence that's positively magnetic. You're not at the top of the mountain yet, but it feels great to have finally laced up those hiking boots and begun climbing! Without a doubt, this is the honeymoon phase of your venture. Bask in its glow for as long as you can!

Loneliness

Needless to say, all honeymoons come to an end. As the days turn into weeks and the weeks into months, your enthusiasm may begin to wane. During this critical time, your feelings of isolation and loneliness can be intense. You may have the sensation that you're in limbo, with one foot and half your psyche in the past while your other half struggles to find a foothold in the future. It's easy to feel cut off from everyone and everything you care about, to feel that you've fallen off the face of the earth. Your old structure—the round of phone calls, meetings, lunches, and projects that once defined your day—is gone. You're just beginning to create a new one to take its place.

Leslie Smith, associate director of NAFE, captures this feeling of isolation graphically in an *Executive Female* article she wrote called "Home Alone, the Sequel": "Every day, there are more refugees from the corporate world—women starting their own businesses, women spending part of the week working at home, part in the office, women on maternity leave or embarking on a job search from home. All of them risk insularity—losing touch with the business world. When I began my maternity leave about two weeks before my daughter was born, I fully planned to work several hours a day at home until her birth. What I was not prepared for was the panic that set in that first Monday of my leave. I sat at my dining room table, looked at the large clock on the wall that read 9:00 A.M and suddenly noticed the silence. Every morning for thirteen years, I'd gone to an office filled with the bustle of doing business—phones ringing, colleagues stepping in, meetings. Even though I looked forward to my job as a mother, I didn't feel grounded at home and worried about losing touch with the working world."

Leslie's home-based work situation was a temporary one. But she expresses very well the shock of suddenly finding yourself alone and adrift at a time when you haven't yet discovered and embraced new working rhythms and patterns. Another entrepreneur describes her strongest feeling as having been one of "disconnectedness." She felt uprooted and out of touch with the rest of the world; it took almost a year to reorient herself and feel comfortable in her new work environment. Another woman talked about the panic that swept through her as she opened the door to her apartment–turned–home office and was overcome by the sensation that it had been invaded by an alien being—her entrepreneurial self! She turned to her dining room table, littered with papers, and suddenly felt pressured to make an immediate business and personal decision: should she sit down and get to work right away, or go to the kitchen, make a tuna fish sandwich, clear a space for herself at the table, and eat first?

Barbara Brabec finds that people in her home business network often cite isolation as one of their major problems. "Used to the social life of an office, they may find working alone at home to be almost unbearable at times. That's why it's so important for home business owners to develop their own networks," says Barbara. "They need a group of people they can communicate with on a regular basis." Since this is a major issue, we'll talk later on about some of the tools you can use to handle the problems of feeling lonely and out of touch.

Image Anxiety

If and when strong feelings of isolation and loneliness hit you, you can find yourself in the midst of a minor—or major—identity crisis. If you no longer have a title, a "real" office to go to, or a budget, then who exactly are you? Businesswise, where do you fit into the scheme of things? Apart from your family and friends, who really cares about this momentous step you've just taken in your life, and why should they? How should you plan your time? What should you do first? What's most important and what can you afford to let slide? When you start asking these kinds of questions, it's easy to begin feeling that you've cut yourself adrift and fallen through the "black hole" that Joyce McClure talked about earlier. Confusion about your professional identity can begin to erode your sense of judgment and your self-esteem.

Getting a handle on your new professional identity is complicated by another tough challenge you'll face in the first three months of your venture: learning to live with the fact that the line between your professional life and your personal life is blurred. To put it even more strongly, that line is now nonexistent—your personal and professional life are one and the same; *you are your business and your business is you.* As you gain more experience and perspective, you'll undergo a separation of these two domains; suddenly you'll realize that you are not your business any longer, just as you were not your corporate job. But for now, it's vital that both you and the people close to you realize that the personal and professional aspects of your life are going to be intermingled. As we'll see, you can set some boundaries, but they'll be shifting, sometimes without warning, until you've reoriented yourself.

Practically speaking, this may mean that you'll be working long and crazy hours and may not have much of a personal life at all for weeks and even months at a stretch. It may mean turning down lunch dates with friends because you don't have enough money and explaining to them that you don't have as much time as they think you do. It can mean facing your family's frustration when the house is a mess because you're frantically trying to meet a deadline, real or self-imposed. Or maybe it will mean making your husband understand that the private time you once enjoyed together after work is, for now, a thing of the past. In fact, *after work* is a meaningless phrase for many entrepreneurs during their start-up, when every waking hour is devoted to nurturing their new business. At a time when family support is critical, coping with these pressures can be very stressful for everyone involved.

Insecurity over Finances

Insecurity is a mild term to describe your feelings about money at this vulnerable stage; *fear* might be more accurate. If you have relied one hundred percent on a paycheck throughout your career to date, then the risks you've assumed by giving up a steady source of income can hit you like a ton of bricks. Even seasoned moonlighters, used to the ups and downs of project work, find it a shock to realize during a business start-up that cash flows only in one direction: out of their hands and into someone else's. During the first days and weeks of your new working life, you'll soon learn just how quickly the dollars add up and fly out the door when there's a price tag attached to everything—every paper clip, every pencil, every chair, every piece of computer software. Not to mention your phone bill, which is likely to go through the roof. Watching whatever income you have to work with melt away before your eyes can truly be frightening, especially considering that female-owned businesses are often seriously undercapitalized.

Even if your short-term financial picture is strong, you can easily succumb to feelings of insecurity when it comes to money. Although she had two clients and forty thousand dollars in billings in hand, Debra Oppenheim often found herself staying up nights in the early days of her business worrying about how she would pay the bills, her lack of disability and health insurance, and why she had chosen to put herself at financial risk in her fifties, at a time when she should have been building a nest egg rather than depleting it to underwrite her new firm. And although she and her partner were extremely cautious about their overhead, they still made mistakes and wasted money. Lorraine Gerstein's business was brisk during the start-up stage of her rehabilitation consulting business. Nevertheless, she found her revenues draining away because of a shortsighted management decision—putting people on staff rather than hiring them as independent contractors proved to be a costly, unnecessary expense. Joyce McClure started her cottage life with a substantial financial cushion after selling her house at a hefty profit. In spite of her financial savvy when it came to real estate, Joyce quickly saw her money consumed by the cost of day-to-day living.

For each of these women, concern about money was a very real issue. At the same time, each of them ultimately realized that some of that concern stemmed from feelings of self-doubt and insecurity about their decision to take total responsibility for their earning power. As soon as you begin to question your ability to handle the demands of the entrepreneurial life, you open the door to vulnerability on the money front. When this happens, it's easy to become preoccupied with what you've given up by leaving your corporate job: the steady paycheck, the profit sharing, the bonuses, the insurance, the money for vacations and all of the little extras that make life fun. Just when you should be focusing on finding business and keeping the pipeline filled, you can sap your financial drive by dwelling on lost income rather than your potential earning power.

Energized and Intensely Alive

As you struggle to redefine your professional identity and keep the lid on your financial anxiety, it may be hard to remember that you are equal to the challenges you face. But you are, if you really do want to make the cottage life work. One of the most powerful signs that you're on the right track is the energy you'll release as you focus on surviving your first three months. The capacity for work you display when you are totally committed and push past your fatigue may surprise you and everyone around you. It may allow you to perform small miracles, overcome disappointments that would once have devastated you, and win the help of total strangers with just a phone call. It can make you seem obsessed and irritable and drive you to do things you never would have dreamed of doing in your corporate life.

Pamela Mauney started her confectionery business, Pam's Blue

Ribbon Toffee, as a moonlighting venture, cooking after five and on weekends in a commercial kitchen she rented from a local caterer. Yet, even after putting in a full day at her post office job, she would find herself experiencing a second wind once she started making her toffee. "I've gotten a lot of positive feedback from my family and friends and this has been a real great energy booster," says Pam. "Often my energy level hasn't been very good, due to one thing or another. This is different. I don't know why I have more energy, but I do. There's been so much positive feedback from people—it's been unbelievable. This has really helped keep me going. . . . Of course, I get tired, but it's a different kind of fatigue—the kind you feel after you've worked hard and accomplished something. I like what I'm doing, so when I'm finished, I feel good about it."

The energy Pamela tapped into during her start-up also helped her develop a more positive, expansive self-image. "I definitely do have more confidence about myself. I was extremely timid when I first went in to sell my product. I wasn't sure about pricing—that was a big thing. I didn't want it priced too high, yet I had to make a certain amount. When I started, I was pretty unsure and not forceful. Today I'm more confident about what I'm doing. I look at myself differently now. I know that I can succeed and I'm not intimidated by someone else's views. I can hold my own. To me, this is very important. I've also learned about marketing. I've always enjoyed working with customers in my post office jobs, but still, going out and selling is something I hadn't done before."

Pamela's experience is by no means unusual. Time and again, many of the women I interviewed—Karen Fried, Melinda Pancoast, Debra Oppenheim, and Lorraine Gerstein, to name a few—described the surge of energy they experienced in the early days of their venture and how incredibly productive this period was. As we'll see when we talk about your first one hundred days, this energy is a powerful motivator; the positive feelings of self-confidence and strength it triggers will be tremendously helpful in handling the inevitable problems you'll encounter.

Planning Your Success Strategy

No matter how many inspiring success stories you've read or how many other entrepreneurs you talk to, everyone's start-up is different. Basically you're in a survival mode: it's sink or swim. Of course, if you're busy from the word go, then the demands of running your new business may force your emotions to take a backseat. And if your enthusiasm and passion are strong enough, they can overpower any negative thoughts that crop up. But if you're feeling lonely or financially strapped, then you have to act quickly to stabilize yourself emotionally. Otherwise you run the risk of losing faith in yourself, your skills, and your staying power. The result? You can easily lose your momentum and feel deflated; where the seeds of hope once flourished, fear can quickly begin to take root. Here's some advice from women on the front lines on making the first three months of your new venture as productive as possible:

Remember That Even Positive, Life-Affirming Changes Are Stressful

Myrna Ruskin, an entrepreneur who's started many small businesses, took an interesting route to her current career as a stress management consultant: she began as a wedding planner. In this role, she saw firsthand just how distressing and nerve-racking even a happy event like preparing for a wedding could be. So much so, in fact, that she found herself deriving more satisfaction from the stress-relieving effect her counseling had on nervous brides and mothers than she did from orchestrating the actual weddings. Ultimately this interest led her to the field of stress management. As Ruskin is quick to point out, even the happiest, most rewarding types of change can trigger tremendous stress, because you are called on to "adapt, cope, and tap all your resources."

When facing the deep changes involved in your start-up, Ruskin urges you to nurture your self-esteem and give yourself credit for the strengths you bring to the process. As she puts it, "You can be beautiful, bright, talented, empathetic, and have a wonderful sense of humor on Saturday. If you leave your job on Monday and decide to strike out on your own, do any of those things change? No! You are still bright, talented, and empathetic, with a great sense of humor! You are who you are. You just don't have the job that you had before. You still have all the same strengths. Now you have to channel them in the new direction you've chosen."

The message? You'll find it a lot easier to handle this stage if you aren't too hard on yourself about the way you're feeling. Keeping your sense of humor also helps. Without it you can quickly lose your perspective just when you need it most. So do whatever it takes to help take a walk on the sunny side of the street—call a friend, do something a little crazy, wear something bold and bright, or, better yet, write yourself a phony check for a million dollars! Lighten up and make it a point to enjoy yourself. After all, isn't having fun part of what it's all about?

Come to Terms with Why so You Can Focus on How

As you work through the first three months of cottage life, you can easily get caught up in asking yourself lots of open-ended "why" questions about what you've done: Why am I making this move? Why did I decide to make it now? Why do I believe it's right for me? Why should I be able to beat the odds? It's critical that you make peace with these issues as soon as possible so you can focus on figuring out the steps you need to take to make your new venture work. In her counseling sessions, Jackie Farley often enjoys quoting a saying of Nietzsche that goes something like this: "If you can answer the question why, you can endure the hows."

During this start-up stage, one of your major goals should be to come to terms with *why* so you can focus on *how*. To reach this point, you need to accept, respect, and be honest with yourself about your real goals and ambitions. You need to move beyond your fantasies about success and turn inward to discover exactly why you're doing what you're doing, what sacrifices and trade-offs you're prepared to make, and what the end game really is for you in starting your venture. Remember, *intention creates opportunity*. Once you've come up with a why that satisfies and sustains you, you can concentrate on how to reach your goal. And that forward motion will help you gather the support and recognize the opportunities you need to succeed. But if asking why continues to baffle and absorb you, you'll end up spinning your emotional wheels when you should be in gear and on the road.

Create a Personal Mission Statement

One way to deal effectively with why so you can get on with the "hows" of business survival is to develop what Jackie Farley calls a "personal mission statement," a brief sentence or paragraph that acts as a kind of emotional umbrella for your life and work. Writing the mission statement is "as much a process as it is a product," says Jackie, and "it's detected, not invented." It also should be inspiring and challenging. In writing the statement, concentrate on the big picture—your values, your beliefs, and what you really want to achieve. Focus on your personal growth targets, because the statement is really a life-planning exercise rather than a business plan.

Once your ideas and insights begin to jell, capture them in a rough draft and then live with it for a while. Don't worry about wording or specifics, just focus on getting down on paper what you want to do and how you want to spend your time and energy. When you feel reasonably happy with your first effort, hang it up in your home or office where you can easily see it while you're working. Leave it there for a couple of weeks without changing it or judging it. Then gather your new thoughts and revise it until it really begins to reflect the direction you want to take. Keep it on hand as a touchstone for your planning and be flexible, changing it as needed.

A personal mission statement can support this stage of your venture in several ways. First, it will help you stay focused and directed and screen out extraneous activities that might deflect you from doing what you need to do to make your cottage life-style a reality. And second, it can make it easier to balance priorities and schedule your time effectively. As Jackie Farley is fond of saying, "time management should be purpose management." Your mission statement can help you decide what to say yes to—and what to say no to—based on the goals you've set for yourself. It also can be a powerful source of inspiration during those inevitable moments when you question your sanity and feel tempted to pull out the want ads.

Make Your First One Hundred Days Count

There's an old Chinese proverb that says, "The beginning and the end reach out their hands to each other." How true this is! You are making a fresh start and entering an exciting new phase of your work life. It's the perfect time to let go of old patterns and create new ones that will serve you well in the future. Make the most of this precious time and you'll be setting the stage for success; let it slip through your fingers and you'll lose powerful momentum. So whether you're starting your venture in May or July, make a New Year's resolution—a new business resolution, if you like—and promise yourself to keep your hand on the tiller and proceed full speed ahead. And however stormy your sea of emotions proves to be, resolve to stay your course for at least one hundred days. You'll be amazed at the strength this simple, but powerful, decision will give you.

Remember that the fantasies you have about working on your own are rooted in desire, not reality. While those fantasies can be powerful motivators, they also can cloud your judgment when it comes to the practical side of setting up your business. Resolve to approach the first days of your new venture with an open mind and without any preconceived notions about the image you should present, how things should work, or how much money you should be making. After all, you're new to the cottage life, and for you, its seas are uncharted. So expect the unexpected, do your homework, and reach out for help when you need it.

As you plan the first three months of your venture, remember that big changes are made up of small changes. "Most successful change," notes Dr. Brian Schwartz, "takes place in increments. If you make too big a leap, you can place yourself in jeopardy." So don't try to do everything you want to do at once; it's self-defeating and often a recipe for disaster. You can scatter your energies, bog down in details, and lose sight of the big picture. Instead ask yourself where you want to be after your first three months and then set some priorities. Choose three—or, at most, five—key goals you want to accomplish and then drive toward them every day. Keep them realistic and doable within your time frame. Be specific; focus on what you *want* to do, so you can set some targets. Be clear on *why* you want to do it, so you'll stay motivated. And finally, think through *how* you can achieve each goal you've set, so you can map out a plan of action for getting there. Put both your goals and your strategy on paper so you'll feel committed. And don't forget to reward yourself every time you make real progress.

Karen Fried's approach to the first three months of her company demonstrates just how much you can accomplish in a short time if you're extremely organized and goal-oriented. Karen, you may recall, is the inventor of the popular word game Think-It Link-It. She launched her venture in September 1991, while she was still working as a highly successful executive in one of New York City's leading commercial real estate firms. To give you a firsthand look at the incredible energy and drive Karen's new venture unleashed, on the opposite page is a list, taken from her own notes, of the major steps she took during her first thirty days.

Mind-boggling as this list is, it reveals how powerful the ability to zero in on a clear-cut goal can be. While at first glance it looks as if Karen was going off in many different directions at once, in fact, she was extremely disciplined and focused. All of the tasks she accomplished during the first hectic thirty days of her new venture focused on three key goals: structuring her business and protecting her idea; game design and manufacturing; and marketing and merchandising.

During the first three months of her start-up, Karen literally lived a double life, closing several major real estate deals while mastering the ins and outs of game design, manufacturing, marketing, and merchandising. By the end of her first one hundred days, not only had she researched the field thoroughly, talked to scores of people in the industry, and planned a business strategy, but she also had designed and produced one thousand game prototypes and generated orders for the game from Toys "R" Us, the country's largest toy distributor, as well as Bloomingdale's, FAO Schwarz, and Kiddie City. She accomplished all of this by using negotiating and communications skills she had fine-tuned in her real estate business. She also did her homework, quickly gaining hands-on experience in the game industry. While Karen's drive is exceptional, the message here is one that any new business owner can benefit from: get organized, stay focused, and set realistic targets. These steps can make your first one hundred days satisfying and rewarding.

GAME
SEPTEMBER 18—OCTOBER 18, 1991

- Chose name of game, wrote and rewrote rules.
- Bought a copyright book and learned about the process.
- Ordered and received copyright information from the fed.
- Found a copyright lawyer, hired him.
- Found a tax lawyer, hired him.
- Chose a corporate name, incorporated.
- Performed a copyright search. Ordered an extended search.
- Applied for trademark protection.
- Produced a prototype and refined it.
- Decided on all specs for game components: box size, card size, etc.
- Requested prices for box, board, printing, cards, pad, timer, etc.
- Negotiated final prices for timer, pencils, playing pieces.
- Wrote 500 LINKS. Hired a graphic designer to fine-tune design.
- Bought and examined competitive games for color, size, copyright information, design.
- Met with industry experts about the licensing/distribution game.
- Spoke with S.P. about the marketing/promotional investment.
- Met with M.F.—discussed the investment aspect.
- Made a commitment to Toy Fair, read information.
- Put together a preliminary budget for prototypes/legal, Toy Fair.
- Created the game, including the "draw" spaces.
- Decided on recycling concept and theme for game/marketing.
- Met with the American Cancer Society to discuss donation.

Set Boundaries in Time and Space

In making the transition from corporate executive to entrepreneur, you must anchor yourself, both emotionally and professionally. Setting boundaries in the early days of your start-up is one of the best ways to do this. As a first step, create a work space devoted exclusively to your business. Be sure that your phone, files, contact lists, and everything else you'll need during the day are instantly at hand. If you're working at home, keep your personal and business paperwork in different places; mingling them can create an organizational nightmare. Separating the functions in your life is really critical, believes psychologist Barbara Mackoff. As she points out, "It seems like the most obvious thing in the world to say, 'Have a separate office,' yet you'd be astonished at how many people choose a separate room or even a garage to work in, but still take a pile of work and sit down at the kitchen table. I suggest strongly that when you set up a business, you have a place where you only work. You don't make personal phone calls there and you don't play there. You also don't take work to places where you play. If you decide to take time to marinate a steak or sort your laundry, then fine, call it a coffee break, leave your office to do it, and then return! Mixing functions is like a mixed metaphor—it makes it hard to set limits on your work and your personal life. To separate your work space, create a ritual of entry for yourself. I sometimes suggest that people actually put a lock and key or a latch on the door to their office. This is a way of symbolically turning out the lights on your work and signaling to yourself that you're making a transition into another part of your life. It's also important to do something physical to throw off the adrenaline from your workday—the same kinds of things people might do during a commute."

In her book *Leaving the Office Behind,* Dr. Mackoff offers many other helpful techniques for creating a transition between your business and personal lives. If you work at home, she suggests that when your workday is over you do something that gets you out of the house, so that when you return, in your own mind, "you don't work there anymore, you live there." Take a fifteen-minute break to review your day and unwind before you begin your evening. Close your office door and walk around the block, or take a shower, relax with a glass of wine, or run an errand. Try to keep regular hours and avoid returning to your office once you leave it for the day; if you work late, call it overtime. Have a separate office phone and let your phone machine take messages once your workday ends. If you're under intense deadline pressure, get extra child-care help.

"In addition to setting boundaries for yourself," says Dr. Mack-off, "it's also important to set boundaries and communicate them to customers, clients, vendors, family, and friends. You have to educate them about what to expect from your new work situation. Keeping regular hours is one of the keys to this; not answering your personal phone line during the day is another. Otherwise people don't know the difference between working at home and being at home. Friends will come over and ask you to watch Jimmy or your mom will call at two o'clock to chat. Let everyone know that you work between the hours of eight and six. You also don't have to take calls at ten o'clock at night to prove you're serious about your business. Some women worry that their male customers will think, Oh, she's not working, she's giving her child a bath. Well, let them fantasize! You're using your time after work to renew yourself so you're as sharp as you can be when that person calls at eight in the morning.

"Setting up a structure where your business has its limits is also very important in balancing your home and work life. It allows you to give total concentration to your work and then focus on all the rest of your life, which includes your family and children, your community, spirituality, music, or football, or whatever else is important to you. You can say, 'Until six o'clock, this project has my full attention. But when I walk out of here, I'll give myself a transition, and then pay attention to the rest of my life.' When I'm here, I'm focused on work, and when I'm there, I'm focused on family—even if 'there' is just three feet away. Finding this balance takes real skill."

Create a New Operating Structure

Establishing a well-disciplined work pattern to replace your old corporate routine will help "ground" you while allowing you to discover new, and often more efficient, work rhythms. It also will raise your comfort level about taking the risks associated with entrepreneurship and make you feel more in control of your time and resources. During your corporate career, the structure of your workday was more or less imposed on you. It was built around meetings, phone calls, memo writing, project planning, and deadlines. Now you need to forge a new structure on your own to keep you productive, motivated, and attuned to your market.

Planning your daily and weekly routines to ensure that you make the most of your time is one of the keys to survival during this stage. Time is yours to use or misuse now as never before, and it's easy to procrastinate and waste it when you're the only boss you have. If you work with a computer, then be sure to investigate some of the time-saving small business software that's available. There are electronic calendars and tickler files, business proposal packages, and mailing list and label systems that can save you time and keep you organized. There are also on-line services that can allow you to use your computer to conduct research, access electronic bulletin boards, and join industry groups. Just remember that all of this support costs money, and be sure to watch your budget.

Finding the work style that's best for you, given the nature of your business, energy level, and logistics, is also essential. In 1991, Cheryl Williams made the decision to start her own firm, ReArt, and run it from her apartment. As a consultant, she provides support on all facets of small business management for individuals and creative arts companies. After ten years in financial services with a number of companies, Cheryl found it very challenging to plan a new work routine and use her time most productively. Here's how she handled it: "Initially my structure emerged from my journal writing. It was the first thing I did in the morning, as a way of collecting my thoughts and paying attention to the intuitive side of me that had, in essence, been dormant or suppressed for so long. Out of that daily hour and a half or two hours, I began creating a framework, so I didn't wake up feeling, Oh, my God, I have absolutely nothing to do. It's me and the soaps and the refrigerator."

Today, some three years after starting her business, Cheryl has fine-tuned an efficient and personalized work strategy. She works from her Riverside Drive apartment in upper Manhattan and still starts her day at about eight in the morning by writing in her journal, which is now on her computer. Typically she spends the rest of her morning researching information, reading periodicals to keep up-to-date on industry trends, and talking on the telephone. She stays in touch with former clients, touches base with current ones, and follows up new business leads. Since she prefers to build her business by word of mouth, this marketing effort is an ongoing one. The rest of her day is spent on planning and implementing projects for her clients, either at home or at their offices. At some point during the day, Cheryl also tries to take time out for exercise, using equipment in her apartment. She also makes it a point to attend a networking meeting, conference, or other business-related event about once a week.

To keep herself focused, Cheryl tries to stay with the same work flow from week to week. She usually sets aside one day a week, typically Monday, for the business of running her business—billing, filing, correspondence, trips to the post office, and so on. She also tries to build some planning time into her Monday, if possible. Tuesdays, Wednesdays, and Thursdays are devoted to client work—planning and research, meetings, setting up systems. Friday is usually spent following up leads, taking care of overflow paperwork, and mapping out the coming week. If her work load is especially heavy during a particular week, Cheryl will devote Monday afternoon and Friday morning to servicing her clients, still leaving herself Monday morning and Friday afternoon—one full day—to handle administrative tasks and paperwork.

Cheryl's weekly work pattern may give you some ideas you can adapt to your own situation—or it may not strike a chord with you at all. What's important is that her operating structure evolved naturally and reflects the nature of the consulting business she is building. Some entrepreneurs find that they thrive only when using a very different approach, one that Jordana Simpson calls the "work-play mode." This work style is based on intense periods of planning and concentration followed by creative time off to reenergize. After refueling, you shift back again into the work at hand, extending your workday into the evening, if you choose. Whatever approach you take, creating a work structure to anchor your day and week is essential. As your structure evolves, you may find that the core of your workday follows the classic nine-to-five corporate pattern. In fact, most entrepreneurs spend much of their time doing exactly what they did at their corporate jobs—planning, making calls, attending meetings. The real challenge here is taking advantage of the flexibility your new work situation gives you while creating a disciplined framework around it. As you'll see when we talk about traps (see pages 240–43), it's also important to guard against overspending when setting up your office. While you want and need to feel organized and professional, do it on a tight budget.

Conserve and Channel Your Energy and Enthusiasm

Being excited and energized about your new venture is a wonderful, uplifting feeling. If you do find yourself enjoying a honeymoon period, when everything seems to be going smoothly, then try to bottle it. If you are lucky enough to feel this way, it's only natural that you'll want to share your excitement with family, friends, and former colleagues. By all means, go ahead, but with one caveat: don't get too carried away. Why not? Why pull in the reins when you've just charged out of the starting gate? There are several good reasons.

For starters, spending too much time talking to anyone and everyone about what you're doing and planning to do can dissipate your energy and enthusiasm at a time when they should be directed exclusively toward the job at hand: getting your business off the ground. Talking about starting a venture is one thing; getting on with it is another. So try not to spend precious time on the phone or over long leisurely lunches rhapsodizing about your risk-taking skills, your ambitious plans, and how great it is to be on your own. Just *do* it. Conserve your energy and excitement, pour them into your new business calls and renewing your relationships with valued suppliers and former clients. This is the route that Karen Fried took. After spending many hours discussing all kinds of business ideas with her friends, when her big idea for a word game finally hit, she decided to pursue it quietly and on her own. She didn't tell her friends or anyone at work. Not only did this help keep Karen focused, it also made it easier to keep herself going, despite the obstacles she faced. She felt freer to make mistakes, because no one else knew about them. She went public only after she knew the word game could succeed and felt totally committed to it.

There's another powerful reason to be somewhat guarded in expressing your feelings of optimism. Although it may be hard to accept, being overly enthusiastic can sometimes cause problems with family and friends. Your optimism may be so infectious that people around you want to climb aboard your train before it leaves the station. In situations like this, your move may not only spark their imagination, it also may fuel feelings of discontent and dissatisfaction with where they are and what they're doing. They may begin to see your venture as a vehicle for helping *them* escape the rut they're in, and they may begin fantasizing about taking the plunge, too, using you as their lifeline. Suddenly they'll raise the possibility of going into business with you or putting you in touch with someone they know who can give you inexpensive advice or office space or whatever. And before you know it, you'll find yourself hooked into a commitment that won't work for you. Given the right chemistry, working with a friend or relative can be a positive move. But it's definitely not one you want to make lightly or in response to someone else's dissatisfaction.

Enlist Support from Family and Friends

While it's important to harness your energies and make every minute count during your start-up, that doesn't mean cutting yourself off totally or sacrificing valued friendships to your business. The loneliness you may feel in the early days of your new work life can dampen your enthusiasm and cloud your judgment. So while you need to set some boundaries early in the game, don't be afraid to reach out for support and encouragement. Remember always that wherever you are and whatever you do, you don't have to go it alone. During this start-up phase, your goal should be to organize a cheerleading squad for yourself, a small band of believers who will bolster your confidence and nourish your self-esteem. There will be plenty of time once you're better established for tough, unsparing counsel and periodic reality checks. Right now you need encouragement from this team more than you need lots of well-meaning but diffuse advice and criticism about what you're doing and how you're doing it. This doesn't mean, of course, that you don't need professional help from lawyers, accountants, and other professionals; their expertise may be vital to your venture's successful launch. What we're talking about here is the kind of emotional sustenance you should look for from the people who are closest to you and whose attitudes can influence yours the most.

Family involvement and interest in your business can be a blessing or a burden, a source of strength or a minefield. Your family has an enormous, if invisible, stake in your business. Its members are emotional investors in your potential success—or your failure. Their belief, or lack of it, in your ability to make your new enterprise work is the currency with which they purchase a part of your dream or reject it. So set the ground rules for their contribution to your venture in its infancy. Decide what kind of help you want from each family member, and then let them know, clearly and tactfully, how they can support you. This holds true for friends as well. Assigning a specific task to every member of your cheerleading squad is a good strategy. It will help you, it will set some limits, and it will give the people around you a stake in your success. If your mom is a media maven, then ask her to be on the lookout for ideas and trends that might fuel your venture. If your sister is an ace marketer, then put her to work designing a brochure or doing market research.

Without the help of family and friends, says Pamela Mauney, "starting my business would have been impossible." Having her family actively involved has been a real plus. They've provided both practical and moral support and have come to appreciate the amount of work and time it takes. Remember, though, that your family's first and most important job is to help keep you motivated and support your can-do spirit—not in a Pollyanna-like way, but with zest. Apart from this role, your best bet, at least initially, is to keep your family's contributions clearly defined, limited, but productive. You may or may not want to have your family influence your start-up decisions. And appealing as the idea may seem, give careful thought to bringing family members, however well-meaning and skilled, into your fledgling enterprise on a more formal basis.

It's also important to spell out as clearly as you can to family and friends how your business will affect your personal life—and theirs. Barbara Brabec believes that this is especially crucial if you have children and plan to work at home. She advises anyone in this situation to "sit down with your family, especially your spouse, and make sure at the start you have the family's full support. A new business is stressful enough,'' she adds, ''without being burdened by family complaints that meals aren't as good as they used to be, the laundry isn't done on time, and the house is a mess because it is strewn with 'business' from top to bottom.'' While these are all hot topics, they are likely to be the tip of the iceberg. As time goes on, many far more emotionally charged issues are likely to emerge. At this stage, however, it's important that you begin to give both your friends and your family, especially if you're married, a realistic sense of the demands your business start-up is going to make on all of your personal lives. Your domestic duties are only one danger zone. The amount of time and budget you have for socializing, the out-of-synch-with-the-rest-of-the-world work pattern you may find yourself in, and the stress you'll be experiencing—all need to be put on the table and discussed.

Start Building Bridges

During the early months of your venture, building bridges should be high on your priority list. You must maintain your contacts with key business colleagues, clients, and vendors. Yes, you may have left your job and former employer behind, but staying in touch with people you worked with and care about should be part of your start-up game plan. Make it a point to call people regularly, drop them a note, or send them a news clip you think they might enjoy— whatever comes most naturally to you.

After relocating to Maine, for example, Joyce McClure made week-long visits to New York City every few months to get a quick dose of urban energy and keep up with friends and contacts. She also encouraged people to visit her in Maine. As a result, several years after she'd left a high-paying public relations job, Joyce was still receiving calls from headhunters trying to lure her back into corporate life. Even today keeping that door open is important to her. Debra Oppenheim left her corporate partnership on good terms with her colleagues, many of whom were very supportive of her new venture. Less than a year after she left, her old employer started referring clients to her. Jordana Simpson and her partner, Valerie Rosenoff, also launched their business by approaching a company they had worked with for another designer. Over time, other clients and friends gave them leads, which led to several projects. Former suppliers also can be a valuable source of new business. One entrepreneur generated a number of assignments through the graphic designers and video producers she had worked with at her old corporate job. While all of this may seem obvious, it's still worth saying: staying in touch with former clients and colleagues is a must. And the time to begin doing so is in the honeymoon stage of your new venture, when your enthusiasm is highest.

Beware of Old Spending Patterns

If money is tight, you easily can fall into one of two traps: You can fuel your financial fears by micromanaging to the point where you're literally obsessed with every penny instead of focusing on planning, client service, and networking. Or you can go to the opposite extreme and attempt to solve your financial problems by ignoring them and hoping they'll go away. In this frame of mind, you easily can overspend when you should be economizing or endanger your business by putting your financial affairs in the hands of an accountant or consultant who doesn't really have any stake in your success but simply eats up more of your money.

You also may respond to financial anxiety by clinging to old personal spending patterns that can seriously hamper your chances of success. In her corporate job–holding days, for instance, with paycheck in hand, Jordana Simpson recalls assuaging her feelings of work dissatisfaction by treating herself to something special—a silk scarf, a new bag, an expensive pair of shoes. When she started her own business, she had to give up this luxury and find new, less costly ways to calm her anxieties and reward herself. Doing this is never easy, but it's essential. At a time when you should be on a belt-tightening personal budget, old money-spending habits can be dangerous. Debra Oppenheim, for example, found that it took her a while to accept the fact that she had to rein in her personal spending and adjust her life-style in response to her start-up's fragile finances. For a while she continued spending money as she had when she was a partner at her old executive search firm, a pattern that easily could have sabotaged her new business. As we'll see later, overspending on costly equipment, hiring help instead of doing everything yourself, and unnecessary image-building expenditures are all financial traps you can fall into so easily during your start-up phase. Each of these mistakes can quickly put your new business at risk. Awareness is essential here. Knowing the emotional hungers and fears that fuel your spending patterns and anxieties can be the key to taking better control of this problem.

Celebrate Your First One Hundred Days

If you've survived the first one hundred days of your new life, then you deserve a badge of honor. You've had to battle loneliness and cope with loss. You've had to set goals for yourself and force yourself to persevere in achieving them, even when you were feeling down and adrift. Transitions are never easy, and you've had to work through a major one. When you hit the one hundred–day milestone, let yourself go! Celebrate! Reward yourself! Be amazed at your resilience and stick-to-itiveness! And when the confetti settles, take stock of what you've learned about the demands of your start-up. Make an honest, clear-eyed assessment of exactly what appeals to you—and what doesn't—about the new work style you're shaping for yourself. What do you really love about it? Is it the freedom you have to work at your own pace? Is it the flexibility your new life gives you and your family? Is it the satisfaction you get from putting yourself on the line and being forced to master new skills—skills you never even dreamed you had? Then look at the flip side: What is it you really hate, procrastinate about, and wish you could pay someone else to do for you, even though you can't afford to right now? Is it the paperwork, or the constant marketing? Or the sixteen-hour days? Or feeling too out of synch with the rest of the work world?

As you create a balance sheet of the joys and burdens of being your own boss, take a close look at your personal mission statement and see if it's still on target or needs some fine-tuning. Then take a deep breath. You're entering exciting but dangerous territory as you move into the next three months of cottage life. While you're in for a rocky ride, if you know you're moving in the right direction, your newfound skills and confidence will help light your path.

7

STAGE THREE:
FACING REALITY—MONTHS FOUR TO SIX

*Going into business for yourself is a little like knowing
you want to be a ballerina. You get the tutu, the shoes,
the cassette tape of Mozart—all the right stuff. But that's
not what makes a ballerina. What makes a dancer is
getting out on the floor and dancing.*

—*Jordana Simpson*

Your first three months of cottage life probably have been exciting, confusing, hectic, and more than a bit surprising. If you've used your time well, then you've taken some important steps to anchor yourself emotionally. You've created a personal mission statement to help keep you focused and "on purpose." You've made some basic decisions about where and how you plan to work. Your new work space, whether it's at home or outside, is beginning to take shape. So far you've managed to survive without the nuts-and-bolts support your corporate life once provided; you even have a rough idea of the overhead costs you'll have to cover each month. Your personal life may be on the lean side, but your days certainly are flying by and more interesting than ever; you'd have plenty to talk about at a cocktail party, if only you could go! All things considered, you're beginning to think that this whole cottage idea might work after all. The sense of freedom and flexibility it's given you is really intoxicating. You're just about hooked.

Then, *wham!* You're knocked flat. Even if you started out with a great idea or one or more anchor clients, as you move into the fourth month of your new life, alarm bells may start ringing. It's easy to feel that you're all dressed up with nowhere to go—you've put on your shoes and the cassette tape of Mozart, but no one is asking you to dance. Yes, the start-up project that launched you has been exciting, but it's drawing to a close and you've been too busy giving 110 percent to it to drum up new business. Yes, a handful of clients have made the corporation-to-cottage move with you by giving you work, but they could disappear overnight, and then where would you be? Yes, the research for the new product you want to produce has been very encouraging, there really seems to be a market for it. But what should you do next? And where will you find the money? You're trying hard to stay upbeat and productive, but it isn't easy.

What's going on? In a nutshell, your fantasy is colliding with reality. You've become the entrepreneurial risk taker so many magazine articles wax eloquent about, and it's proving to be a risky business. As the hours turn into days and the days into months, it's beginning to dawn on you that your corporate experience really hasn't prepared you for the ups and downs of starting a business. It's as if you began this new phase of your work life wearing a pair of rose-colored glasses and then, without warning, someone grabbed them away from you. Suddenly you find yourself facing an enormous chasm—the gap between the fantasy you had of running your own show and the day-to-day reality of doing it. As that reality sinks in, some aspects of the cottage work style you may have once brushed aside may begin to trouble you—the demands on your personal life, the financial worries, the time required, the rejection you may face, the sense of having to do everything and never being able to do enough. During this stage, it will be essential to keeping these anxieties under control while staying focused and pushing forward. Your main goals in the next three months will be to

- maintain your confidence in the face of self-doubt;
- find your "secret motivator" and create a renewal strategy;
- refocus your support system and adapt your networking style;
- make your beginner's status work for you; and
- stay focused, despite the obstacles you encounter.

WHAT YOU CAN EXPECT TO FEEL

As reality sets in, the excitement and energy that fueled your first weeks may seem to drain away. The novelty of your business start-up may be wearing off, both for you and for the people around you. Your new business isn't news anymore. Dealing with the day-to-day challenges of building a business from scratch can start to feel like pushing a rock uphill. As a corporate executive, you may have cheerfully juggled several projects, managed a large staff, handled big budgets, and faced countless deadlines. Even with all of this experience under your belt, being in business for yourself can tax your emotional and physical resources more deeply than you ever imagined. You may find that you aren't as efficient on your own as you were on the corporate job and that your time management skills aren't as strong as they could be. Yet, despite these challenges, if you stay balanced and take decisive action, this can prove to be an exciting time of personal growth and self-discovery. As you move toward the six-month mark of your start-up, here are some of the feelings and concerns you're likely to encounter.

Mixed Signals

The next three months can be especially demanding because you can find yourself buffeted by contradictory feelings. You may be encouraged because you've survived your first three months and begun building a new base of operations. At the same time, you can find yourself battling serious bouts of self-doubt about your business skills. You may have started your venture with a bang, but as things wind down, fears about lack of work can undermine your sense of accomplishment. You may have burned up the phone wires in an energetic quest to do your homework and renew contacts. But instead of equipping you to take action, all of your research may make you feel like a babe in the woods. Information, which once seemed to be a key to your success, suddenly seems to be a barrier; you now know enough to know exactly how much you don't know about what you want to do. And you're smart enough to be anxious about it.

Pushed and pulled, like Joyce McClure, you may find yourself vacillating between fear and optimism about your future. During her move from New York to Maine, Joyce found herself dwelling on two conflicting feelings: On the one hand, she sometimes felt as if she had plunged into a "black hole" by giving up a fast-paced and comfortable career for the uncertainties of small-town living. On the other hand, she also felt the hopefulness and liberation that a new beginning often offers; her decision gave her a "clean slate" and the chance to reshape her life.

Conflicting feelings like those Joyce experienced can make you feel at war with both yourself and your professed new business goals. What's really happening here? The answer can be summed up in three words: *you're testing yourself.* And perhaps you're also being tested by those around you. In the first three months, you dipped your foot into the water of entrepreneurship. Now you're being forced to face some of your shortcomings and fears and decide whether you really want to take the plunge. Are you managing your time well or letting it slip through your fingers because there's no one to crack the whip or hand you a paycheck? Are you forcing yourself to find new business or just treading water? Can you acquire the new skills you need to survive? Can you handle the financial strain? These are some of the questions likely to crop up during this time of testing. What's really at issue, however, is not simply your business acumen, but your *emotional stamina.* What you're really asking yourself is, Do I want this enough to make it work, whatever it takes? Am I willing to accept the setbacks and disappointments that will come my way? Is there enough joy, passion, and fun in what I'm doing to keep me motivated? Do I have the staying power my venture demands?

As Jordana Simpson candidly admitted during a discussion of her graphic arts business, "My biggest fear isn't lack of experience, it's lack of endurance. I'm very good at the start-up stage and very powerful in creating a lot of energy and enthusiasm when a project is getting off the ground. I'm like a short-distance runner—very fast through the gate. But sometimes I'm afraid that I'm not one of those people who have the strength to go around the track again and again." Right now you may be feeling exactly the same way.

Performance Anxiety

The pressure to perform, both self-imposed and from those around you, is likely to escalate during this stage. As you move into the fourth month or so of your venture, you may find that your anxiety about how well you're doing takes a quantum leap. Lack of feedback becomes a problem—without a paycheck, a boss, or promotions, how do you measure your progress (or lack of it)? The need to produce results—or to sustain them at an unrealistic level at this stage of your business—also can become an issue. This is especially true if you start out with a big project, a hot idea, or a strong initial market response. Everyone, including yourself, expects you to keep up the pace. You know all of the statistics about small businesses needing from one to three years to break even or show a profit, but somehow you expected—or were expected—to beat the odds virtually overnight. When work doesn't come in but the bills start piling up, you can feel compelled to rethink your game plan, sell beyond your comfort level, or take on any kind of project, just to survive. At this time, you also may begin to feel that your personal support system—namely, your family and friends—really doesn't understand what you're going through and how hard it all is. You may begin to feel underappreciated and even abandoned. Emotionally you're in for a pound, while the people who should be investing most heavily in you seem to be in for a penny. Your spouse, for example, who pledged his enthusiastic support during your venture's honeymoon, may now feel ambivalent. He may begin to resent the amount of time your work demands or the pressure he feels to make more money. In short, your cheerleading squad seems to be packing up while you're still out on the field and it's starting to rain.

The anxiety you're feeling may be intensified by the fact that you've reached a critical juncture in your venture's infancy. For lack of a better phrase, let's call it the "fall-apart phase." If you look closely, you'll probably recognize all of the signs from your corporate experience. If you're in public relations, it's the day of reckoning, when you submit a painstakingly prepared media campaign, only to have your client complain that you weren't listening and your concept is totally off base. If you're a writer, it's that sinking feeling you get when you submit a first draft to your editor and she tells you, however tactfully, that she doesn't like it and you have to throw it all out. If you're a product designer, it's the moment you discover that the initial specs you were given have changed drastically and the whole project has to go back to the drawing board.

You get the picture. This stage seems to be a natural point early in the life cycle of many major projects in which you invest heavily in terms of time, talent, and energy. Just when things seem to be coming together, something hits you from left field, everything falls apart, and you have to pick up the pieces. Once you've experienced this phenomenon a few times in your corporate life, you come to realize that it's simply part of the process you're engaged in, your professionalism kicks in, and you know enough not to take it personally. If and when your new business goes through a parallel upheaval, however, the stakes are much higher; your livelihood may be at risk. How you respond can make or break you. You may feel down and discouraged, but as we'll see, you simply have to push past this stage in order to regain your balance and sense of control.

Self-Doubt

Jackie Farley, who has worked with many business owners at her CenterPoint retreat in Aspen, finds that many women in the early throes of making the move from employee to entrepreneur are extremely vulnerable. Even after their start-up is launched, they continue to express a lot of self-doubt about themselves and their staying power, and tend to "concentrate on what they're losing" in leaving the corporate world. Jackie notes that "they begin asking themselves questions like, How do I know if I'm doing the right thing? How can I trust myself and my vision?" When self-doubt hits, you may find yourself second-guessing or waffling about even the simplest decisions and trying to keep your options open by procrastinating or turning to other people for advice. Far from fantasizing about your potential success, you may begin replaying old, long-forgotten situations in which you failed to reach a goal you had set for yourself. You may begin thinking back to other moments in your life when you took a big risk and suffered the consequences. When this happens, it's easy to start rewriting history and romanticizing the job you left behind, reliving the fatal moment when you "cut the cord," and wondering why you didn't have the presence of mind to realize that your old work situation wasn't all that bad.

Self-doubt also can lead you to dwell on the issue of timing—maybe you should have waited until the economy picked up, you put away more money, or your personal life was in better shape. If you start thinking this way, your response may be to retreat—to begin hedging your bets and treading water for a while. When this happens, your seemingly firm resolve to make the entrepreneurial life work for you at any cost can begin to crumble. You can find yourself in a test-the-waters mode; instead of a full-out drive to build your business, you may adopt a wait-and-see attitude toward your new life. You may be tempted to put out some feelers in the job market, just in case things don't work out the way you had planned. More often than not, however, this approach can backfire. Instead of relieving your anxieties, exploring job options at this stage can make you feel confused and fragmented.

Deeply Committed and Determined

While months four through six may test your patience and energy, there's nothing you'll face during this time that you can't handle, *if you stand your ground*. Yes, you may still have moments, and even days, of real self-doubt when you think about giving it all up and getting another corporate job. But these flashes of self-doubt will pass—*if* the entrepreneurial bug has bitten you. Why? Because during this stage, you'll discover a precious gift that will sustain and uplift you: a sense of deepening commitment. When this happens, you'll find yourself crossing an imaginary line. There are no signposts to guide you and the moment it happens may go unnoticed. Yet it is a major milestone in the brief life of your new business, because crossing that line means that you truly have become emotionally invested and identified with your fledgling enterprise. You've moved beyond having an intellectual concept to making an emotional commitment, from thinking to yourself, This idea could really work, to feeling, I want to make this happen and I will do whatever it takes to succeed. Cheryl Williams describes this as the moment when you "take off your corporate cloak and assume the mantle of the entrepreneur."

After test-marketing her toffee, for example, Pamela Mauney remembers saying to herself, "I know I can make this work." As the result of her initial success, two months after she started, she made the decision to turn what had been a hobby for many years into a commercial business. Karen Fried's moment of emotional commitment came about four months into developing her game, when she at last went public. After several months of living a kind of double life, juggling her demanding real estate job and her game business, Karen finally walked into her boss's office, told him about her moonlighting venture, and asked him for a leave of absence. Ultimately he opted to keep her on board and give her more flexible hours. But Karen remembers feeling that by telling the head of her company what she was doing, she was putting her eight-year real estate career on the line. She took this step only when she felt completely absorbed in making her game a success.

For many entrepreneurs-in-the-making, this moment of commitment comes toward the end of their first three months; for others, it occurs around the four-month mark. But the precise timing isn't important, it's the event that counts. When this time comes, and you become emotionally invested in your venture, then your decisions take on a new urgency. You no longer just think you can create the business you've envisioned. You're hungry, and you *need* to make it work. This is an exciting moment but a challenging one, because you've upped the ante. You've raised your stake in your business's success—or failure. Making it happen has really become a test, not just of your ability and experience, but of your self-esteem. You really *have* become your business, and your business has become you.

PLANNING YOUR SUCCESS STRATEGY

Without a doubt, you have a lot to handle during months four to six of your venture. You're definitely still in a survival situation, but the pace and the pressures you're facing have changed. While the intense activity that fueled your first three months may have slackened, your emotional drive is gathering force. As you approach the midpoint of your first year in business, here are some specific steps you can take to push ahead:

Begin Thinking Like an Entrepreneur

As you move ahead with your venture, it's vital that your mind-set changes from that of employee to business owner. But how, exactly, do you make this happen? How do you mentally accept yourself in the role of entrepreneur? First, you need to begin thinking about yourself differently, and second, your actions and the way you communicate with the rest of the world must reflect your new self-image. Here's how Cheryl Williams describes this process as it unfolded for her:

"Having control over my time, realizing that I could make a difference, realizing that my business skills didn't have to be used only in a corporate setting, and recognizing that, yes, I could be creative—for me, these were all part of beginning to think like an entrepreneur. The issue of creativity was a big one for me. I realized that I could be involved with creative organizations, tap into their energy, and perhaps draw on that energy to use my own talents more fully. This was a real turning point for me. When I first started my business, I told people that I was really an intermediary. I spoke accounting and legalese, but I also spoke creatively—and as a result, I could work with temperamental artists but also deal with accountants, bookkeepers, and attorneys.

"In 1991 I fully accepted, so to speak, 'the mantle of the entrepreneur.' When you do this, it puts you in an entirely different space emotionally in terms of how you carry yourself, how you perceive yourself, and how you present yourself. This is really important, because it all comes across when you're meeting people. Every time you meet someone, there's a possibility that business can result. That's not really the case in corporate America, unless you're in a sales position. It's a totally different dynamic. When you have your own company, you're selling yourself, particularly if you're in a service business. You are unaffiliated with a corporation. You *are* the corporation.

"You realize, 'I am in business. I am in business to make money.

This is my livelihood now.' And as a consequence, you begin to put structures in place to support this new view of yourself. You begin to look actively for situations in which you can meet people. You sometimes determine that there are organizations you need to weed out, because they don't provide the opportunity to meet potential clients. You really begin to look at your time differently. Time becomes of the essence, because while you are out doing whatever it is you're doing, you are also selling. You are constantly selling. Time is also of the essence because most of us don't have the luxury of support staff—we literally have to do everything ourselves. Until you get to a point where you are flush with cash, you are continually doing a trade-off analysis: Is it worth it for me to spend the time to go to the post office now, or can I do it while I'm doing something else? You're constantly making these kinds of judgments and making adjustments.

"You also never want to totally sever yourself from your corporate background. But you need to use it in a new way. And you should never be reluctant to ask for help. Sometimes we feel that if we don't do it all on our own, then there's something wrong with us and we aren't cut out to be in business for ourselves. I think that knowing when to ask for help is extremely important. It can come in the form of taking classes, visiting the library and doing research, and, of course, talking with other people. So you really aren't alone as an entrepreneur. Or you're as alone as you choose to be."

PERCEIVING and presenting yourself differently. Realizing that you can make a difference and that you can leverage your corporate skills and use them creatively to build a business of your own. Accepting the need to market yourself and your skills. Realizing that your business is your livelihood. Putting structures in place to support your new self-image. Managing your time differently and constantly making trade-offs about your work and resources. Reaching out for information and support in order to find out what you need to know. All of these factors come into play as you begin shaping a new image of yourself as an entrepreneur. As a corporate executive, your role was largely that of facilitator; your tasks were determined by your boss's and your corporation's agenda. Now you must take the lead by creating your own agenda and then planning and executing the steps to make it happen.

Take Control of How You Respond to Your Feelings

When all is said and done, the courage and discipline you need to transform yourself into an entrepreneur comes down to endurance. A business owner who faced a rocky road during her start-up once shared her secret of survival with me. "Not giving up. That's the real key," she said. "If you don't give up, then one way or another, you *will* succeed and make your business work." "The ability to keep going, no matter what happens"—that's how another business owner described the ingredient all entrepreneurs have in common. If you have the energy and the will to keep moving and figure things out as you go along, then you'll manage to survive, whatever obstacles come your way. On the other hand, if you don't have the flexibility and emotional resilience to push ahead and keep on pushing, then all the creativity and resources in the world won't guarantee your success.

Emotional highs and lows are part of the path to entrepreneurship. At the same time, it's important to realize that you don't need to surrender yourself totally to negative feelings of self-doubt or anxiety when they hit you. There are some specific techniques you can use to help change your mood, lift your spirits, and regain the momentum you need to move toward the business goals you've set for yourself. In fact, when it comes to chasing the blues away, some strategies are far more successful than others, according to a recent study conducted by a psychologist at Case Western University and published in *The New York Times*, December 30, 1992. In research with more than four hundred women and men of all ages, Dr. Diane Tice took a close look at the range of approaches people tend to use to dispel bad moods when they hit.

What works best? Taking action to solve a problem or deal with a disturbing situation is far and away the best method for shaking the blues, according to this study's results. So if you're stuck, then the single most important step you can take to get yourself out of a rut is to do something positive. Pick one specific task you can begin immediately, and then just *do* it. Be sure it's something very concrete and absorbing but easy to achieve quickly. Working hard to meet a small challenge—one that will give you satisfaction and pleasure when you complete it—will do wonders for both your psyche and your self-esteem. A task that requires you to take physical action can be especially helpful. Even something as simple as cleaning up your desk, getting your files organized, or actually sitting down and writing that pitch letter you've been thinking about can help clear away the mental cobwebs and improve your outlook.

Interestingly, even though taking action seems to be the best way to chase away the blues, most of us don't use this approach. When we feel down, we're more likely to respond by getting together with friends or talking about our problems on the phone. Yet, socializing in this way isn't usually much help; often it provides only temporary relief. Think about your own experience. After receiving a bad piece of news or hitting a major hurdle, how many times have you reached for the phone and called someone—your mother, your sister, a friend—and given them an earful about what's just happened? Or gone out for drinks and spent most of the evening dissecting a problem in excruciating detail? Sounds familiar, I'm sure. But when you've vented your feelings and hung up the phone or paid your dinner bill, how much better do you really feel? All of the unfocused talking you've done is more likely to fuel your bad feelings than it is to dispel them.

Starting your new business gives you the perfect opportunity to create some new working patterns for yourself. Why not start here? The next time some bad news hits you, try an experiment. Make a decision not to tell anyone about it for at least twenty-four hours—not a soul! If a friend or family member calls, then take a tip from the movie *All That Jazz* and tell yourself, It's showtime! Put on a private performance. Act as if you are on top of the world and not down in the dumps. Sound cheerful instead of beleaguered. Radiate confidence instead of fear or concern. "Act as if and you shall become," an old saying advises. There's no better time than now to test whether or not this is true. If you stay with this approach for a couple of days—or better yet, a few weeks—you'll be amazed at the results. Not only will you begin feeling a lot better more quickly when the blues hit, but the positive energy you radiate will be reflected back to you from the people around you. If they think you are doing well and are on top of things, then that's exactly how they'll respond to you, and their energy will feed into yours.

On the other hand, as Cheryl Williams suggests, reaching out for help right away may be the most productive step you can take. If you find that talking about a problem really helps you think it through and cut it down to size, then make the decision to do it. But discuss it in a businesslike manner and context, not in a social setting. Call a friend whose judgment you respect and run the problem by her or him. Use the friend as a sounding board to explore your options. Or get in touch with someone through a professional association who may have run into the same roadblock and ask for advice. But above all, resist the temptation to sit around feeling sorry for yourself. While this advice may seem too simple to be effective, it works for many people and it can work for you, too. The key here is to use some easy-to-apply techniques that will help you get past the temporary slump you may find yourself in, so you can get on with the business of making your business work.

Find Your Secret Motivator

It's only natural that going the distance is a big issue for small business owners. Staying motivated and focused, especially when things go wrong, is one of the biggest challenges that any entrepreneur faces. As Barbara Brabec notes, "It's having the staying power and endurance to keep things going and figuring out how to keep yourself up when everyone else in the world is telling you, 'This isn't working. You can see for yourself that this isn't going to work. You are going to fail.' It's amazing how often friends and family will tell this to people. So before you start your business, know what you're going to do when you get down."

One of the keys to tapping your staying power is to find your own personal "secret motivator," the emotional tool or technique that will give you the strength to keep going when you feel like giving up. In Barbara Brabec's case, reading works best. "As a writer," she says, "I've found that reading the right material can do more for me than anything else in the world. I read what other people believe in and preach, and suddenly there's a spark inside me. I see something that I didn't see before that sets me off on a whole new track." For Cheryl Williams, journal writing is her secret motivator; it's a source of inspiration and strength. Also, the need to feel that she's "making a difference" through the work she does as an advisor to small businesses is a powerful incentive for Cheryl. Caroline Hull finds that talking with other working mothers who are successfully balancing their work and families energizes and inspires her. For Judith Grant Palma, listening to self-help tapes is a good way to stay upbeat and hopeful.

Myrna Ruskin is a strong believer in the power of affirmations—brief success statements that can help keep you focused and positive. She often works with clients to formulate one or two of these statements and asks them to repeat them with passion and feeling several times a day. Some of the affirmations that Ruskin finds very effective include: "I have all the tools I need to be successful in my new business." "My thoughts for my new business are excellent." "I love my new business and the fulfillment it gives me." "I love the sense of control working for myself provides." "Risk taking excites and energizes me." Ruskin suggests that you write these statements on three-by-five-inch index cards and keep them where you can see them—by your Rolodex and telephone, for example. Some women find that success statements like these work well as secret motivators. Others find that donating part of their new business income to a worthy cause or volunteering their time helps keep them going when they hit a rough spot. Here again, the specific formula or tool doesn't matter; what's important is finding a motivational technique that works well for you.

Make Your Beginner's Status Work for You, Not Against You

As a new kid on the entrepreneurial block, you have lots to learn about the nuts and bolts of running a business. This process is doubly challenging if your venture involves breaking into an industry that's totally new to you. But wherever you are on the learning curve, being a newcomer can be either a handicap or an asset, depending on how you handle it. If your beginner's status makes you afraid to ask questions and overly concerned about making mistakes or appearing unprofessional, then it can hold you back. If, on the other hand, you use it to question conventional wisdom, take a fresh look at how things are done, and come up with innovative solutions, then being a novice can be a real benefit. In fact, it can be a key to your success.

In her article "Off to a Flying Start" (*Executive Female*, January/February 1993), Patti Watts talks about the Zen concept of *shoshin*, or "beginner's mind." Although Watts uses the concept in reference to starting a new corporate job, it can be a powerful tool in building your business as well. As one Zen master describes *shoshin*, "In the beginner's mind, there are many possibilities; in the expert's mind, there are few." As a beginner, you are free to explore, to experiment, and to challenge. Your mind is open and unencumbered by preconceived notions about how things should work. If you take this idea to heart, as Karen Fried did, then you can use your lack of experience to powerful advantage. When Karen began her business, she knew absolutely nothing about designing or producing a game. But eight years of success in commercial real estate had fueled her self-confidence and business skills, so Karen plunged headlong into her venture. Along the way, she broke just about every rule in the book: "I did so many things wrong," she recalls. "If you listed all the 'don'ts' of trying to develop a new game, you'd see that I did them all." But in the process, she learned a powerful lesson: "Never let people tell you definites about what you're doing, because there aren't any."

Instead of feeling overwhelmed by the experts she talked to, Karen listened and "soaked up everything like a sponge." But she didn't let their expertise discourage her or make her feel inadequate. One expert, for example, told her that Toys "R" Us was the biggest game retailer in the country and the hardest store to get into. "They write the rules," he said, adding that they would never even look at a new, untested game like Karen's. Instead of running for cover, Karen picked up the phone, called information, got the number of the Toys "R" Us headquarters, and managed to reach the chief buyer. After grilling Karen for twenty minutes, he agreed to meet with her. Before the meeting, Karen did her homework. She visited Toys "R" Us stores, talked to salespeople and customers, and prepared a ten-page marketing plan for launching her game. After discussing Karen's strategy, the buyer agreed to market Think-It

Link-It when it went into production. She took the same approach with other retailers, including Bloomingdale's and FAO Schwarz.

Karen used the same combination of confidence, curiosity, and creativity to plan innovative ways to design, package, and manufacture her game. She also used her fresh perspective to market her game by coming up with new and appealing angles for TV and newspaper reporters who covered the toy industry. But remember, your beginner's status will take you only so far. Although Karen Fried used it to open doors and question the way things were done, she was also extremely disciplined about doing her homework. She sought out expert advice and learned as quickly as possible about every aspect of the game business, from design and manufacturing to distribution and marketing. Gaining experience in every phase of the industry you want to enter is critical to success, in her view. It's also one of the best ways to protect yourself from being ripped off or taken advantage of during your start-up, when every penny and every moment counts. Feeling confident enough to make mistakes, learn from them, and transform them into opportunities is also key.

Use Your Downtime Constructively

During your start-up, one of the toughest challenges you'll face is keeping your productivity at high pitch. This is especially difficult when you run a service business that is totally dependent on client demand. Often you can find yourself in a feast-or-famine work cycle in which you juggle several assignments for short, intense periods of time and then suffer long droughts, when business seems to dry up. How do you use these fallow periods to greatest advantage and avoid becoming totally reactive, instead of proactive? Cheryl Williams believes that these lulls "happen for a reason" and that you should work with them, not against them. She suggests that you see this not as downtime, but as "creative time" in which to recharge your emotional batteries. You can use these periods to rethink where you're going and fine-tune your business strategy. You can seek out new sources of information that may spark a new idea or direction. You can update yourself on industry trends. You can organize yourself more efficiently. Expanding your marketing efforts is another perfect way to use this time. You can gather new marketing data, for example, or map out a way to repackage your services and create a new product line for yourself. In-between periods also offer a chance to solicit feedback on your performance. In fact, Cheryl suggests that you follow up every assignment with an evaluation form asking your client to identify the benefits received from your work and pinpoint any problems. These can serve as great recommendations when new business comes along.

Other ways to make your downtime more rewarding can include taking a course related to your business and networking with people outside your industry in order to gain a new perspective on it. One entrepreneur used the time between projects in still another creative way: he researched and wrote several articles about key issues his industry was facing and then sent them to the editors of several trade journals. One was immediately accepted and provided him with a powerful marketing tool for new business calls. The key to making these quiet periods fruitful is to structure the time as carefully as you do your project-driven hours. If you don't, then whole days can slip away without any real progress being made. You can also end up finding yourself unprepared or burned out when the pressure hits again.

Adapt Your Networking Style

In your corporate life, networking was probably a major asset in your career; reaching out to other professionals gave you valuable contacts, visibility, and industry data. As you move from employee to entrepreneur, your networking skills are more important than ever. A strong professional support system can help you expand your client base, identify promising new market niches, and learn the ropes by talking with experienced business owners. Equally important, networking can give you feedback and ease your isolation.

During her transition from corporate executive to consultant, Cheryl Williams found networking invaluable. "Throughout this time," she recalls, "I stayed actively involved in all kinds of organizations, including NAFE, the National Women's Political Caucus, the Financial Women's Association, the Black Retail Action Group,

[and] the Mount Holyoke Club of New York. This definitely grounded me emotionally. Having a strong network of friends and associates was very helpful in starting my business. . . . If you work at home, like me, then you sometimes miss the opportunity to bounce ideas off someone else or take a breather and talk to someone besides your cat! Friends and family are important, but if they aren't in business for themselves, they don't always fully understand your situation. So it's very important to develop your professional network.

"As an entrepreneur, you'll find that the kinds of organizations you find yourself associated with are different. I was never actively involved in the National Association for Women Business Owners, for instance. Now I go to their meetings. I had been on the mailing list of the Financial Women's Association but had never joined, because so many of their activities were geared to women in the corporate world. As a result of changes in the nineties, many more of their members are entrepreneurs, so two years ago, I became a member."

It's also important to realize that the dynamics of your networking will change when you make the shift from employee to entrepreneur. When you networked as a corporate executive, you operated with a clearly defined framework and status—you had a title, responsibilities, and resources. Many of the people in your network may have wanted something from you—contacts, entrée to your firm, a project assignment. Now the shoe is on the other foot: *you* are in a business-seeking mode, and you want from your network precisely what you were once in a position to give. Where you once solicited bids from and gave work to suppliers—a designer or printer, for example—you may now be turning to these same people for leads or help in selling a new project. When you enter the start-up phase of your new business, you may find that the balance between giving and receiving shifts dramatically: you may need more help than you are able to offer, at least initially.

Remember, however, that successful networking is a two-way street; it always involves an exchange of benefits. And even if you no longer have a corporate title or budget, you still have valuable resources you can leverage. You can barter your skills and expertise, for instance, or provide a networking contact with an insider's look at your industry. Or you can offer to include a networking contact in a new business proposal, if appropriate. Whatever approach you take, be sure to handle your new situation sensitively and resist the temptation to sell yourself too aggressively. It's also wise, at least initially, to cast as wide a networking net as you can; you never know where a new business lead might come from. When she and her husband relocated to North Carolina, Susan O'Hara-Brill reached out to a handful of people she knew there to learn about the job market and generate business. When Joyce McClure moved to Castine, Maine, she didn't know a soul. But she immediately became involved in the community and began telling people about her background and her plans. Ultimately she hooked up with a man who was very well connected in the town and with members of the state government. He became Joyce's mentor and gave her entrée into the state's economic development program for small businesses.

As your entrepreneurial network evolves, you also are likely to experience a common, but often upsetting, phenomenon: the shrinking Rolodex. When you make the move from employee to entrepreneur, be prepared to find that some of the most valued members of your current network no longer return your phone calls or take the time or interest to support your new venture. One new business owner who left a high-powered editing job found that most of her contacts simply melted away when she started her own company. The emotional impact proved almost as hard to deal with as the loss of professional resources. In addition to feeling isolated, she felt abandoned and even betrayed by some of the friends and acquaintances she had counted on most for support in surviving her transition. When Ann Hull left her position as conference director of the Modern Language Association, she experienced much the same thing. "I was a very favored customer with the people I dealt with professionally who were suppliers," Ann recalls. "And when I left the MLA, it was very interesting to see the people who remained very close to me, as opposed to the ones who never called. Nobody was ever unfriendly, but some of the people I thought were really good friends never gave me any support; others surprised me by staying in touch and even passing on leads."

Tough Out Your Fall-Apart Phase

If and when you find yourself hitting the fall-apart phase in the early months of your new business, it's vital that you mobilize your defenses quickly and forcefully. This isn't always easy; just when you think you have things under control, you can be blindsided—your rent goes up, a proposal bombs, a production snag slows you down, you lose a client, you run out of money, you're hit with an unexpected tax bill. Needless to say, when this time comes, your ego takes a beating and you feel like quitting. In most cases, you can salvage a fair amount of your work, but it feels as if you have to start over. During your corporate life, you could at least take solace in your paycheck. Picking up the pieces is a lot harder when it happens on your own dime. It can really knock the wind out of your sails.

Karen Fried vividly recalls reaching the fall-apart phase. It was about five months into her game venture. A few months earlier, she was a whirlwind of activity. She had taken her concept to the prototype stage, convinced several major retailers to give her orders, and committed herself to an April launch date for a full production run. Then in February she "hit a wall." She needed to raise a huge amount of money to begin manufacturing. There were two traditional avenues open to her. She could license the game, turn over control to an established firm, and receive a percentage of the profits. Or she could retain control by raising investment capital herself; at least $500,000 was needed for the launch. Both approaches were risky; about 95 to 97 percent of all games fail on the drawing board. Initially Karen decided to retain ownership and pursue the venture capital route. This is when reality set in and she reached a low point.

During the first three months, as Karen describes it, her game had "taken on a life of its own—everything that happened just happened. All of a sudden I started asking, 'Okay, how many of these things should I make?' I had become friends with five or six inventors and had their business plans and partnership agreements. One night, about two weeks before Toy Fair, I was on my computer. It was three o'clock in the morning and I was looking at their numbers. And they didn't make sense. . . . At that point, I hit a wall and I thought, I'm all excited about this, but it doesn't work economically. No one is going to make anything. So it's a bad business decision. All of a sudden, the cold, hard facts came to light. At this point, I said to myself, I wish someone had told me this on day one. Now what am I going to do? I've talked to these stores, I've made a fool of myself, I've basically quit my job. I was miserable. I had already spent twenty thousand dollars of my own money, let go of my source of income, and done it in a big way by talking to all the big players and telling them I was going to launch the game in April. Now I have to raise money in about a week and go into production. It was Pressure City."

At this juncture, Karen decided to explore licensing, her other financing option. She won appointments with every single acquisitions executive at all of the top game companies. "All of them liked the game and took it all the way down the road," recalls Karen. But in March she hit another roadblock: the licensing companies weren't biting. Exhausted, she flew to Vancouver and went bicycling. "I just took a break," she recalls. But the day before her trip, she told herself, " 'You have to either believe in this game or not. Because if you don't, it's going to fail. If you do, you can make it succeed.' And I thought, I love this game. Everyone who sees it loves it. These toy companies have made mistakes before. If I have to raise the money myself, then how can I do it?" By the time she left on her trip, Karen had decided to move forward on her own.

Going away proved to be a wise decision. After she returned, things began to fall into place. First, she decided to improve the game's design, and asked nine designers to create mock-ups for the new version. She decided an April launch didn't make sense, so she delayed it until the holiday season and let the retailers know about the change, despite her concern that they would think she didn't know what she was doing. Instead everyone felt she had made a smart business decision and agreed to stay on board. Next she decided to finance a limited production run using her own money and then test-market the game before trying to raise venture capital. Ultimately the game debuted in New York and Chicago, was sold in 150 stores in 22 states, and proved to be a hit during the holiday season. Through creative marketing, the game began to finance itself and by early the next year it reached the break-even point.

. . .

A great story, isn't it? But it's more than just inspiring. Karen's experience and how she handled the roadblocks she encountered offers powerful suggestions for surviving your own venture's fall-apart phase, if it occurs. First, as Karen said earlier, you need to remember that there are "no definites." Regardless of what industry experts say, there's always another way to do things. The trick is to find it. Karen explored the traditional financing option, but when neither raising capital nor licensing proved attractive she didn't throw in the towel. Instead she beat the odds and found a third way to finance Think-It Link-It by underwriting a test run with her own money.

Second, at a critical point, when things looked hopeless, Karen recommitted herself to her venture and made it happen. Third, after intense emotional involvement, she stepped back and regained her perspective. This enabled her to couple her energy and passion with what she had learned and figure out a way around the financial roadblock she faced. Next she went back to the retailers she'd contacted, admitted she'd made a mistake, and restructured her game plan. She also timed the launch for the holiday season, ensuring maximum impact. Then she went back to the drawing board, redesigning the game from start to finish. She leveraged every dollar by limiting her production run and test-marketing the game. Since she didn't have money for advertising, she used word-of-mouth and personal appearances to build excitement and generate publicity.

Karen Fried's approach shows the kind of staying power and ingenuity you'll need to survive the trial by fire your venture almost surely will face during its infancy. Hitting a wall is never easy, but once you push through it—or find a way around it—you're stronger and better equipped to face your next hurdle. Believing in both your idea and your ability to bring it to life are absolutely critical to success. With this belief, it's almost impossible to fail, whatever the odds. And no matter how many mistakes you make along the way, you can still make your business work. At any moment, you can pull back or push ahead. But remember, there's always a way to move your business forward. And it's your job as an entrepreneur to find it.

Plan a Renewal Strategy

"When you're in business, finding time for yourself is almost impossible; your private time is the first thing to go." That's how Kathy Lloyd-Williams sums up one of the biggest problems entrepreneurs face. At the same time, as Jackie Farley puts it, "You can't keep yourself going without refilling the well." How do you handle this dilemma? How do you find time to reenergize yourself, emotionally and creatively? You *make* the time. That's the answer I heard again and again. Like new business development or marketing, a renewal strategy has to be built into your start-up game plan.

There are many ways to refill your wellspring of ideas and energy. "All of them," says Dr. Barbara Mackoff, "have to do with expressing aspects of yourself that you can't really give free rein to during your working hours, when you are trying to grow your business." One key is giving yourself the private time you need to relax, get in touch with your intuition, and reward yourself in ways that have nothing to do with work. Exercising is one of the tools women mentioned frequently as a great antidote to stress and a way to build your stamina. Meditation is another tool many women use to free themselves from daily tension and tap into their inner resources. Listening to music and cooking are two other popular relaxation activities. For many women, volunteer work is a rewarding way to relax and recharge themselves, both emotionally and spiritually.

Another important aspect of renewal involves preserving and nurturing your most enriching and satisfying personal relationships. Devoting time and energy to your friends and family is especially important in helping you handle the major transition that a move from corporation to cottage involves. These "intimate connections" are essential to your well-being and success, notes Barbara Mackoff. "Freud said love and work are the keys to satisfaction," she adds. "Other people use the phrase, 'mastery and attachment.' Mastery is what you achieve through your business—that clear sense of enterprise, accomplishment, and excellence. Attachment is what you receive from and give to your family, community, a lover, and friends. These are the arenas in which you are free to be silly and sexy, political, or mystical and spiritual.

"Humor is another wonderful source of renewal. My book *What*

Mona Lisa Knew is all about using humor. Most women say they aren't funny. So I recommend cultivating the art of silent comedy—taking a stressful event in your business environment and relabeling it with a kind of comic twist. In the midst of a tough situation, you can ask yourself, What does this remind me of? What's the perfect music to describe it? Is it the theme from *The Twilight Zone?* Or what situation comedy does a problem remind you of? Is it the candy episode in *I Love Lucy,* where everything is pouring out faster than she can handle it? Or do you see yourself in the *Perils of Pauline,* tied to a railroad track? Picturing something funny about a tight spot and then relabeling it is one form of humor that can really be helpful."

Having taken the plunge, it's only natural that you yearn to feel and act like a creative dynamo, a powerhouse of ideas, energy, and action. Given this idealized image, it's hard to accept the fact that you'll often feel overwhelmed and overextended. Remember the saying quoted by Barbara Brabec (on page 13), "An entrepreneur is someone who's willing work sixteen hours a day for herself in order to avoid working eight hours for someone else"? Well, during this stage, you'll find out all too quickly just how true this can be. Unless you renew yourself on a daily and weekly basis, you'll quickly run out of steam. Giving yourself the gifts of time, love, and laughter is one of the smartest, most productive business decisions you can make.

8

STAGE FOUR:
BUILDING MOMENTUM—MONTHS SEVEN
TO EIGHTEEN

I believe women can be their own best resource, once they discover that they know what they need to know. Someone once joked that God gave us two ears and one mouth so we would learn to use them in proper proportion. The key is balance in the face of distraction, listening within as well as without.

—Jackie Farley

If you find yourself at the six-month mark of your new venture, then you've passed another major milestone in your entrepreneurial life—and it's one you should be proud of. So should your family and friends. In order to reach this stage, you will have responded to the changes and problems you've faced with a flexibility and staying power that may have surprised you. And just in the act of surviving, you've exhibited a certain degree of grace under pressure. You've come a long way! You probably have never worked harder in your life. The seeds of this work may not be bearing fruit yet, but the rewards of your labor will come as surely as day follows night, *if* you can find the staying power you need over the next twelve months. What's driving you on? The quest for freedom. The field you've plowed is your own. Whether the business you're creating is a sole proprietorship, a partnership, or a full-fledged company, it's yours to grow and nurture for your own personal fulfillment and your family's future. A rewarding feeling, isn't it?

The next year is a critical one for your fledgling business. Yes, you're still in a survival situation and in a total action mode, and finding time to plan and reflect is as difficult as ever. Sometimes it seems impossible, for all of your energy is consumed in getting from one day to the next. And you always seem to be behind; there's never time to do everything you should be doing. But though survival and making ends meet are still top priorities, you are definitely much farther along the learning curve than you were three months into your new venture. You've moved past the start-up stage and into a building phase, and the decisions you'll face will be more complex, more outer-directed, and often more costly. You'll find that your business has a rhythm and a life of its own that you couldn't have predicted when you started it. And, as we'll see later, sometime over the next twelve months, your market will find you and begin to redefine your business for you, often in surprising ways. This redefining process is something you'll encounter periodically during your venture's life cycle. When it happens at this stage, your major challenge will be to let your business grow in its own way and at its own pace. Over the next twelve months, your key goals will be to

- listen to yourself and maintain your emotional balance;
- leverage your existing resources and plan for growth;
- redefine your network while building new alliances; and
- rev up your marketing motor creatively and cost-effectively.

What You Can Expect to Feel

During this period of intense activity and change, you're likely to feel pushed and pulled in many directions. First, there is an intense drive to work more and do more as your emotional and financial stake in your business grows. Now more than ever you feel that there's no turning back. Whatever direction your business ultimately takes—wherever the winds of change may blow you—you are tied to your venture like the tail of a kite. At the same time, you may be heading into some serious storm clouds on the personal front as your family and friends take a backseat to your business concerns. Here are some of the concerns that are likely to dominate your next year in business:

The Jill-of-All-Trades Syndrome

At this stage, you're safely past the start-up phase and beginning to feel more like a business owner. In fact, your corporate life seems to be receding into the distance; sometimes it feels as if you've been running your own business—or it's been running you—forever. Separating your personal and professional identities continues to be a major issue. To a large degree, you are still your business and your business is you. You've probably settled into a regular routine, and though you're still working crazy hours, you no longer feel guilty about using the flexibility that being your own boss gives you. You're freer to express your own work rhythms and manage your time more fluidly. Right now, in fact, time may be one of the ways you're paying yourself.

In terms of your self-image, it may be a little shocking and even disconcerting to learn that the outside world has discovered your business. The market has a need and you've agreed to meet it. You're expected to be professional and to deliver, day in and day out, regardless of any problems and obstacles you may face. What began as an idea is now an obligation and a responsibility. If you're writing a newsletter, then your subscribers want the next issue in their mailboxes on time, whether or not your kids have the chicken pox. If you're manufacturing craft kits for children, the retailers carrying your line absolutely, positively must have that product delivered well in advance of the holiday season, or your reputation may suffer irreparable damage. If you're providing benefits consulting services to corporate clients, then there are regulatory deadlines to meet.

In theory all this is fine. After all, you went into business precisely so that you could offer a service or make a product that meets market needs. And you're certainly no stranger to deadlines. But having to do everything singlehandedly, often with very limited resources, may be much harder than you expected. It can make you feel inadequate and overwhelmed—a jill-of-all-trades and mistress of none. It also can make you feel boring and one-dimensional. Karen Fried recalls seeing this sign in a business owner's office—EAT. SLEEP. WORK. EAT. SLEEP. WORK. EAT. SLEEP. WORK. These three words may describe your daily grind exactly.

So where's all the fun you're supposed to be having? Where's the glamour and glitz? Anita Roddick of The Body Shop stars in American Express commercials talking about women and beauty. Martha Stewart publishes her own magazine and appears on the cover of nearly every issue holding baskets of flowers from her garden or baking pies in her gourmet kitchen. And what are *you* doing? You're crouched on the floor of your garage, stuffing envelopes. Or chasing the Federal Express truck. Or double-checking your bank statement for the tenth time, trying to figure out why your balance is so incredibly low. Or staring at your phone, waiting for a new and exciting client to call.

You've taken the plunge. You've put everything on the line. You've given up vacations and expensive lunches and a dozen other indulgences, small and large, that made you feel good about yourself and the life you were leading. Now you're longing to feel entrepreneurial with a capital *E*. You're in the midst of the "before" stage of launching a successful business and seriously wondering whether the "after" will ever arrive. Will anyone ever interview *you* about your business start-up for *Working Woman* or *The New York Times*? Or even the *Humboldt Beacon*? Will you ever be big enough to move out of the garage or the basement so that you can see daylight like everyone else? Are you going to have to keep your business going until you're eighty because you can't afford to stop? As your day-to-day routine becomes more predictable and the problems you face become clearer, these kinds of questions are likely to surface. Once you begin to settle in, the high you enjoyed in the first days of your start-up seems gone forever. The danger here is that you may find yourself doing things to try to bring it back, to recapture some of the excitement that seemed to make all of this work worthwhile. When this happens, you can find yourself becoming entranced with risk taking and putting yourself on the line in order to keep your adrenaline pumping and your psyche motivated. Your ego may be very vulnerable at this stage: highs and lows are extreme, you're easily wounded by setbacks, still afraid of failing, and you may be prone to inflating any bit of recognition or success that comes your way.

Financially Constrained

Six months into their businesses, many women find themselves facing troubled financial waters. There's no mystery here—small businesses generally start on a shoestring and operate on the financial edge. Most people have enough reserve funds to survive at least the first six months, with the help of savings, severance pay, family support, and short-term project work. Somewhere around the seventh month of their venture, however, funds may reach the low-water mark. In many cases, just the cost of functioning day to day can be far more expensive than anticipated—phone bills, equipment, stationery, health insurance, and research materials can burn through your bank account like wildfire. If you've poured all of your money into your start-up but have little to show for your efforts so far, then self-doubt may rear its head again. At this stage, both you and your family may be wondering whether you are investing in your future or simply throwing good money after bad.

If you're in a service business, then no matter how vigorously you market, it will take from six to eight months to keep the pipeline filled. So if you've been zealous about your effort to generate new business from day one, you should start seeing results right about now. If, on the other hand, you've devoted the lion's share of your time over the past six months to researching your market, goal setting, and organizing yourself, allowing your new business effort to take a backseat, you may find yourself forced to scramble for funds to keep going. And if you've launched your business with one or more anchor clients, overdependence on them may already be a liability. Instead of being proactive about broadening your business base, you've spent your time catering to the needs of existing clients. In failing to find new sources of income, you may be limiting your growth and allowing one or two key relationships to define your business for you.

If your venture involves manufacturing a product, when you reach the six-month point, you may find you've exhausted your start-up funds in testing the market, developing prototypes, finding distribution outlets, and negotiating with suppliers. In order to execute your plans and produce your product, even on a trial basis, you may need a substantial infusion of cash. At this point, you may be in a race against time. In order to seize the moment and maximize your product's chances of success, you need to get to market quickly. You also may have made delivery commitments to retailers in return for their orders. Now you have to manage not just the manufacturing, but also find more money—fast. Is venture capital a realistic option? What about a bank loan? Should you take the F and F (family and friends) route and find investors close to home? Given the nature of your business, does it make sense to approach potential suppliers for help in underwriting your start-up? What other funding outlets should you be exploring? Do you have a workable business plan you can pull together in order to tap outside sources of capital? These are the financial questions likely to keep you awake at night during this stage.

Stretched to the Limit

In the best of all possible worlds, having embraced the entrepreneurial life, you'd like to be able to take it easy, to coast a little, the way you did once in a while at your corporate job. But give up this idea; it's not going to happen for some time to come. Right now, the worst thing you can do is to sit back and relax. Your only option is to fuel your business's growth by stepping on the gas. You'll also find that time is even easier to waste or mismanage than money. Getting the most out of every day will be a constant battle, a battle you'll often feel you're losing. Being on top of things is a foreign concept; there are just too many balls in the air for your two tired arms to catch.

Creating new work patterns to replace your old ones, pacing yourself, and mastering the unfamiliar skills you'll need to nurture your new business all require enormous amounts of energy and concentration. It's easy to push yourself too hard and sap your strength, especially when you have to do everything without help. Unless you give even greater attention to reenergizing yourself, the stresses and strains of your start-up stage, worries about money, and fears about your future can catch up with you. When this happens, your health, energy level, can-do attitude, and business judgment all may suffer. Taking care of business also means taking care of yourself. Building time into your day and week for renewal is especially important during this stage.

As your business consumes more and more of your time, the toll it takes on your personal life may increase, making you feel seriously out of balance emotionally. Your family may feel, not without reason, that your business is taking your best and leaving them to pick up the pieces. Your friends may feel neglected, too. After giving you support and encouragement and being there when you needed them, now they find that you don't have time to return the favor. In short, the intimate connections Dr. Barbara Mackoff spoke of (page 186) are becoming ever more fragile. The irony of this situation may be almost unnerving. After all, one of the prime reasons you went into business was to gain greater flexibility and bring the personal and professional aspects of your life into greater harmony. Right now this idea may seem like wishful thinking.

More Confident and Knowledgeable

As we've found in every other stage, this one has a silver lining. As you enter the next twelve months of your venture's life, the groundwork you laid during your start-up phase begins to pay off. Despite the ups and downs you've encountered, you're likely to feel more confident about your chances for survival and success. There are many valid reasons for this growing belief in your abilities, and it's important that you acknowledge and build on them during this time. You've come a long way since you first made the decision to strike out on your own, and you've grown stronger in your inner resources and outer experience.

First, you've probably realized just how important—and empowering—doing your homework can be. Over the past six months, you've invested enormous amounts of time analyzing likely markets for your product or service and learning the mechanics of running a business. The experience of Kathy Lloyd-Williams is a case in point. After years of working for large companies, Kathy decided to leave the corporate world and start a business of her own. As a mother of two young girls, she found herself drawn to the idea of creating a company that would focus in some form on children and family issues. She spent months exploring potential ventures; once she had conceived the idea for xoxo international and her first product line—"make your own fun" card kits for children—she spent several more months investigating the toy market, possible distributors, and manufacturing logistics. Looking back, Kathy feels that "researching my market was the smartest thing I did. It made me feel confident about my idea's potential and my ability to sell the product I wanted to create."

Second, you're likely to find that your expanding experience and the confidence it creates will enable you to reach a new level of business sophistication and marketing savvy. Enthusiasm wedded to your newfound expertise can prove to be a powerful and exciting combination. And finally, your growing confidence is also the product of the new and improved self-image you develop as you successfully overcome the hurdles to building your business. During this stage, you are likely to become more and more adept at applying your corporate skills to your entrepreneurial venture—not just because this makes sense, but because you have to; you need every ounce of training and experience at your command to make your new business work. You also may have a clearer picture of both your strengths and your weaknesses as a businessperson. Your skills in servicing clients may be your major asset, but time management is a problem. You may be strong on new business development but weak on follow-through. You may be a pro at negotiating contracts but a procrastinator par excellence when it comes to doing paperwork.

The shortcomings and pressure points you've identified over the past six months may be cause for concern, but they also offer the incentive for improvement. After all, if you can just get past the survival stage, you'll be in a position to shore up your weaknesses by hiring outside help or finding someone with complementary skills with whom to work. At this stage, the true strengths you bring to your venture are also emerging; by now you have a far better idea about your most valuable assets than you did on day one. Even more important, you've probably zeroed in on aspects of the business that excite you and hidden talents you want to nurture.

Planning Your Success Strategy

This twelve-month period promises to be exciting and action packed. If things are going reasonably well, your business should be gaining momentum while you're gaining clarity about both your abilities and your goals. Apart from the pressures you face, you also may experience a sense of rhythm and harmony; you and your business are beginning to unfold and grow together. This is a time of tremendous opportunity and important choices. The decisions you make about direction, markets, product development, manufacturing, personnel, size, and structure will be more demanding and require a deeper business knowledge, sophistication, and savvy than your start-up stage involved. Once again you've upped the ante, both professionally and personally. Here's some valuable, front-line advice about handling the business and personal challenges you'll face:

Listen to Yourself and Tap into Your Centerpoint

"I believe women can be their own best resource, once they discover that they know what they need to know. . . . The key is balance in the face of distraction, listening within as well as without," says Jackie Farley. This chapter opened with these words, and I think they're worth repeating here. Being your own best resource, learning to listen to yourself, and finding balance in the face of distraction are all vitally important in gathering the emotional resources you need to stay your course over the next twelve months. Let's explore each of these ideas briefly.

BE YOUR OWN BEST RESOURCE

Sounds appealing, but what exactly does it mean? Being your own best resource means that you, and you alone, are the expert when it comes to planning and running your business. Yes, you may need help from other professionals, like lawyers, accountants, and perhaps even an experienced entrepreneurial mentor, to be sure that you don't hang yourself. But their job is to help you stay on course, not to determine that course for you. That's your role as the owner of your business and the mistress of your fate. As we'll see (page 249), letting other people take control of your business is one of the biggest traps you can fall into during its formative stages. Being your own best resource also means that even though you may feel inexperienced and uncertain about your next steps at any given point, *you are never totally lost and without direction.* Deep down, as Jackie noted, you do "know what you need to know" to achieve your vision and make your business succeed. Either you have the answers within yourself or you have the power to reach out in ways that will draw them to you.

Karen Fried certainly found this to be true in developing her Think-It Link-It game: "It's amazing to me that I was able to make the right decisions about the game at a critical stage. I didn't have my father, who was an entrepreneur, there to tell me what to do—which is a luxury that some people have and it's a wonderful thing. I had to figure it out. I don't know anyone who's done this the way I have. It just came into my head that this was absolutely the right way to do it. I'm not sure it would have been right for anyone else. But it turned out to be totally right for me."

LEARN TO LISTEN TO YOURSELF

This means doing your "inner work" as well as your outer work—creating a strong foundation to support your day-to-day activities, decision making, goal setting, and problem solving. Listening to yourself also means being nakedly honest. It means having the courage to ask, Just between me and my secret self, what decisions am I about to make for the wrong reasons? Because I'm feeling insecure and need to show off? Because I've bought into an image of the "entrepreneur" that feeds my ego but has nothing to do with where my business is right now? Because I'm desperate for money to keep myself afloat? Because I've set quotas and goals for myself I can't achieve but am too invested in to give up? Because I'm trying to prove myself—to myself, my husband and family, my friends, my old boss, my old coworkers, my mother, my father? And finally, listening to yourself also means stepping out of the "action mode" long enough to quiet your mind and your anxieties so that you can hear your inner voice and tap into your intuition.

FIND BALANCE IN THE FACE OF DISTRACTION

This means finding the eye of the storm, or what Jackie Farley calls your "centerpoint." Regaining your emotional balance is something you can and must try to do every day, wherever you are. It doesn't have to involve going off into the mountains for four days. As Jackie explains, "It simply means taking time for yourself in an environment that is soothing to you. It can be a room in your house, or a walk in the country or wherever you happen to be. Or it can simply mean turning down the volume in your brain. I am fond of saying that with too much thinking, one can become deaf.

"Most people understand the concept of having a centerpoint. I describe it as a source within of serenity, confidence, wisdom, and strength. One of the ways that we try to find our centerpoints while on retreat is to look for a metaphor in nature—a sound, or smell, or an image of a tree, or a stream, or a flower—that we can each use to tap into our inner sense of strength and intuition. That metaphor can give you a way to migrate mentally back to your centerpoint whenever you need to, whether you're sitting at your desk or simply trying to reenergize yourself. There are many ways you can do this. Some people meditate, some people listen to music. It really comes down to finding a way to take care of yourself that keeps you in touch with your instincts—something that's incredibly important for entrepreneurs."

Let Your Market Find You

As discussed earlier, two very exciting and unpredictable things are likely to happen during this twelve months. First, your market will find you and begin to redefine your business for you. This redefining process is a very natural, organic one and it will occur periodically as your business grows and matures. It may throw you off balance when it happens, especially this first time around, but it is really a very positive development. It means that your business has begun to find its market and the market has begun to find your business. When this happens, your job—and it can be a tough one—is to let your enterprise evolve rather than trying to control it. Letting your business's natural rhythm emerge, rather than subjecting it to a forced march based on an artificial timetable you've concocted to meet your own needs, isn't easy.

Finding the flexibility and ego distance to allow your business to reshape itself can be a challenge. This redefining process may involve a shift in direction, accepting different kinds of work, or rethinking your views on exactly what business you're in. When it occurs, you'll be forced to make some choices about the trade-offs required to keep your venture afloat. What sacrifices do or don't you want to make? Are the compromises you're considering realistic and workable? Do they move you in the direction of your vision or are you panicking—taking anything that comes along in order to survive? Should you say yes or no to a particular project? Should you take a part-time job or find a retainer situation to underwrite your company's financial future? Will moving into a new market leverage your resources or deplete them? These are the questions you may find yourself facing as your business evolves and changes.

Letting the market find you is the key to surviving and benefiting from the direction your business takes during this stage. When Caroline Hull began *ConneXions*, her newsletter for home-based working mothers, her original plan was to build its circulation base through subscriptions rather than through advertising, as she was concerned about ensuring the integrity of the products and services she advertised. It became apparent over time, however, that increasing circulation via subscriptions was going to be a slow and painstaking process; the real answer to making the newsletter viable was attracting advertisers. In short, Caroline began by thinking that her primary source of growth and her target market would be her readers. But once she had created an attractive publishing vehicle, another market found her—namely, advertisers who wanted to reach her audience. Caroline also decided to build on it by creating a consulting service, The ConneXus Group, to help corporations and organizations deal effectively with work and family issues. Despite her efforts to promote the service, demand wasn't as high as Caroline expected. However, another market has begun tapping her expertise: small businesses, which have sought her out for help with their strategic planning and marketing.

Another publishing-related example: When Barbara Brabec first began writing about home-based businesses more than twenty years ago, much of the information she provided focused heavily on the crafts field and small, cottage-based manufacturing businesses— Barbara's short how-to guides, her quarterly *National Home Business Report*, and her book *Homemade Money* all had a strong product-based flavor. Over time, however, more and more people interested in starting service businesses began reading her publications, sharing their experiences, and asking for advice. When this happened, Barbara discovered a whole new market in her mailbox. She responded by reorienting her publications to reflect more fully the special needs of service-related concerns. In fact, the fifth edition of *Homemade Money* was totally revised with these needs and the future business outlook in mind.

When Debra Oppenheim and her partner, Jane Phillips, opened their executive search firm for nonprofits, they started with a handful of anchor clients. And over the next eighteen months their business grew dramatically, largely through word of mouth—the market found them and responded to their expertise and strategy of offering professional, high-quality search services to nonprofit organizations and foundations. As Debra points out, "You never know what people really think of your skills until you open your own business. Suddenly I found people calling us with new business because they'd heard of my work for many years. I didn't really pay much attention to what people thought or to building a reputation. Yet, the fact that people have sought both Jane and myself out has really had an impact on me. Although I wouldn't advise other people to do this, we have done very little marketing."

When Melinda and Malachi Pancoast began Milestone Management Consulting Services they were working with small companies in Vermont and focused mainly on training programs to increase productivity and profitability. As their client base expanded to include both manufacturing and service businesses of varying size, a new market began tapping their expertise: married business owners. Like Melinda and Malachi themselves, many of the companies that sought out their services were owned and run by couples who had very special demands placed on them by their dual roles as business owners and marriage partners. Milestone Management responded to this market by creating a special program for married business partners. Among the topics the course covers are: what women want, what men want, appetite and production, more fun at home and at work, creating a powerful new organizational design, translating vision into action, and handling breakdowns. Today, several years after the market found them, this concept still offers an exciting avenue of business.

By now you should have a fairly clear idea of the many different ways in which a business can redefine itself in response to market demand. Allowing this to happen is one of the keys to entrepreneurial success. But it requires both a great deal of confidence and flexibility. As you think about your own business and its evolution during your start-up stage, do you see any connections here? Did you start out thinking you were going to do one thing and find that you are doing something else? Did one market you hoped to tap prove unrealistic and another emerge to take its place? Did you broaden your vision of what you want your business to be to give you more options for both survival and expansion? Have you pinpointed any new market trends that your company could respond to without changing course totally, but by adjusting its direction? Are there markets within markets that could benefit from your services the way that married business owners have benefited from Milestone Management's expertise? One of the keys to answering these kinds of questions is to begin monitoring your business closely by "taking its temperature" on a weekly basis. What's working well? What's not? Where are the most serious internal bottlenecks? What external roadblocks are getting in your way? What market or audience seems most receptive to your business? Are you advancing closer toward your goals, however slowly, or do those goals seem to be receding or out of synch with the work you're doing?

Manage Your Growth Carefully

This sounds like a bit of a contradiction, doesn't it? We just finished talking about the importance of letting your business redefine itself, and now we're focusing on managing growth. If you think about these two concepts for a moment, though, you'll see that they really go hand in hand. Yes, you should allow your business to reshape itself, but you need to guide and nurture that process. Certainly there are more resources around than ever before to help you build your venture successfully. There are books like *Growing a Business,* by Paul Hawken, and *Our Wildest Dreams,* by Joline Godfrey, for example, as well as conferences and training programs across the country. But even with all of this support, relatively little attention seems to be paid to managing growth from an emotional, as well as a business and financial, perspective. That's what we're going to focus on here, by looking at how two entrepreneurs handled their growth in the first eighteen months of their ventures in ways that bolstered their self-esteem and kept their anxieties within manageable limits.

Let's start with Karen Fried. You may recall that she launched her game with a small production run in a handful of test markets. By the time the holiday season had ended, about sixteen months into Karen's business, Think-It Link-It was available in hundreds of stores and had been featured on the *Today Show* as the hottest new game for Christmas. Karen also had broken even on her investment. As the result of marketing, a TV game show possibility, and other developments, Karen now believes that she "might not have to raise money for another year. I can let the game refinance itself. As long as I don't take money out, I can let the game grow itself, which is really exciting.

"From now on, I think a lot of amazing things will happen, but they're not going to if I lose interest or walk away. You have to stay focused; you're always at a critical stage in your business. My days start now with faxes from toy stores asking me for the game. But I have to be really careful, because I don't want to just flood the market. So there are a lot of decisions you find yourself making. Which marketing vehicles should you use—TV, radio, cable? At some point, I'm going to have to raise money. But there are so many ways to move forward. I want to blast the game out in a couple of areas. Each step of the way, there are millions of decisions and lots of risks. Twice a year, I hit a juncture where there are all these choices and I have to pick a direction. Last week I sat down and thought, I have twelve great ideas, but I can't physically pursue them all. Right now I have three interns working for me, looking at radios, cruises, and high schools. I could have fifteen people working for me and it wouldn't be enough."

Karen's test-market strategy allowed her to finance the game's initial run through commissions she had earned as a real estate broker. Keeping ownership and financial control of her concept was both an emotional and a business decision; it energized her, tested her ingenuity, sparked her creativity, and helped her handle the pressures she faced. It also relieved her of the enormous pressure and tension she was feeling about raising huge amounts of money from outside investors. It allowed her to test the game's salability in a way that leveraged her ownership position. And finally, it freed her to experience firsthand the fun and enjoyment her game created—she was able to give live demonstrations in her test-market locales. All of these steps helped Karen realize her vision and market her game in a way that enhanced her self-confidence and fed her enthusiasm for the product she was creating. In the process, she grew along with her business.

Like Karen Fried, Debra Oppenheim has enjoyed great success in launching her own business. When I first interviewed her, she and her partner, Jane Phillips, had been working as a team for about six months. When they first opened their doors, Debra and Jane shared a one-room office on Fifth Avenue. A few months later, they rented more office space and hired an administrative assistant. I interviewed Debra again about a year later, when she had been in business for about eighteen months. During the twelve months between interviews, she'd faced firsthand many of the practical—and personal—challenges involved in building a small company.

"I started with two clients," Debra recalls, "and now we have clients coming in the door. The kind of growth we've experienced was totally unpredictable and completely unplanned. The business just took off and mushroomed into something larger than Jane and I ever anticipated it would be. When you have a small business, I think the most difficult thing to do is to manage it effectively. And we still haven't gotten our hands around that. That's our biggest problem. In a way, we're in the same position as someone who sets out to manufacture a product. You put it on the market and begin to get orders, and you have to keep your manufacturing process going in order to fill those orders. I think a lot of small businesses fall apart because their operating structures can't keep up with demand.

"Whatever your business, you are only as good as the work or the product you produce. If you are giving your clients value for their dollars, I think you'll always have business. But if you can't produce at the same level, you run into problems. As quickly as word gets around that you're terrific, word gets around that you're not. But how do you support a business that's growing as quickly as ours? That's my biggest single worry. This is a wonderful position to be in, as opposed to having no clients, but we have to wrestle with it.

"Another real problem we're facing is that so much money is going into our business. It's unbelievable. There's always something. Not just rent for an office, but the data base, the computers and other equipment, the furniture. The best thing we did was to start slowly. We sublet one office and took another one only when we could afford it. We had a temporary support person who's now full-time. So there are three of us and we're planning to hire a receptionist. In addition, we have three people working on a project basis. We've also made a decision to bring a colleague into the business who operates out of Washington, because we are probably going to open an office there soon. We'll give her support and the use of our firm's name, and she will ultimately become a partner in the firm. But her office will be set up as an independent profit center.

"I've seen many small search firms start as spin-offs of larger firms that felt they needed fancy offices and furniture, support people and systems people, and so on. They start out with an overhead that isn't sustainable or creates a tremendous amount of anxiety. We are trying to avoid this by moving forward little by little. We've been very cautious about overextending ourselves; that's why we have people working on a project basis. Even so, the decisions you have to make about systems and bringing people on board full-time are monumental and they soak up more of your profits. We now have health and disability insurance. All the spending is a source of constant anxiety. But we have to be able to support the business with good professional help, because two partners alone cannot handle the volume we have, since we are directly involved in each search."

The dozens of decisions Debra and Jane faced in the eighteen months since their business began have been very demanding from a business standpoint. During this time, Debra also has been very concerned about managing growth in a way that works for both her and her partner on an emotional level. In her view, every business decision is also a personal decision. The choices they make at this stage can dramatically affect their quality of life by robbing them of precious personal time and forcing them to expend enormous amounts of energy supporting their overhead.

"Emotionally," says Debra, "there are several factors we're dealing with at this stage of our business. We have to decide how big we want to be. Do we want to try to stay where we are or grow just a little larger, with the capacity to support what we have intelligently? Do we want a much larger business? Do we want to become a mega search firm? That's possible. But it takes an enormous commitment, emotional as well as financial. I don't know whether I want to do that. I don't want to be a mogul. I just want to do good work, make sure we have good people working with us, and enjoy what I'm doing. As my partner put it, 'Let's make sure we have fun with this along the way!' Otherwise, you're just working longer and longer hours; that's not the quality of life either of us wants. I cherish my personal life. I don't want to work seven days a week or spend my time going to parties, sitting down with the guys, and discussing business."

Forge Creative Alliances to Keep Yourself on Track

Earlier on, we talked about the need to create a cheerleading squad and adapt your networking strategy to your new role as a business owner. As you move forward, it's time once again to restructure your support team. After weathering the first six months of your new work life, your needs in this area have changed. You're beyond the point where you need cheerleaders to boost your confidence and spur you on; in fact, their boosterism can be dangerous. It can shore up your ego and keep you from being scared at a time when it's vital that you take off your rose-colored glasses, look your future firmly in the face, and make the tough decisions required to survive. So let the cheering squad go and forge a new, more sophisticated support system for yourself—one whose mission is to help plan your business strategy rather than hold your hand.

To build this new support team, seek out talented and experienced professionals in a range of industries who can keep you focused and provide reality checks on a regular basis. There are many creative and exciting ways to begin forging alliances that will help you move your business to its next level of growth. Let's take a look at some of the approaches that have worked well for other women whose needs may be similar to yours. As a first step, you can borrow a leaf from the corporate world and find a mentor or coach who can give you one-on-one advice and feedback. To find someone whose background matches your needs, you might consider joining a formal mentoring program offered by the SBA, which teams up a budding entrepreneur who's reached a critical phase of growth with a seasoned business owner, who acts as a coach and sounding board.

Or you might take the route that Joyce McClure chose and use networking as a way to identify someone. Joyce recalls, "When I first started to find some direction, I was never afraid to ask someone for the names of other interesting people to talk to. And they would say, Gee, I think you ought to go see this guy or that one. So I would send a letter and resume and then go talk to them. Along the way, I met a retired executive, George, and his wife, who've lived all over the world. George had taken over a local group of retired executives. He resurrected it and made it a success. So he knew a lot of people. So I went to see him with my resume and he looked at it in amazement. And he became my mentor from that point forward. I went to the Governor's Conference with him. He took me under his wing and introduced me to everyone he thought I should know. I happen to be very shy by nature, but once you get out there and start meeting people, it can be delightful."

As a variation on this theme, you can set up a "kitchen cabinet," an informal group of professionals whose judgment you trust and who are willing to meet with you from time to time. This is a strategy that Lonah Birch of the SBA believes makes a great deal of sense for a small company during its formative stage. She recommends that you consider asking your accountant and your attorney to join—and even a friendly banker, if you can find one. You can use this group as a forum to review and fine-tune your business plan and as a source of ideas about marketing, new business, money, and other hot topics you are dealing with. One business owner has made this approach pay off by organizing her own advisory board of people in different fields who enjoy one another's company. She taps their expertise by inviting them all to dinner for creative brainstorming sessions, which she structures loosely around an agenda that she sends everyone in advance.

Another way to forge effective alliances to support your growth is to find or create a networking group geared to your specific needs. Caroline Hull did exactly that when she and Linda Blake started MATCH, a nonprofit organization built around the special issues facing home-based working mothers. Monthly meetings provide the chance to network and cover a wide range of both professional and personal topics, from choosing a computer and government contracting to balancing business and family needs. Today MATCH has more than one hundred members in Virginia and has generated interest among women in other parts of the country who find its approach to combining motherhood and work both refreshing and unique.

Finding a "partner who's not a partner," to use Jackie Farley's term, is yet another technique you can adopt to gain valuable professional advice or expertise. As the phrase suggests, this is someone who will team up with you temporarily to fill a specific need. Debra Oppenheim and her partner used this strategy to redesign their operating systems. As Debra says, "We don't have the business mechanisms in place to support our business; there are many more sophisticated tools that we should be equipped with. What we've done is to bring in outside help on a barter basis. We have a colleague who's an ex-McKinsey consultant and works with nonprofits. She has her own small business and is an expert in the kind of long-range thinking we need at this stage. She's facilitated several sessions with us to help us with our planning and financial systems. In exchange, we've given her free access to our office when she's in New York. This has been a good way to get the advice we needed without spending too much."

If this concept sounds promising to you, then you may want to consider creating what Caroline Hull calls a "cluster," by hooking up with someone who has a skill that you lack—marketing or accounting, for instance—and then building an informal team that comes together on an ad hoc basis. By joining forces in this way with other small business owners, you can leverage your time and

resources without breaking your budget. To work effectively, however, you need to manage this type of relationship as carefully as
any other business connection, or you could find yourself receiving
only erratic support and missing important opportunities.

Make Marketing a Key Part of Your New Business Agenda

The first step in creating a marketing mind-set is to recognize how
important this activity is to your business survival. Having a good
product or service is only half the battle; letting people know about
it is the other half. Like many entrepreneurs, you may feel that
quality is the key to success—if you offer a high-quality product,
the thinking goes, then you can't help but succeed. In the real world,
however, things don't always work this way. Barbara Brabec recalls
the story of one woman who didn't know anything about publishing
but had a good idea: a periodical designed to put people in the crafts
industry in touch with shows and retail shops. She borrowed five
thousand dollars, bought a computer, and spent a lot of time and
money creating an attractive brochure and a handsome publication.
But she didn't know how to get subscribers. She had a beautiful
product but she couldn't sell it, and a year after she started, she was
out of business and deeply in debt.

"In this case," adds Barbara, "it took about six years and great
emotional turmoil for the woman who started this venture to pay
the five thousand dollars back to the people who invested in it. She
created a wonderful product and gave it her best, but she made the
mistake of thinking that a good product was all she needed. She
poured all her money into appearance up front but didn't know
lesson one about how to find customers for the product she designed—or whether anyone really needed or wanted it. One of the
biggest misconceptions about marketing is that if you have a good
product, people will beat a path to your door. They will do that only
if you get out there and work like the dickens to market yourself,
get publicity, and tell the whole world what you're doing. You can't
just create a good product, place one ad, sit back, and wait to
get rich."

Know your market and how to reach it—that's one message this story offers. Another is, reach out to that market early and often. To have a real chance for success, your marketing program has to be proactive and consistent. This means that you have to see marketing not as a one-shot promotional blitz, but as an integral part of your business. As Barbara Brabec pointed out, you can't just take out a single ad and expect orders to flow your way. More often than not, the results of this stop-and-go marketing are very limited. The real key to success is slow and steady progress—learning to use new tools, building relationships over time, networking on a regular basis, and experimenting by trial and error. To succeed in this arena, you have to be prepared to devote substantial time to mastering the skills required. Often it's the time-consuming demands of contact and follow-up that small business owners, who are already stretched to the limit, find the hardest to deal with when it comes to marketing. But this comes with the territory. In order to reap the benefits of your work, you may need to commit a few hours each day, or even a whole day or more a week, to communicating with the outside world about what you have to offer. Without this kind of persistent effort, the walls of your cottage can quickly begin to close in on you.

If you happen to have a strong corporate marketing or sales background, then you may find that your on-the-job experience is transferable to your entrepreneurial venture. Judith Grant Palma, for example, began her ten-year banking career as a customer service representative but spent the last eighteen months in a high-pressure job as a sales and training manager for a branch bank. When the bank laid her off, she spent some time searching for a new corporate slot but ultimately decided that she wanted to open her own small business as a skin-care specialist. When she made that decision, she found that "the year and a half of all the pressure and stress I'd experienced in my last banking job really came in handy, because I felt very comfortable when it came to marketing—selling myself, advertising, contacting local papers, and thinking up new promotional ideas." Judith was fortunate in being able to find a direct marketing link between her corporate training and her new venture. In general, however, the main advantage that professional marketers have in this area is a healthy appreciation for the powerful leverage that marketing can offer their new businesses. When it comes to the actual skills they've acquired in a corporate setting, many marketers find that they still have a lot to learn—or unlearn. As Barbara Brabec points out, "Marketing a home-based business is very different from corporate marketing; it requires a totally different mind-set. You may have a tremendous service or product, but you won't have an ad budget or corporate identity behind you. You have to figure out a winning strategy that will work now that you are home-based and have a limited budget. The average tools for the home-based business are word of mouth, inexpensive brochures and flyers, co-op mailings, and publicity. I know a lot of businesses that have built themselves on publicity alone. When I started my own business, I didn't have any money to advertise, so I learned very quickly how to get my name into print. If I hadn't done this, I never would have survived. While I work to be known nationally, most small businesses need local exposure. Most business owners need to master skills like getting involved in the chamber of commerce and community projects. They need to know bankers, accountants, attorneys, and people in fields where good word-of-mouth publicity will connect them with the prospects they're looking for. It's more than likely that the first dozen things you try won't work when you first begin your marketing. You may get a very poor response when you start out. Then somewhere along the line you'll hit on something that really works and you can use it to build your business."

Barbara has built her publishing venture largely through publicity. Although she didn't have either a journalism or marketing background when she first started nearly fifteen years ago, she's been highly successful in positioning herself as an expert on home-based business. The result has been extensive national exposure in magazines and newspapers. Barbara has cultivated her media contacts in a number of very creative ways: by becoming a vocal advocate for small businesses, by developing a lively and informative two-page press "tip sheet" on hot small business topics, and by acting as a resource for reporters who want to get in touch with small business owners across the country. Using these approaches and through her books and public speaking, Barbara has become a widely quoted authority in the small business arena. Her success is a prime example of how powerful creative marketing can be, even on a small budget.

Like Barbara Brabec, Caroline Hull didn't have any marketing or writing experience when she began her newsletter *ConneXions*. Yet, she, too, has been able to build local, and even national, awareness of her business. While she invested part of her limited marketing budget on designing a very professional brochure and other direct mail materials, she has never spent a dime on ads for *ConneXions*. As Caroline puts is, "This is a shoestring operation, and I don't really have money to advertise." Instead she's taken the same route Barbara Brabec used and built her subscriber list mainly through free coverage she's received in the local and national press. The first article on her new venture she says, "resulted in a whole slew of responses. Since then I have actively played the press connection whenever and wherever I can to promote my business."

If you, too, make a strong commitment to expanding your repertoire of professional skills to include marketing, then you'll find that, like everything else, practice makes perfect. The more you do, the better you'll get. And the more confident about your success you become, the more successful you'll be.

Nurture Your Personal Life

During this stage, when you feel stretched to the limit, challenged by more complex and expensive decisions, and more committed than ever, it's tempting to put your personal life on hold. Usually this means that you don't take private time for yourself, and you let your business overflow into your time with family and friends. Balancing the personal and professional sides of your life may seem impossible, just as it was when you labored in the corporate vineyards you've now abandoned. *Don't give in to this feeling.* Renewing yourself emotionally and spiritually becomes more and more important as your business changes and grows. A full personal life will enrich and enliven your business; sacrificing that personal life will impoverish and diminish it. So once again, as discussed in stage three, it may be time to recommit yourself to the idea of setting boundaries. At this stage, the lack of boundary between yourself and a boss becomes a pressing issue. As Dr. Barbara Mackoff points out, "When you had a boss, the boundaries between yourself and that person were very clear. There were some things you could not say or do. He/she was in charge of certain decisions. Now you have no boundaries between yourself and the boss; there is no space between yourself and the major decision maker in your business. This is where people most often fall into the trap of an uninterrupted horizon of work. They forget that even the most Neanderthal manager would not expect anyone to work as many hours as people working at home do. How do you set limits in this situation? How should you spend your day? What's most important for your survival? What values does your business express?

"As a way of handling this issue, I ask people to take a look at the kinds of consideration that even the toughest boss would give them. Think about what your regular office hours should be, what your policy is about weekends and holidays. What your vacation time policy is. How you will compensate yourself for overtime and reward yourself for outstanding work. I also encourage people to sit down and write out what I call their own 'theory of productivity' as it relates to time on the job. What makes people most productive? Most women will find that one of the keys to productivity is having the ballast of a rich private life. To work with the intensity needed to make their business grow, they need time for themselves and time to enrich their family life. Setting up boundaries is one of the best ways to balance the demands of a family, a spouse, and a small business."

Yes, you want your business to grow and prosper; it's an important part of who you are and who you hope to become. But the relationship between business success and your personal life doesn't have to be a win-lose proposition. You don't have to sacrifice one to build the other. There are many creative ways to refill your emotional well and strengthen your ties with family and friends. Make the issue of balance a priority and you'll find a way to achieve it, at least most of the time. Let yourself be pushed too far and fast from those you love and all the business success in the world won't fill your empty nights. Remember, you're not just building a business, you're creating a life strategy, one that satisfies not just your need for fulfilling work but also your need to feel happy and whole.

9

FROM NET WORTH TO SELF-WORTH

Our society equates worth with wealth. But those of us making the change from corporation to cottage are saying, in essence, that we no longer measure our entire value based on how much we make. We're willing to take the risks and go through this transition to come out with a greater sense of self and a greater sense of comfort about the lives we choose to lead.

—Cheryl Williams

With money in your pocket, you are wise, and you are beautiful, and you sing well too." In many ways, this old proverb is surprisingly up to date, isn't it? In a few words, it captures the feelings of comfort, power, and success that our society associates with money. As a fledgling entrepreneur, however, you are marching to the beat of a different drummer. By choosing to leave the corporate fold and start your own business, you are voluntarily emptying your pockets, perhaps for several years. Your vision of financial success is a dream deferred; you are trading paychecks in hand for the potential earning power your new business offers. In taking this step, you are making a pivotal financial decision. At a time in your working life when many people around you are enjoying steady incomes, saving for a rainy day, and building their retirement plans, you've chosen to give up this kind of security and fall behind financially, at least for the immediate future. Not an easy decision, by any means. Also a very risky one, for however carefully you plan your move, anticipating exactly how much money you'll need is always difficult, if not impossible. As Caroline Hull puts it, "If there's one thing you can count on, it's that starting a business always takes far more time and money than you ever imagine."

Your challenge on the financial front is threefold. First, you need to take control of your start-up assets and make your money work harder and smarter than it ever has before. Second, you need to be honest and realistic about your emotional attitudes toward money and what it means to you. And third, you'll need to find satisfying nonmonetary ways to pay yourself so you can stay motivated, build your self-esteem, and feel good about the work you've chosen. A tall order, isn't it? Especially in the belt-tightening 1990s, when start-up dollars for small businesses seem scarcer than ever. But don't let today's economic climate be a barrier to business ownership. Other women have found ways to finance their dreams, and you can, too.

Not having enough money can be either an opportunity or an obstacle, depending on your attitude. As most successful entrepreneurs will tell you, if you really want to make your business work, then you'll find the money you need—somewhere, somehow. Doing this will require ingenuity as well as stretching and straining on your part, especially when it comes to giving up some old financial patterns you may be very attached to. As you'll see in Appendix 3, there are books, magazines, newsletters, and training programs around to help you identify and tap promising funding sources. While this chapter will explore briefly some of the ways in which other women have financed their ventures, finding start-up capital isn't my focus here. Helping you understand your attitude toward money so that you can take the most positive and productive approach toward leveraging the dollars you have is really what this chapter is all about. My goal is to inspire you to think more creatively about the start-up capital you need, reassess some of your feelings about money, and recognize that your relationship to it will change as your business evolves.

FINANCING: ALWAYS AN ISSUE

You may be dreaming of starting a mail-order business for kids, running a gourmet-to-go service for commuters, or launching a newsletter with an eye toward the greening of corporate America. You may plan to go solo, start a partnership, or build a huge multimillion-dollar company that will land you on the cover of *Inc.*, *Working Woman*, or *Fortune*. But whatever business you envision, large or small, product- or service-based, a sole proprietorship or a cast of thousands, there are three things about money you probably have in common with many other female entrepreneurs:

1. Money isn't the key driver behind your decision to start your own business. As noted earlier (pages 18–20), it's fifth or sixth on the priority list of most female entrepreneurs, and it's probably the same for you. Your quest for independence, control over your own destiny, flexibility, and personal fulfillment is likely to be more important to you than money, especially during the start-up phase of your business. Yes, you hope and plan to earn more money on your own than you ever would if you stayed at your corporate job, but passion, not pay, is the key to your move.

2. Whatever the amount of money you start with, you're going to feel it's not enough and that you'd have a better chance at beating the odds if your bank account was bigger. However successful you are during your start-up, it's likely that you will spend lots of your time and energy worrying about money—finding it, making it, spending it, saving it, wasting it, wanting it. You're going to be thinking about money more than you ever did at your corporate job, and it will make you anxious. Sometimes very anxious.

3. As an entrepreneur, your emotional relationship with money is going to be more intense and powerful than it was when you were an employee. Whatever the nature of your feelings about money and your money management style before you started your business—good, bad, or indifferent—those feelings and style will be amplified when you make the move from corporation to cottage. Recognizing this, renegotiating your relationship with money, and changing old financial patterns will be among the hardest—and most liberating—entrepreneurial challenges you'll face.

"Money is always a critical issue for the women I work with," says Lonah Birch of the SBA. "They never seem to have enough."

This comment accurately sums up the financial picture for most female entrepreneurs. As you probably know all too well, female business owners tend to be undercapitalized and operate on a shoestring. One SBA study, for example, found that 80 percent of all women started their businesses from scratch and had no financial cushion to fall back on. Interestingly, however, the SBA also found that 80 percent of all men were in exactly the same boat. And regardless of whether their ownership is female or male, the vast majority of businesses—over 90 percent, in fact—employ fewer than twenty people and generate less than $1 million in revenues. Yet, when it comes to annual sales, female business owners tend to lag behind their male counterparts. More limited access to money may be one reason; the relatively higher number of female-owned firms in the start-up stage may be another.

The persistent lack of financial resources continues to be one of the key reasons why women tend to start service-based businesses—both the initial investment and the overhead required are low. Service-based industries, such as consulting and advertising, also encourage many women to make the move by taking on contract work as sole proprietors. Today, in fact, more than 95 percent of all female-owned businesses are one-woman bands. But by taking this route, women may pay a price: while they may eventually earn more money than they would in a salaried job, they never have the opportunity to generate the escalating profits that can come only from building and running a company. Traditionally, many women starting small businesses opted for this income replacement approach rather than viewing their venture as a company with a life of its own that they could transform into a strong, profit-generating vehicle. Today, however, this appears to be changing as more women move into capital-intensive businesses and bring greater management experience to their enterprises. But while attitudes toward building a company may be changing, one financial reality hasn't: women continue to have a harder time than men when it comes to bank loans, a major source of funding. Barbara Brabec's experience in starting her newsletter is a case in point.

"If you dream of launching your own business, especially a home-based one," says Barbara, "then you'll have to find the funds to do it yourself, because bankers will not give you a loan. When I first started my publishing business, for example, I thought I had a good idea and would get a loan. I had a nice financial presentation, designed a beautifully typed little folio, went to a banker and told him I wanted five thousand dollars. He never even opened my plan. He said, 'What's your collateral?' We were living in a rented house and all we had were the material possessions we owned. Here I was holding down a full-time job, I had a good salary and great credit, but the bank wouldn't even look at my plan.

"About seven years later," Barbara continues, "I went in to a local banker and asked for a ten-thousand-dollar line of credit. When he asked, 'What's your collateral?' I pulled out my financial statements and said, 'You're looking at it. I have a business that is seven years old and has turned a profit from the first day it opened.' And he said, 'OK,' and gave me the credit. So if you have been in business for a while, you might be able to get a line-of-credit loan on your signature. But that affects your personal credit, too. Women in particular are often astonished to find that, even today, many bankers want their husbands to cosign with them. If you need a big sum, like a couple of hundred thousand dollars, then the SBA might be able to help. But most of the people in my network really do start on a shoestring: five hundred dollars to one thousand dollars are very typical start-up figures. That money buys your first batch of printing, or a mailing, or an ad. That's why most small businesses grow so slowly; the initial investment is so small that it takes a long time to expand."

Kathy Lloyd-Williams agrees with Barbara's assessment. Kathy financed her company start-up and the prototypes for her "make your own fun" craft kits for children with her own money. When the business began to grow, in order to add new product lines and handle its increased manufacturing costs, she raised money for expansion through private investors and began exploring joint ventures. Even with a strong corporate finance background as a former executive with IBM, American Express International Banking, and Rothschild Ventures, Kathy found that raising funds to support her business was "more difficult than I expected. Our biggest challenge has been financing. We've financed our growth through private investors. There are not a lot of good vehicles for funding start-up companies; most banks won't look at you unless you have three years of profitable operating history. I actually come from a finance background and I still found it incredibly difficult at times. It's a shame, because there are lots of very talented people out there but it's not easy to get access to capital. We're only coming out of the hand-to-mouth situation now. It hasn't been easy."

Barbara's bank experience and Kathy's difficulties in raising money are not unusual. And the problems they've faced probably have less to do with the fact that they are women than with their desire to start home-based businesses—small retailers, service firms, and even small manufacturing companies all represent higher risks for lenders than do larger businesses and manufacturing-based firms with lots of tangible assets. But the real point here is the catch-22 situation in which many small businesses seem to find themselves when it comes to bank financing: they don't have the collateral needed to borrow cash for their start-up, and they can't build collateral unless they have the cash needed to get their businesses going. For many start-up ventures, this situation makes bank loans an unlikely and impractical source of funding. Looking on the bright side, this actually may be a blessing in disguise.

SUBSTITUTING BRAINS FOR BUCKS

As Barbara Brabec pointed out, most of the people in her home-based business network, both male and female, start their businesses with relatively small amounts of their own capital and grow slowly. Though it may seem surprising, as a female entrepreneur, this funding pattern can actually work for you rather than against you. In fact, the lack of capital that most women face often proves to be an asset rather than a liability once their businesses are up and running. Because they typically have trouble getting loans and are more likely to start small and operate with minimal budgets, many female-owned ventures keep their overhead low, are not dependent on bank credit, and run a tight fiscal ship. A 1991 survey by the National Association of Women Business Owners (NAWBO) found that 75 percent of female entrepreneurs surveyed had started their ventures with their own money, 40 percent had no bank credit, and more than 50 percent had expanded by reinvesting their profits.

This pattern of growth was similar to that which I discovered in my interviews. Most of the women I talked with launched their ventures through savings, by investing their earnings, by moonlighting, and by going the F and F route, borrowing from family or friends. For example, Sue Laris-Eastin and her first husband started their newspaper, *Downtown News,* working on their dining room table with fourteen hundred dollars Sue borrowed from a bank by telling them she was remodeling her kitchen. Pamela Mauney launched her specialty food business, Pam's Blue Ribbon Toffee, with her salary from her day job as a postmaster. Four months into her venture, Pam and her family had invested about two thousand dollars and anticipated that she would break even in about three months. Debra Oppenheim began her partnership in a nonprofit executive search firm with forty thousand dollars from two clients, her savings, and money borrowed from her "significant other." When her business exploded during its first year, she and her partner supported its rapid growth by reinvesting their profits; Debra handled her own personal expenses by "living on overdrafts" until she and her partner could begin taking out a little money from their revenues.

All of these women started relatively small, and most of them ran their businesses for the first six to twelve months and even longer with little or no outside funding. In taking this route, they actually may have strengthened, rather than limited, their chances for success. As Barbara Brabec points out, "The advantage of having little money with which to start a business is that it forces one to think more creatively, often in more profitable directions. In short, one learns how to substitute brains for bucks. If businesses short on cash tend to grow more slowly, they nevertheless grow steadily. Each small step seems to generate the extra cash one needs to get to the next level. Anyone who is willing to develop a business slowly over two to three years has a good chance of experiencing real growth by the fourth or fifth year. Patience and perseverance are high on the list of essential qualities for success, and a head for business is vital.

"Based on a quick look at some of the reports from my network members, I would say that the average part-time enterprise may gross around $30,000 a year and net about $15,000. If you are working full time and especially if you are working with a spouse, then you can start grossing $120,000 to $150,000 and then perhaps hire an employee. According to my network members, the money they bring in runs the gamut from a few thousand dollars a year to over half a million or more. It is absolutely astounding to see the amount of money that some people are making from home-based businesses."

Slow and steady growth, fueled by brainpower and ingenuity rather than dollars, is an approach to building a business that clearly has worked well for many women, including those I interviewed. From an emotional as well as financial standpoint, this strategy has many advantages: It allows you to keep control of your resources, keep your anxiety about money at a manageable level, and keep yourself hungry enough to be motivated. At the same time, slow growth and a step-by-step approach to generating the cash you need to expand forces you to think strategically and to market creatively and constantly—two prerequisites for success during the start-up stage of any business. A modest bank balance also compels you to get more bang for each and every buck you spend. It also ensures that any financial mistakes you make will have a high price tag attached to them and aren't likely to be repeated. The real message here is both hopeful and challenging: lack of money doesn't have to be a stumbling block to success in starting a business. If it seems to be one for you, then you may need to do some soul-searching about how committed you really are. In the end, most of us find the money to do the things we really want to do. If we don't, then it's probably lack of desire and drive, not lack of dollars, that is holding us back.

GIVING UP A PAYCHECK MENTALITY

Jane Adams, the author of *Wake Up, Sleeping Beauty* and *Women on Top*, has researched women's psychological money styles and interviewed both corporate executives and entrepreneurs about their views on money and success. She believes that these two groups of women have very different approaches toward making money, just as men and women do. These different attitudes are shaped largely by childhood and our experience in the work world. Says Adams,

"Money definitely has gender characteristics. For men, money is something you get for what you do. They learn that as kids, when they get paid for mowing the lawn. Girls get paid for being good. As women, we tend to undervalue our services. We see money as relational and affectional, as something we get for who and what we are, not for what we do or know. Money is a reward for adhering to standards and meeting expectations. Women tend to think of corporations in terms of 'Big Daddy.' We get money from him for how we behave and not what we do—for being a good manager, or for getting along with people.

"If you've been in a corporation and are thinking about becoming an entrepreneur, the key thing you have to come to terms with is how you think about the corporate paycheck you've received. You have to be able to see that money not as a reward, but as a payment for your skills. If you take this approach, then when you move into your own business, you can see it as payment for the product or service you produce. What's important is that you understand that the salary you get is instrumental—that you get it for the skills you have as opposed to the kind of person you are. This is the primary mind-set switch you have to make in order to get your values about money in synch with being an entrepreneur."

Most women who work for corporations, as Adams pointed out, tend to view money as relational and affectional and to treat their paychecks as a "reward." They see money as a measure of how successful they are in their on-the-job relationships and how well they behave as team players and managers. Men, on the other hand, as well as accomplished entrepreneurs, both male and female, tend to view money as *instrumental*—as a tool that allows them to make something happen. The tendency we have as women to undervalue our skills and to view money as a reward rather than payment for our skills can be a major emotional, as well as financial, barrier to making the transition from corporation to cottage. There are several other "insidious traps" that women must be especially careful to avoid during this transition, according to psychiatrist Edward Hallowell, coauthor of *What Are You Worth?*

"I think that women in general are more ambivalent about feeling independent than men are," says Dr. Hallowell. "Without knowing it, some women feel guilty about the idea of being financially independent. They may also be afraid that financial independence may affect their ability to find or stay in a relationship. At an even deeper level, they may feel that they are violating a fundamental taboo, that making money will put them in a place they shouldn't be. As a result, they may have a hard time negotiating their fees, or take on a partner they don't need, or share a business that they really don't want to share. Consciously they may see themselves as the new woman, ready to take the risks and jumping into entrepreneurship. But psychologically, old patterns die hard. So for some women, the intense outward desire for independence is accompanied by an unconscious desire to feel more comfortable, to be dependent, to be taken care of the way they were when they had a paycheck. When this happens, they can hurt their chances of success by behaving in ways that look as if they are afraid, as if they don't deserve to have a business, or as if they are guilty. Men, on the other hand, have the opposite problem: they are afraid of dependence and often won't enter into relationships that would benefit them."

How you talk about your desire for financial independence and what you really believe may be very different, cautions Dr. Hallowell. It's these hidden messages that you need to guard against: "What you are telling yourself to psych yourself up is one thing," he says, "but watch out for what is laid down in your bones. Watch out for what you feel in spite of yourself. What you wish you could deal with but feel afraid to. The key to handling these emotions is to try to get them out of the subconscious, to get beyond the taboos, to demystify your feelings about money, so you can get them out on the table where you can see them and deal with them."

According to Dr. Hallowell, another money pitfall for women to avoid during their business start-up is adopting what he describes in his book as a "dodger mentality." This money style is one of avoidance, of not wanting to deal with finances or feeling that you are somehow stupid or inadequate when it comes to money management—that "I'm good at business, but I can't handle the financial end of things." Women who have this attitude can "emotionally disqualify" themselves from becoming financially secure and actively supervising money matters by setting up situations in which they become very dependent on their accountant or financial officer. In some cases, the dodger mentality can have very dangerous consequences. It can lead women to use money problems as evidence that they are incompetent and doomed to failure by saying, I don't have any money, so I can't make it. I'm not really qualified to do this. I don't really know anything about business. Where did I get the crazy idea that I could make this work? As a result, they may be tempted to give up their venture too soon and for the wrong reasons.

"Some women have to watch out for the need to use money as an excuse or proof that they should never have started their business in the first place," warns Dr. Hallowell. "As proof that their father was right and they had no head for figures or couldn't make it on their own. Or that their husband was right when he told them they couldn't handle it. Feeling this way can make you overlook the fact that every start-up has financial problems in the beginning and that you are only encountering what everyone encounters. It doesn't mean you can't make it."

THE FOUR STAGES OF MONEY MANAGEMENT

In the course of interviewing female entrepreneurs about their experiences and attitudes toward money, I found that some intriguing patterns emerged. Just as these women passed through different emotional stages on the road to building their businesses, so they passed through what seemed to be four different stages in their relationship to money. As their businesses started, evolved, changed, and matured, so did the way they handled money. During the start-up stage, as you might expect, money was viewed almost exclusively in terms of the emotional (as well as financial) investment it demanded; for many, it was a source of anxiety and discomfort. As these women became more attuned to the ebb and flow of entrepreneurial life, they became more relaxed and secure about their ability to generate money to keep their businesses alive.

To get a better handle on your own approach to money, let's take a look at the stages the women I interviewed seemed to go through as their businesses developed. Needless to say, everyone's money style is highly individualistic and the product of a complex mix of conditioning and personal initiative. As a result, the guidelines offered here are broad and may or may not be relevant to your situation. It's also quite possible that you'll bypass one or more of these stages as your entrepreneurial life unfolds. Nevertheless, the four stages outlined below should give you some useful food for thought.

Stage One: Money as an Emotional Barometer

In this stage, money is closely tied to self-esteem; it is seen as an indicator of success and self-worth and the ticket to independence. Net worth and self-worth are interwined. Money is an emotionally charged and very sensitive issue. The fact that the move from corporation to cottage involves major financial sacrifices—surrendering a steady paycheck, benefits, insurance, pension benefits—often triggers self-doubt and fear about regaining lost ground. In order to compensate for this loss, some women may push themselves to the edge in an effort to beat the odds; they seem unwilling or unable to accept the two- to three-year break-even financial cycle that characterizes most small business start-ups. The result may be financial self-sabotage—they set themselves up for failure by overspending on nonessentials or setting unrealistic growth targets. Slow and steady growth doesn't meet their criteria for success; fast and flashy is what they crave as proof that they can make it.

During this stage, the feast-or-famine work pattern most start-ups experience, and the cash flow problems it creates, can have a direct impact on your sense of emotional well-being and self-esteem. Your mood swings may be closely tied to a day-to-day financial scorecard—you'll tend to feel anxious and down in the dumps when money isn't coming in and upbeat and hopeful when a check finally arrives in the mail. Breaking this link between your emotional behavior and your fluctuating bank balance won't be easy, because your paycheck days have conditioned you to respond in this way.

In the work world, the accepted standard of success is financial earning power. And in the early days of your new business, it's more than likely that you'll find yourself applying this same standard to your new work life; for better or worse, it's the only success indicator you have to work with. And it's the one that everyone else uses, so why shouldn't you? The answer isn't hard to find: because now you're not like everyone else, you're different. At this point, you have two choices. You can embrace the old measure of success and run the risk of feeling depressed and out of synch with the rest of the world. Or you can begin to redefine success in nonfinancial terms and focus on the psychic payoffs that your business is giving you—the chance to do work you really enjoy and value, more flexibility and control, and the opportunity to test yourself and learn new skills. Uncoupling your feelings about your self-worth and net worth may not be easy, but it's the first step to seeing money as instrumental, as a tool and not a measure of your self-esteem and accomplishments. Only by gaining this emotional distance from money can you begin to use it in ways that will allow you to truly succeed as an entrepreneur.

Stage Two: Money as the Enemy

During this stage, your business is needy and insatiable. The more money you feed it, the hungrier it becomes and the more it wants. You can find yourself spending your hard-earned dollars and perhaps those of the rest of your family on things you never dreamed you'd need before you started your business. As you struggle with cash flow, you can find yourself growing more and more anxious about your bank account and how you are going to make ends meet. However large the nest egg you may have used to launch your venture, you'll find that it's shrinking by the minute. The larger it is, the faster it seems to go. At this stage, you may be forced to rob Peter to pay Paul and to juggle your dollars in a way that's totally foreign to you. You may find yourself borrowing more money from family and friends just to keep afloat.

   In these circumstances, it isn't hard to see why you may be feeling that you're in way over your head and gasping for air. Given the struggle you're going through to make ends meet, it's understandable that you should begin to see money differently. Where once it seemed to be the ticket to your independence and a more rewarding lifestyle, it's become the enemy, a barrier to your business goals. It's the problem, not the solution. In this frame of mind, your lack of money takes on larger-than-life proportions. It looms over you like a dark and forbidding mountain; it's in your way. If you had more money, you could afford a more professional image, you could buy better equipment, you could have a real office instead of a closet or the corner of your bedroom, you could get a better wardrobe so that you'd make a better impression, you could afford to hire help so that you wouldn't be bogged down licking stamps when you should be strategizing. The list of money-related woes goes on and on.

What's happening here is similar to the testing time that we talked about earlier (page 167). Your emotional stamina and staying power are being stretched to the limit. You're letting money control you instead of the other way around. You've given money power over your emotions and perhaps even your business judgment, and now you have to wrestle with it in order to regain what you've given away. In this situation, money is a kind of emotional scapegoat; lack of it can be used to explain away or justify some of the fears and self-doubt you may be feeling as you struggle to let go of the past and reshape your professional identity. Apart from deluding yourself about what's really happening, the real danger here is that lack of money will begin to immobilize you instead of energize you. It can become an excuse for inaction and for not doing things you have to do but may not feel comfortable about, like drumming up new business or renegotiating more attractive terms with key suppliers to help you regain your financial footing. Using lack of money as an excuse also can prevent you from confronting the real and very legitimate fears that you may have about failure—and success.

How do you handle this stage? As a first step, you have to de-personalize money. You have to force yourself, however hard it is, to accept the fact that money isn't the enemy—that just as it won't solve all your problems, so it isn't the source of all your problems. Some of them, yes. But all of them, no. You have to begin to see money as a neutral force, one that has no will or energy of its own. It can neither enslave you nor empower you. Next you have to look beyond your lack of money and the stress it has triggered and try to find out what's really going on. Is lack of money just an excuse for not dealing with other, deeper fears you may be harboring—fears about your ability to run the business you've started, to be the kind of person you think a successful entrepreneur should be, to provide for yourself and your family? And finally, you need to defuse lack of money as an emotional trigger by substituting brains for bucks. You need to get beyond your lack of money by reaching deeper into yourself and tapping your creativity and ingenuity.

Stage Three: Money as Protection

By the time you've reached this stage, you've begun to overcome your fears that you're not going to make it financially. You've weathered some pretty serious storms and managed to stay afloat, so you've become more comfortable, not just with the entrepreneurial life, but with your own personal style as a business owner. Your confidence is growing and your business has begun to find its own rhythm. You've begun to separate a little from your business emotionally; your business may still be you, but you are no longer totally and completely your business. Your personal identity and professional image, once so closely intertwined, are now beginning to unravel themselves. One of the most positive results of this process is that having and spending money becomes less an issue of survival and more a by-product of success.

Only after you have been in business for a while will you begin to see money as a means of protecting yourself. Understanding and appreciating the protective nature of money is a major step toward thinking about it rationally rather than purely emotionally. During this stage, you'll make exciting progress in renegotiating your relationship with money. As you begin to learn and fine-tune your survival techniques and how to manage your cash flow more effectively, the balance of power subtly shifts between you and your earning power—money is no longer your enemy, but your friend. You begin to realize more fully that just as money isn't the source of all your problems, so it isn't the solution to many of them. You begin to see money more clearly, not just for what it is, but for what it can and can't do. It can insulate you, give you a cushion, and buy you time. It also can give you more control over the work you do by giving you the freedom to say yes to projects you want to be involved in and no to those you don't. At the same time, money can't buy you emotional freedom or prevent you from making mistakes. It can allow your business to grow, but the decisions you make about how and when that growth should take place will ultimately be responsible for whether or not you expand successfully. It can allow you to exert more control over your professional life, but it can't compensate for the lack of attention you may be giving your personal life.

Stage Four: Money as a Tool

When you reach this stage, you'll know that you've really earned your entrepreneurial wings. Your attitude toward money will be very different from what it was when you first launched your business. You'll have stopped being afraid of money and it will be devoid of emotional content for you. You'll see it and treat it as a medium of exchange and a vehicle for enacting your business decisions. At this stage, money has become transactional and fluid; it's fuel for accomplishing the things you need to do to move your business in the direction you want to go. You still have a value system attached to money, but as Jane Adams would say, it's one in which money is instrumental rather than relational. That is, you see it in terms of its capacity to help you achieve things, not as a measure of your personal or professional success.

By now you've begun thinking in terms of value exchanged for money, and you've begun to use money as a tool that can help you leverage your resources—to negotiate a contract, build a relationship, produce a product, market your services. You'll also find that you have a more realistic understanding of the real meaning of money as independence. Money can give you financial freedom to work when and where you want to, it can give you access to new and exciting talent and projects, and it can allow you to grow your business from within by releasing you from dependence on outside sources of funding unless you choose to use them. Here's how Jane Adams describes this mind-set: "The successful entrepreneurial women I've talked with really understand that money is a tool; it doesn't carry any emotional baggage for them. It doesn't have any 'memory,' as Ned [Dr. Edward] Hallowell would say. For entrepreneurs, money is a tool that can buy them independence. When it's a tool, it has actual value. It does something—it's used to buy a piece of equipment or purchase a service. Entrepreneurial women also realize that you'll never get rich working for a corporation. I think for corporate women, money still has symbolic rather than actual value. Money, for them, is a symbol of compliance. When they begin to understand that money is independence, that's when they quit their jobs.

"Men see money as independence very early on. It takes women longer to see that money can make them independent of and from the restrictions of being a woman in our society. For entrepreneurial men, once they get past the break-even point, money is just a way of keeping score. I think that most entrepreneurial women never get beyond seeing money as independence and never reach the point where they see it as a measure of competitive success, a way of keeping score the way men do. This may be changing with younger women. For younger women in the nineties, I think the entrepreneurial sector is very appealing. They see security as an emotional issue and something they won't find in the corporate world."

To outline more clearly the money-as-a-tool entrepreneurial style, let's take an example that one business owner used to illustrate her changing attitude toward money. As part of a major ad campaign, she commissioned an expensive photographic shoot with a well-known photographer. When the photos arrived, she found that she wasn't happy with them. Early in her business, she would have been very upset and emotional about the results produced. She would have blamed herself for choosing the wrong person for the job and focused her attention on her lack of judgment. When this incident actually occurred, however, she had been in business for a while and was no stranger to the problems associated with using free-lance creative talent. She also had a more businesslike relationship with money.

As a result, instead of letting her emotions get the best of her and cloud her judgment, she found herself zeroing in on the steps she needed to take to fix the problem and get the artwork she wanted. She immediately realized that she had three options, each with a different price tag: she could persuade the photographer to reshoot the photos for her at cost; she could negotiate a kill fee with him and hire someone else to redo the job; or she could contact a stock photo house, order a search, and then pay for the use of existing prints. When she first started her business, the entrepreneur recalls, she never would have been able to think in such clearheaded, unemotional terms about a project bottleneck like this. But by the time it happened, she was well-equipped to handle it with cool professionalism.

When you reach this stage, you see more clearly, perhaps than ever before, what money can and can't accomplish from a business perspective. You understand its value as a shield against some of the slings and arrows your business may encounter, but you also have a healthy respect for its limitations. You've begun to come to terms with money; you've come to view it with emotional detachment as a kind of valuable but invisible employee. You're freer to let it do its job while you do yours. It has a powerful and important role in your business, but its role is also a passive rather than an active one. You are the piper who calls the tune and money does the dancing.

Understanding and Managing Your Money Mind-set

For better or worse, all of us, women and men alike, have strong feelings when it comes to money. The way we think about and handle the dollars we have—or expect to have—has lots of emotional baggage attached to it. Money represents independence and freedom, security and protection, self-esteem and success, and a dozen other powerful and evocative feelings and desires, most of which have little to do with what dollars can and cannot buy. On the flip side of the coin, lack of money can have a powerful and sometimes destructive impact on how we feel about ourselves and our work. But there is hope! Again, your relationship with money is dynamic, not static; as your business develops and changes, so will your money management skills. One of the keys to handling this change and making it work for you instead of against you is to understand the emotional wellspring from which your attitude toward money flows. In my interview with Dr. Edward Hallowell, he outlined six very helpful steps you can take to acknowledge and manage your own personal "agreement" with money in ways that can make the move from corporation to cottage easier and less stressful from both an emotional and financial perspective:

One: Understand Your Emotional Responses to Money

Separating money from your emotions and seeing it as a neutral tool rather than an index of your self-worth and success is a difficult, and sometimes even a painful, process, but it is an essential one when you start your own business. How do you get there from here? The answer lies in understanding what money means to you and how you arrived at that meaning. Once you understand what you expect from your earning power—and what it can and cannot do for you— then you can begin to renegotiate your relationship to money.

"The most fundamental piece of advice I would give anyone," says Dr. Hallowell, "is to look at your emotional responses to money and your money style—the way you handle it. This is the point where most people stumble: they don't take the emotional aspect of their money style into account. And so they focus all their energy on the numbers, the graphs and spreadsheets, without any awareness of their psychological attitude. They never ask, 'How have I handled money in the past? What mistakes have I made? What are my weaknesses when it comes to money?' I can't tell you how many people—both men and women—are shooting themselves in the foot because of psychological issues surrounding money that they haven't addressed. The desire for freedom, stress, insecurity—all these factors can play themselves out along financial lines.

"For example, some people tend to overspend. They throw money at problems as a way of solving them. In starting up a business, they might take the attitude, 'I have to go first class,' and make the mistake of buying equipment they can't afford. These people are trying to handle their feelings of inadequacy by overspending on image; as a result, they put themselves in a hole they can never get out of. But if they could catch this tendency early on, then they might be able to rein themselves in. At the other extreme, some people are just naturally afraid to take a risk. They are naturally tight with their money and may have a problem getting off the dime because they won't want to spend enough to make the initial investment their business requires. They are too scared. So they never get out of the starting gate.

"Both these problems, overspending and underspending, are really psychological and not financial. If you can use insight into your money style to counteract patterns like these and to understand how you behave around money, you have a much better chance of succeeding. When you are calling the shots, the way you handle money can make or break you. If you are a 'gambler' and you don't know it—if you become impulsive when you are financially stressed—then you can blow your whole business in an afternoon. When you are laying out your own capital, your money style, whatever it is, is intensified and amplified. So you have to take stock of yourself. Chances are you are not going to fundamentally change who you are, but you *can* change the way you manage who you are. That's what counts."

Two: Try to Give Yourself Some Breathing Space

How do you give up the attitude of dependency that's associated with working for a corporation and having a paycheck, and begin moving to the point where you are financially equipped to take charge of yourself? How do you make the move without overreacting to the stresses involved and taking foolish risks, as if to prove yourself wrong?

"You have to recognize," warns Dr. Hallowell, "that making this change won't happen at the snap of your fingers. It's going to take time. So you have to find a way to create a transitional period for yourself in which your financial needs will be taken care of, at least for a time. You have to set things up so you can come up for air. This may mean starting your business while you still have a job. Or getting a loan or financial help from friends to tide you over until your business is up and running. If you are forced to leave your job before you can make these plans, then you have to be careful not to overreact and become so terrified that you throw yourself into the fire and go off half-cocked."

Three: "Never Worry Alone"

Talking about money is something that many of us find hard to do. Some experts say we'll talk about sex more readily than we'll talk about our paychecks. But talking about your financial concerns is one very important way to work them out and defuse the tensions that money problems can create. Thinking through different scenarios for financing your business and handling your money can help make you feel more secure and more in control.

"Some of the best advice I ever learned in psychiatry," notes Dr. Hallowell, "came from an old teacher of mine who always used to say, 'Never worry alone.' I think this applies to any sort of change. Don't sit up in the middle of the night worrying by yourself. Worrying alone is not productive. Have someone to bounce those worries off of who can help you find ways to handle them. Sit down with a consultant, for example, and worry with that person; use your concerns constructively. Look at the worst possible financial scenario and come up with a game plan for dealing with it.

"It's also very important to have someone you trust and will listen to when they say you're getting out of line financially. It can be a spouse, a partner, or a secretary. It's very difficult to catch many of the financial patterns we find ourselves falling into. Sometimes it's hard to look at what you're doing and say, Oh, I'm overspending. You can get caught up in the enthusiasm of the moment and lose your perspective. So it really helps to have someone say, Wait a minute! You're going overboard here! But you have to be willing to listen. If there is one practical strategy I would advise more than any other, it would be this: find a trusted advisor and then listen to what they tell you."

Four: Don't Overvalue the Power of Money

During our paycheck days, many of us were lulled into thinking of the corporations we worked for as security blankets that would take care of our needs. In making the move from corporation to cottage, we're surrendering that belief and trying to take charge of our financial destinies. In doing so, we often equate money with independence and can begin thinking of our own businesses as the security blankets we once wanted our corporate employers to be. This kind of substitution can be a dangerous one, because it can make us demand things of our own businesses that they really can't give us—and that we shouldn't expect.

"The real danger here," says Dr. Hallowell, "is in overvaluing the idea of money as independence. What does this really mean? Does it mean feeling good all the time? Does it mean never having to rely on anyone again? Does it mean never having any obligations? If you have these magical and unrealistic attitudes toward the benefits that owning your own business will give you, then you'll be disappointed, just as you may have been when you worked for someone else. Independence carries with it all kinds of responsibilities and burdens. We all tend to exaggerate how great things will be when we have the chance to take charge and call the shots. And that's fine. These feelings can be motivators. But you also want to take a cold, hard look at what you're getting into—and realize that it won't be perfect. And then you need to remember that even if it's not perfect, it doesn't mean you made a mistake and should go back to your old life again."

Five: Make a Healthy Agreement with Money

As discussed earlier (see pages 223–24), the way you deal with money parallels your relationship with your business. When you first start it, you are totally invested in it emotionally. Then, as time goes on, your business takes on a life of its own and you begin to separate from it—you recapture your personal life and gain some emotional distance from the demands it makes. The same is true of money management. When you begin to see money as a tool, then you have fundamentally altered the way you respond to what it can do for you. What is this more positive, more easeful relationship with money like?

"Most people's agreement with money focuses on the amount they want—and that amount always has to be more," points out Dr. Hallowell. "I think a mature, healthy agreement with money focuses on how much is enough, not on making more. A healthy agreement with money also takes into account what money can and can't do. Yes, money can give you certain things you want. But it can't give you other things you may need. It can't give you love or emotional security. It can't give you immortality. It can't give you freedom from disease, or chance, or fate. It can't give you goodness or self-worth. It can't give you the father's love you never received as a child. So you need to ask money only for what it can give you.

It can give you financial security. It can give you food. It can give you a year's tuition for your children. That's all it can do. And that's a lot. What money can do for you is great, but it's also limited. One of the biggest and most dangerous fallacies about money is that your self-worth is measured by your net worth. That's why I called my book *What Are You Worth?* If you have too relational an attitude toward money, then you can begin to think of it as a measure of your goodness, as your just reward. Money is just an inert substance, the by-product of doing things well. It has nothing to do with your inherent value as a person. I think one advantage that women have here is that they don't see money in terms of keeping score. They can work with it instead of becoming totally focused on it as a measure of success."

Six: Find Ways to Pay Yourself That Don't Involve Money

Two of the biggest benefits you gain in starting your own business are greater control over your time and the freedom to run your business the way you want to. Both of these benefits can allow you to pay yourself in exciting ways that have nothing to do with making money but everything to do with feeling good about yourself and the work you're doing. When Ann Hull left her demanding, high-pressure job with the Modern Language Association, she began consulting with the Junior League. This work consumed about 80 percent of her time and gave her the freedom to renew old friendships, to do some pro bono work for a small minority association that needed her help, and to become active in a professional association. When Kathy Lloyd-Williams began xoxo international, she made arrangements to have some of her kits assembled by disabled students in her community. She also made a decision to seek out recyclable materials whenever possible. Karen Fried donates a portion of the money she makes from every Think-It Link-It game to the American Cancer Society in memory of her father. She also has plans to set up a scholarship for teenage entrepreneurs and to take time out from running her business to tour major cities, talking with teens about the rewards of launching a start-up venture. Each of these women is paying herself in a way that meets her emotional needs and is giving herself something that money can't buy. This kind of psychic reward can be a powerful motivator for success.

"The fundamental mistake people make with money," Dr. Hallowell stresses, "is they can never have enough of it and they think that all their efforts should be devoted to getting more. Probably the most common way that people enslave themselves is becoming a slave to money. And you can do that in your own business, just as you can in a corporation. But when you are on your own, you have the opportunity to feel happier and richer while having less money. A patient walked into my office recently, for example, and I felt so moved by her story that I decided to work with her for nothing. She thinks that I'm doing her a favor, but I am paying myself. It will make me feel good if I can help her. Being free to pick and choose what you want to do without being a slave to money, and without feeling that you can't do something unless you get paid for it, really frees you up. You are more in charge. You are increasing your options tremendously. You are motivating yourself through feelings of goodwill, feelings of accomplishment, and a sense of growth. Being your own boss allows you to pay yourself in ways other than money and really points up the fallacy that the only reason we work is to make more of it."

SURVIVAL TIPS FOR MANAGING YOUR START-UP DOLLARS

Cheryl Williams is a consultant specializing in providing organizational strategic planning, and financial advice to small creative arts companies. Since launching her New York City–based firm, ReArt, she has worked with a wide range of entrepreneurs with the goal of sharpening their financial management skills. Here she offers some nuts-and-bolts advice that may prove helpful in planning your financial start-up strategy: "When it comes to getting a handle on their money, I've found that most people, men and women, prefer to live in denial. But you don't have the luxury of operating that way during a start-up. Part of what I'm trying to do with my own business, ReArt, is to show people that they really can manage their money effectively. It can be done effortlessly, once you understand why you need to do it. And it won't kill you. People say that women start out undercapitalized. Yes, they start out undercapitalized because they don't have the cash, but even more so, they start out undercapitalized because they don't know what to do with the cash they have. There has never been a business that has failed for lack of cash. It has failed because of poor decisions. And when you have too much cash, you continue to make those decisions much longer than you should. The key is finding creative ways to leverage the cash that you do have.

"So the survival issue for most start-ups isn't not having a lot of money, it's knowing how to make the most out of the dollars they're working with. People use lack of money as a barrier because they're afraid to confront their fears. If you don't know what you need financially, then you just fuel your fears about what you don't have. Once you confront what you need, it becomes concrete and it's not this amorphous monster *money*. Once you know how much money your business requires, then you can sit down and figure out how to go about getting it. You tell yourself, I need X amount of money. The next question has to be, What do you need the money for? And after you identified what you need the money for, then you can figure out what you can get through barter, what you can get through a loan, or this way, or that way. Then your real cash need becomes diminished. And you see that you have lots of options.

"Really keeping track of what you spend and why you spend it is extremely important. If you do that for a month or two, you'll see where your money goes. Of course, there are fixed expenses. But even among those fixed expenses, there are things that could be handled differently. We think of the telephone, for example, as a fixed expense; when we need to make a call, we just pick it up. But perhaps some of those calls to the West Coast could be made after five o'clock. Little things like that can help you get a handle on your expenses. I think it's very important to make a budget—to look at the money you're going to need, where you might be able to get it— and to evaluate your spending patterns and the budget on an ongoing basis, not just at the end of the year or at tax time. When you're running a business, you need to know where every penny goes.

"Quite often, financial planners tell you when you start to save money to pay yourself first. Most people say, 'Oh, my God, I can't do that. I don't have enough money!' But when you sit down and look at your spending, often you'll see that you're nickel and diming yourself into a corner. And that the money you spend—a dollar here, five dollars there—really adds up. If you were to take those dollars at the beginning of the month and put them into a savings account, you really wouldn't miss them. One area where people get into trouble, for instance, is handling a lump sum payment. They receive a lump sum and forget that, come tax time, they have to pay the government. I advocate taking some portion of any lump sum you receive and putting it aside, not just for taxes, but for those times when business isn't coming in. That's why it's important to know what your base expenses are for the month and what your business expenses are; and within this framework, to know what your fixed expenses are and your variable expenses are. Once you get this kind of financial control over your business, then the odds of your making poor decisions and wasting capital are lowered. At the same time, once you have a budget in place, you need to be continually evaluating where you are and where you want to go and acknowledge that it's OK to change. As a result of keeping track of my own income, before I spend, I ask myself, Why? And if I can't come up with a reasonable explanation for why I really need something, then I put it on the shelf.

"For my creative clients, so much of how they think about themselves is tied up in how someone receives their painting or what kind of review their play gets. If they have a great review, then they are a wonderful person and they're on top of the world. If it's not so wonderful, then they feel they are worth less as a person. As a result, they go out and do foolish things with their money. They go out and buy things they really don't need. If they were in a different emotional frame of mind, they would have thought twice about pulling out the plastic. I've seen people make a lot of poor financial decisions when they are emotionally vulnerable. People overspend the same way that they overeat or overexercise. At the heart of their actions is their self-perception and feelings of self-worth. I think that part of the problem here is that our society equates value as a person with material wealth. But once you reach a point in your spiritual quest where your self-worth is not based on dollar figures, then you can allow yourself to have less materially but at the same time have better control over those assets you do have."

10

SIX BIG TRAPS TO AVOID

Women tend to be service-oriented, very good at detail and follow-through, and intent on making everything just perfect. Often the way they run their businesses is a magnification of the way they deal with people in their personal and family lives.

—*Lonah Birch*

Throughout this book, we've touched on most of the traps that we'll talk about here. But because these pitfalls are ones that surfaced consistently in my interviews, it seems useful to take time now to explore them more fully. In listing the major stumbling blocks identified, I've organized them loosely in order of importance. Based on my research, the first four traps— being overly concerned with image, overspending on equipment and office operations, overservicing clients and undervaluing your skills, and treating your business like a family—definitely seemed to prompt the most discussion and strongest warnings from the women I spoke with. That there are a number of other "hot buttons" that easily could have been discussed here—growing too quickly, for example, or failing to market, falling into old financial patterns, or failing to research. But since all of these issues are explored elsewhere in other contexts, I've confined my traps list to the six you are most likely to encounter during the first eighteen months of your new venture's existence.

TRAP NUMBER ONE: BEING OVERLY CONCERNED WITH YOUR IMAGE

Of all the traps that you can fall into at this point, being overly self-conscious and sensitive about your business image is probably the biggest and the most serious. It can lead you to overspend, over-promise, and oversell yourself. You become susceptible to this trap when you start buying into the myth of the entrepreneur with a capital E and trying to live out your personal fantasy of entrepreneurship before you really have the means to do it. For many people, this fantasy revolves around re-creating the safe and comforting office environment they enjoyed in corporate life, only on a smaller, more intimate, and more manageable scale. Living out this fantasy can be extremely costly not only in dollars and overhead, but in the anxiety and stress it creates. It can impel you to move out of your home and into rented office space before you really can afford to, to buy costly equipment so that you can present a first-class image to the marketplace, and to hire other people to do the draggy, time-consuming jobs you don't want to do so that you can focus on what you do best (translation: what you're most comfortable doing).

The emotional need to appear bigger and better established than you really are also can lead you to oversell yourself and to misrepresent your resources. This, in turn, can induce you to take on a project that is too big and demanding at this stage in your venture's life cycle. This is a tough one to call. On the one hand, you want to stretch and prove yourself; on the other, you run the risk of really getting in over your head. At a time when you're probably under enormous pressure to find new business, the temptation to overpromise may be almost irresistible. If you feel confident that you can pull together the resources you need to make it a success, then take the project on. But make it clear that you're in a start-up mode and you'll be drawing on outside resources to deliver the results you promise. In your eagerness to charge ahead, don't try to make a client think that you are bigger, more established, and better connected than you really are. More often than not, this approach backfires.

Melinda and Malachi Pancoast were careful to avoid this image trap when they began offering training in organizational dynamics to small Vermont companies through their firm Milestone Management Consulting. "What worked for us," says Melinda, "was focusing our attention on finding clients and generating money right away. So we spent our time making calls, making appointments, and building client relationships—and didn't put much into our image. We had a computer and we designed our stationery on it. It was really basic. Then, down the road, we invested in really nice stationery and a more professional look. But in the beginning, we concentrated on figuring out what our business was about and how to find clients. We bought some clothes for sales meetings, but we didn't give too much attention at this stage to our presentation. Instead we focused on sales and on working with our first clients. We paid a lot of attention to them and what they needed. We gave them everything we had."

The real issue here is self-image—how you feel about yourself and where you are at this stage of your venture. Here's how Jordana Simpson describes the trap you can fall into: "Trying to model your business after the companies you've worked for can be a big problem. One of the most crushing things I learned after going into business for myself was that I couldn't match the power of the companies I'd left or even some bigger design studios. The truth is that you're this little acorn and you are promising everyone you are going to become a big oak tree, but you're going to be a little acorn for a long time. I think you just have to be comfortable with that. So you have to stop trying to act bigger than you are and puffing yourself up—and stop making promises that you can't keep and that will keep you up twenty-four hours a day."

Being comfortable with your "little acorn" status may not be easy, but it's vitally important. Otherwise you can get so caught up in the trappings of being in business that you rob yourself of the time, money, and energy you need to actually create the business itself. So don't confuse image with professionalism. Delivering on what you promise, strong performance, and a businesslike attitude and presentation—that's professionalism. This is what clients want. Whether you work out of a closet at home or out of an office on Fifth Avenue is far less important than the work you do. So don't get hung up on the trappings of success, or they'll trap you. Focus on finding new business and servicing your clients and customers.

Trap Number Two: Spending Too Much on Equipment and Infrastructure

Debra Oppenheim and her partner, Jane Phillips, found that the minimalist approach to image building is also the key to avoiding another big trap: overspending on overhead and equipment. When Debra and Jane launched their not-for-profit executive search firm, The Phillips Oppenheim Group, they were very concerned about cost containment. Although they felt that the nature of their business required them to rent office space rather than working at home, they initially settled on a very small space.

"We started out sharing an office about the size of a shoe box and using part-time help," Debra recalls. "That worked up to a point. But then we found that we were climbing over each other; even though Jane still had an office at the Ford Foundation, she was still spending a lot of time here. And so about three months after we started the firm, we hired a full-time administrative assistant and we did take another office for Jane. But we did it only when we felt we could handle the increased overhead. So cost containment is a tricky issue. On the one hand, you have to keep your costs low; on the other, you can't keep them down to the point where you can't function.

"When we first started, both Jane and I did a mailing immediately. We sent out a letter that produced good results. But we didn't print a brochure. And when we do, it's not going to be a fancy one, because I think we can spend our money better elsewhere. You really have to be practical about using your resources. I would advise anyone starting any kind of new business to be very, very conservative about money. That's number one.

"Another pitfall in starting a new business, especially one like ours that is so heavily dependent on a data base, is that people might have a tendency to go out and spend lots and lots of money on equipment. Resisting the temptation to do this is very important. Right now we are doing fine with the primitive system that we've devised. When we are generating enough revenue, if the business warrants it, we may put in more sophisticated computer systems. But we can survive this way."

As Debra Oppenheim suggests, spending too much on your operating structure is one trap it's important to avoid. Keep your systems and equipment as simple as you can for as long as you can, to the point where your client-servicing needs outstrip your physical support systems. Only at that point should you begin to think about investing more money to enhance or replace your existing setup. Taking this approach may require some ingenuity and juggling, but it will allow you to grow at a steady pace while keeping your overhead from becoming a major headache and a dangerous financial drain.

Trap Number Three: Overservicing Clients and Undervaluing Your Product or Service

Service is a tricky issue. On the one hand, it's one of the keys to business success, especially in a tough, competitive marketplace. To see just how much value is placed on servicing clients, you have to go only as far as the nearest newsstand or bookstore. Article after article and how-to guides of every description are devoted to this theme. But there's one aspect of client relationship building that has a definite downside when it comes to business survival: overservicing. Clearly when it comes to providing service, female business owners are strong performers. As the SBA's Lonah Birch points out, "Women actually have a higher success rate at running businesses because they are very service-oriented and pay strong attention to detail. At the same time, I think women tend to undervalue their time, talent, and expertise, and perhaps not be as aggressive or assertive as they could be about assessing the value of what they have to offer. Where a male attorney will charge seventy-five dollars or one hundred dollars per hour, for example, a female lawyer will only charge fifty dollars. I also think that women may not think as big as they might when it comes to projections about the potential profits their businesses can generate.

"Because of the many roles that women have, I also think it is more difficult for them to separate their personal and their professional lives from a service standpoint. It's not unusual for them to get calls from their kids or their husbands about some kind of crisis when they are already up to their eyeballs. Trying to be the pleaser and make everyone happy at home and in their business is one of the biggest reasons why a woman tends to put herself on the back burner and why her stress level may be so high."

As Birch notes, a strong commitment to service is a factor in the high rate of success women have demonstrated in starting small businesses. Yet, when it comes to negotiating the terms for performing a service, women tend to undervalue their time, talent, and experience. The result isn't hard to figure from an economic standpoint; you easily can end up doing one thousand dollars' worth of work for a fee of five hundred—not exactly a winning proposition financially. Not only can this leave you burned out emotionally and raise your stress level, it also can break you. This is probably one of the major problems you'll encounter if you are starting a consulting business, because basically you are selling your time and talent. Determining a fair market price for the skills you have to offer—and guarding against overdelivering to the point where you lose money—will be critical to your survival.

Clearly there's a fine line between going the extra mile and doing the superior work that clients need and want, and overservicing to the point that you jeopardize your business's future. As Debra Oppenheim describes the dilemma, "Of course, you want to keep your clients happy. But what happens is that you get mired down in transactions. I bend over backwards to please my clients, and always have. But now that I have my own firm, I've found that marketing and long-range planning go out the window because we are constantly caught up in worrying about the day-to-day servicing of clients. And that's very bad business when you have your own business. You really have to sit down and ask, Where are my next clients coming from? What kinds of effort do I have to expend to reach them? What should I be doing right now to expand my current base?"

Finding out how to value your time and allocate it so that you don't sacrifice marketing and long-term planning to client service can be a tricky business. It requires ongoing adjustments and cost-benefit analysis on your part. It also demands strong time management skills, which may be an aspect of your business you need to work on. Clearly, outstanding client service should be one of your top priorities. But sometimes in your eagerness to do not just a good job, but a great one, you can find yourself giving 150 percent when 120 percent is more than enough. Knowing how to pace yourself, how much effort to expend, and how to expend it most efficiently are key to making your business work. So talk to other people about their negotiating strategies and service philosophies, spend time researching servicing techniques, and then carefully monitor your own approach to the issue of service. Also keep in mind that the best source of feedback about your skill on the service front is your current client base or customers. So try the approach that Cheryl Williams described (see page 180) and ask your clients or customers to evaluate the services you've performed for them. This kind of follow-up is always appreciated.

TRAP NUMBER FOUR: TREATING YOUR BUSINESS TOO MUCH LIKE A FAMILY

If you are home alone and in a solo situation workwise, then this trap isn't one you need to worry about. But if your business has grown to the point where you are bringing other people on board on a part-time or full-time basis, then be sure to read on. Handling the interpersonal dynamics involved in hiring and managing employees is one of the biggest challenges you'll face—and your decisions are critical. If you develop a smooth-running, cohesive team, then you can leverage your time and energy tremendously. If you make some poor judgments on this front, you can pay a very high price, both financially and emotionally.

On the one hand, you may be motivated by a powerful desire to integrate your business and personal values. In fact, this desire may have been what prompted you to start your own business in the first place. And without a doubt, how you manage employees and the environment you create are major ways to express your personal value system through your work. But bringing your personal values and the needs of your business into harmony is a complex balancing act. It requires knowing when to intermingle the personal and professional aspects of your life and when to keep them separate. It also requires that you be very careful about going overboard in viewing your business as a family and your employees as members of that family. If you choose to adopt an intimate, close-knit family work style, then be aware that this approach can cause some major problems for you down the road; it can be emotionally demanding, keep you from making practical, realistic hiring and firing decisions, and cost you money.

When Jordana Simpson and her partner began their graphic design firm, one of their major goals was to create a supportive, nurturing atmosphere. In fact, one of Jordana's biggest fantasies had to do with how she wanted to work with people. In her own words, she was "going to change the face of the workplace by treating people like human beings and by ensuring that there wasn't an authoritarian relationship between employer and employee. So that people who came to work in my studio would love to get up in the morning.

"What I found out," says Jordana, "was that people are people. You can make the most incredible promises about work, but it takes the commitment of everyone on the team to produce results. We had a young designer working for us. And when she started, my partner and I had made an agreement about integrity, communication, and team partnership. The young designer read the list we'd written, she agreed that's the way it would be, and [she] signed on the dotted line. But what I learned is that you can't make anyone communicate who doesn't want to communicate. . . . When you manage people this way, you get ulcers. . . . The truth is, if you manage people the way I fantasized about it, they come into your life and your heart, and it's very emotional. I went home and worried about the people who worked with me."

Lorraine Gerstein had a similar experience. Because of her background in teaching and social services, the "biggest mistake" she made in starting her business was "thinking I could treat employees from a counseling perspective. That I could be a sort of mother hen, a confessor, a supporter. All of these things, I've found, are not possible in a business setting. I was into the nurturing mode when I began and I didn't realize that you have to push people to work and be productive and get the job done. Just having a therapeutic, supportive relationship with the people who work for you is not going to cut it.

"In retrospect, I made some poor hiring decisions. I didn't scrutinize people carefully in terms of whether they shared my philosophy about my business. Some of those hiring decisions were made out of desperation, because I had the work and I needed to turn it over, and I was afraid that if I didn't have people in place, I would lose the business. I would say that just about all my mistakes have to do with making poor decisions with regard to staff. I'm still fine-tuning this. One of the things I no longer do in hiring is to just interview myself. Now I count on several other people on the staff to interview and give me their input before adding another employee. That has been very helpful."

As Lorraine Gerstein noted, finding people who shared her philosophy about her business and how it should operate isn't always easy. But according to Melinda Pancoast, this type of help is very important. "When you hire people," she advises, "be sure that they have the same kinds of goals that you have and that they can align themselves with the company you want to create. If you don't do this, then you end up with a group of people who have no cohesiveness. Everyone ends up working at cross-purposes rather than in the same direction."

Another major pitfall in this area, adds Melinda, is "hanging on to people who aren't working out or being afraid to talk to them about uncomfortable issues. This happens all the time in small companies. People tend to hang on to the employees they have for fear that they won't be able to find someone else and won't be able to get their work done. But usually this isn't a problem. If you stay true to the vision you have for your company and are enthusiastic about it, then you can always find people who are appropriate."

Sue Laris-Eastin, publisher of *Downtown News*, knows all too well the problems involved in finding the right people. Today she has a staff of twenty-five. Over the years, she has devoted a great deal of time to the issues of managing personnel and creating a productive work atmosphere. "People like to work at *Downtown News*," says Sue. "They like the atmosphere. That's one of the reasons that people decide to join us—it feels good to be here. They come in and say, 'Hey, this is really relaxed, I like this.' In every interview, though, I make it a point to tell people so that they're not misled, 'Don't be fooled by the atmosphere. Yes, it is relaxed, and yes, the people here do like each other and enjoy each other, and yes, we do have a good time, but we all work our butts off. So don't mistake relaxed and amiable for kicking back.'

"I think this is a very tough area. And while it can be a trap, I think the benefits of having a friendly work environment are definitely worth the risks. There's almost an impossible line between being too close and too distant, and you never walk it perfectly. The most consistent mistake I've made in business, and I don't ever seem to learn this lesson, is keeping people much longer than I should. I keep them because I think about them in a vacuum. I think about the individuals and their lives. I could never fire people before the holidays, for instance. And there are all kinds of other things that get in my way. But this is really, really a trap. Because when you keep someone who isn't working out, people think, Oh, isn't this woman wonderful and caring? But that's bull. Because that person that you're not firing is screwing up people who are being productive and people who will do well in the company but can't because you've left this obstacle in their way. You're destroying excellent employees with a bad employee.

"This has happened to me with people who didn't produce the volume of work they needed to. I made the mistake of thinking they had bonded really closely with the rest of their department. I thought that if I fired someone, then everyone else was going to be upset. I was wrong. The truth was everyone resented these people because they didn't do as much work. I find it hard to get beyond this. We've done better in the past year at this, but we have to talk to each other hard about it. Is this person producing what we need them to produce? Have they had enough chances? Have we given them all the training that we can give them? What gets in my way is that I have in my life had incredible success at creating a silk purse out of a sow's ear. I've done it a million times. And I always believe I can do it. I rarely see until it's too late that there's something or someone I cannot transform.

"I do know how to hire to my weaknesses, though. One of my managers, Mary Staffa, is a fabulous woman with wonderful instincts about people, and I trust them more than I trust my own. If Mary says, 'No, don't hire this person,' that person doesn't get hired. But I also never shove people down the throats of department heads. Each department has a manager and they all get a say in who they hire. Thinking back, I'd say that the first biggest mistake I've made is not firing people when I should and the second is not hiring well. I've solved problem two, but I'm still working on number one. It takes a long time to build a good staff. There's one last thing to avoid here: everyone, when they're hiring people, should always, 100 percent of the time, call their references. People nod their heads yes about this, but then they don't do it. I know, because people leave here without anyone ever calling me. Some people have made big mistakes because of this."

TRAP NUMBER FIVE: RELYING TOO HEAVILY ON "EXPERTS"

Seeking out expert professional advice about how to run your business during your start-up stage is often a wise and even essential move. When Karen Fried started her Think-It Link-It game, one of the first moves she made was to seek out a copyright attorney in order to properly protect the game she was inventing. Working with an accountant who's familiar with small business also can be useful in helping you decide the best structure for your enterprise. And if you're in a manufacturing business, for instance, expert counsel about liability insurance and other issues is a must. At the same time, it's very important that you retain control of both what your business does and how it operates. Jordana Simpson learned this lesson the hard way. When she and her partner launched their partnership, they were so concerned about doing it right that they hired experts to map out their strategy.

"When we started out on our own," says Jordana, "we got all the 'right stuff': we hired the best accountant for small businesses and found a 'big gun' management consultant. He developed a big, thick business plan for us, but I never understood what it was all about. For me, it didn't make sense. If the consultant had talked to me about vision, tension, and goals, he would have been speaking my language. But the plan he came up with for us was so formal and businesslike that I don't think it did us a whole lot of good. In many cases, I think you're much better off sitting down with a friend over coffee and saying, This is what I want to have in my life and this is the vision I see. Not only is this probably much more helpful, it's also a lot cheaper."

The key lesson that Jordana learned from her expensive foray into plan design is that *she was really the best expert* when it came to her business. And *so are you.* When you go out on your own, it's natural that you may feel some uncertainty and insecurity about what you're doing. You may even think that since you lack experience as an entrepreneur, you need help from all sorts of experts to launch yourself. So you may be tempted to hire other people, and in the process, you can easily forget that *you* are in the driver's seat.

All too often, you'll find that the advice you receive when you rely too heavily on outsiders to make major business decisions for you is too broad to meet your specific needs. Not only is taking this approach expensive, but it also can give you a false sense of security. But remember, no expert you hire is ever going to have the emotional or financial stake in your business that you and your family have. Outside advisors always operate from a distance—and their meters are always running. So don't disempower yourself. Yes, you may need some advice and experienced guidance, but in the end, *you* are the single best judge of what your business has to offer and how it should be run.

TRAP NUMBER SIX: FAILING TO ADDRESS FOUR ENTREPRENEURIAL WEAKNESSES

When Joyce McClure runs training seminars for entrepreneurs, she often asks people to name the four major reasons why new businesses fail. "Invariably," says Joyce, "someone will say lack of money. While money is definitely a big issue, there are four even more important 'lacks' that can sabotage your success: lack of planning, lack of experience, lack of management skill, and lack of promotion. Even if you have all the money in the world, it's not going to overcome the lack of these four things in your business.

"For many people, it's not lack of money that undercuts their success, it's how they spend the money they do have that is really the problem. And understanding how to spend the money you have has to do with planning, experience, management, and promotion. For example, I've found that when people start their own business,

often the first thing they say they need is a brochure, or they want
to run an advertisement. But they don't stop to think about what
they need a brochure or an ad for. Who are they going to reach? Is
a brochure or ad the best way to reach this audience? One ad in the
wrong publication at the wrong time can use up all their money.
While many people don't have strong backgrounds in management
or promotion, if they are going into business for themselves, then
they need to learn these skills—or know where to go to find them.
Lack of knowledge about how to find information is another big
problem I've seen small business owners suffer from. In my seminars,
I throw out a statistic I read that amazes me: only about 3 percent
of all new business owners ever set foot in a library. That's shocking
to me. Because there's a tremendous amount of information available
through this source—and it's all free."

LONAH Birch agrees with Joyce McClure's view that lack of management, rather than lack of money, is a big stumbling block for
women. "Money is always a major issue for women," says Birch.
"But even more critical—and the biggest cause of small business
failures—is lack of management expertise. Many women have a great
idea, but they are not adept at marketing it. They may know how
to develop a widget, but they don't know how to capitalize on their
product by using some key principles of leveraging. Or they are not
adept in motivating other people. All these problems come back to
the issue of management—that's probably the biggest problem I've
found that women face.

  "If you want to build a million-dollar business—if that's the big
picture for you—then what do you have to do to reach that target?
Life is a series of daily, weekly, and monthly milestones and accomplishments—that's how you reach your goal. People tend to do things
they like to do and are comfortable with. But doing what you want
to do isn't always the most productive utilization of your time. And
that's something an entrepreneur has to train herself to think about
constantly—What is the most effective way to use my time right now?
If she analyzed her day, she might find that 80 percent of the tasks
she does are routine. If she could train someone to take them over,
then she could focus on the other 20 percent of her time that's highly

productive, like building client relationships and long-range planning. But the need to plan, manage, and market is very difficult to communicate to an entrepreneur if what she loves to do is build widgets. Many women tend to get caught up in details on a day-to-day basis and this affects their time management skills. And sometimes they tend to want perfection. But finding perfection isn't always possible."

WE have talked at length about the importance of goal setting and marketing. We won't plow this ground again except to reemphasize that these are key survival issues for anyone, male or female, who wants to start a business. If you find yourself suffering from any of the four "lacks" mentioned here, then there are plenty of resources you can tap to help you develop your skills in all of these critical areas. There are books, magazines, and seminars like those given by the National Association of Women Business Owners and the SBA, all of which are listed at the end of this book.

As a parting note, here are some more words of advice on pitfalls to avoid during your start-up. They are offered by Rica Burton, who provided them in response to the NAFE survey we discussed earlier (page 19). Burton, the founder of Choice Professionals, is a small business consultant and trainer based in Los Angeles. She specializes in helping entrepreneurial women determine and sharpen winning strategies for their businesses.

1. *Have no business plan.* Rely purely on instinct to guide your business. Don't worry about heading straight into trouble.
    If you don't know where you're going, any road will take you there. A business plan helps you focus where your company is going and why, and how you're doing along the way. Creating a plan is sensible, simple, and essential.

2. *Run out of cash.* Live on the euphoria of starting a business, ignore cash flow, and overlook the gap between making the first sale and banking the money.
    A cash flow budget helps you predict highs and lows in time to take corrective action *fast*. Plan ahead to eliminate the killer cash crunch.

3. *Stay ignorant about your customers.* Changes in customers' preferences and your competitors' products will leave you in the dust—with no effort on your part.

   Knowing who your audience and market are, what they want *now* and will likely want *next*, is how your business can stay on top.

4. *Do it all on your own.* You're the key to everything. You can do *everything*. Except *grow* at the same time. Let a small success overwhelm you and a big success bury you.

   Get help. The smallest business needs professional guidance. A banker, a lawyer, an accountant, and, especially in a recession, a marketing professional. Hire the *right* person at the *right* time at the *right* price. Think growth and build toward it.

5. *Ignore your employees.* Unresolved "people problems" destroy morale, productivity, and profits. This is one of the fastest and surest ways to destroy your business.

   Motivating and managing your employees is your greatest challenge. More success means more people and more problems to address. Develop the management skills to match your business success.

6. *Surrender to computer chaos.* Don't bother about harnessing the power of computers. It's easier to have a nightmare of confusion and waste.

   Computers offer many benefits in time and money. Discover the advantages of converting, buying or upgrading, and implementing.

7. *Ignore the idea of profit and loss.* Don't focus on making a profit. It's easier to stay in the dark.

   You need to know where your business stands on a regular basis, with a timely system for recording and analyzing key data.

8. *Promote disorder.* Let things pile up, build up, and grow on their own. It's the "natural way."

   Organization is the *first* building block to success. It's the key determinant of *who's in control.* Build a good work flow system from the very start to position yourself for the flood that comes with success.

11

QUICK TIPS AND SMART MOVES

Eleanor Roosevelt once said something I love: "No one can make you feel inadequate without your consent." When you're on your own, you have many more choices to make. This freedom can be empowering or disempowering, depending on how you handle it. We buy into our own success or failure.

—*Myrna Ruskin*

From dozens of interviews, I've gathered together some quick tips and front-line advice from female entrepreneurs around the country. I hope their words of wisdom will inspire and motivate you as you plan your own move from corporation to cottage.

TIMING

LISTEN TO YOUR INNER CLOCK

Timing your move from employee to entrepreneur is one of the major challenges you'll face. But if this work style is really right for you, then at some point, the pressure to take the leap will become so strong that you have to seize the moment—you'll realize that you can't *not* do it. It make take a while for this moment to arrive, but when it does, you'll know—if you're attuned to your own inner clock. So strategize, plan, research, gather your resources, and do all of the outer work required. But at the same time, make time for the inner work needed, listen to yourself, and let your intuition be your guide.

PLAN YOUR WORK AND THEN WORK YOUR PLAN

Wherever you are and whatever you're doing today, you can begin right now to plant the seeds for your start-up. The more resources you have in place, the better equipped you'll be to recognize and seize the moment when it comes. So start building a freedom fund, look for moonlighting work, take marketing and business courses, volunteer for a pro bono project—do whatever you can to build a strong base and fill in any experience gaps you feel may hold you back.

BE HONEST WITH YOURSELF

Are you temperamentally suited for the cottage life? In the case of a layoff, you may be making the decision to try your entrepreneurial wings on the rebound. Marriage, children, divorce, or other personal events may be major factors, too. But think long and carefully about whether leaving the corporate world is really the answer to the pressures you're facing, whatever they may be. Who among us hasn't had the urge at some point to quit an unsatisfying job cold turkey? But making a major life change solely on the basis of negative motivation can quickly prove to be a dangerous game.

It's tempting to rebound from a job loss or disappointment by falling into a work style that seems to offer greater control, but if you're running from something rather than running to it, you may simply find yourself in a new rut. If you've worked in advertising for ten years and hate it, the chances of successfully running a one-person agency are practically nil. If the desire for more time and more money are major incentives, then be aware that reaping these rewards probably will take longer than you expect.

Whatever you decide about making your move, be honest with yourself about your motives and be sure the decision is yours and yours alone. Yes, your family and friends will all have their opinions, but remember, you're the one who'll be on the line.

DON'T LET A LACK OF CONFIDENCE
GET IN THE WAY OF YOUR ABILITY

Change is indeed daunting and frightening, but the status quo can be worse. Recognize that even positive changes can be stressful and that big changes are made most successfully by moving ahead one small step at a time. Nurture your self-esteem. Acknowledge and build on the experience, talent, and resources that you bring to your venture. Bolster your self-confidence through research, networking, and family support. Don't let fear hold you back—harness it and let it energize you and push you to do more and be more.

DON'T LET YOUR AGE KEEP YOU FROM TAKING THE PLUNGE

Many of the women I interviewed were in their forties and even their fifties when they made the decision to take control of their time and create a new work style for themselves. So wherever you are and whatever you've been doing, if you find the drive within you to embrace the cottage life growing stronger and stronger, then go for it! Prepare yourself as carefully as you can and recognize the many changes it will demand. But don't let the opportunity slip away because you feel that time has passed you by. As one woman told me, "I never wanted to look back and say, I could have, should have, would have."

ENLIST THE HELP AND ADVICE OF THOSE AROUND YOU

Husbands, friends, relatives, children—the cottage life is going to affect your relationships with everyone you cherish and rely on. Support from your family and friends can make all the difference in the world. Take this into account when deciding when to make your move. Be as open and as forthright as you can about the time and financial demands that your new business start-up will make on both you and your family. Let the people around you know that they, too, have a stake in your success. At the same time, be aware that their emotional investment in your business will never be as intense as your own. Recognize that their support and enthusiasm may ebb as time passes, and be prepared for this inevitable shift.

What Kind of Business Should You Start?

GREAT IDEAS ARE AS MUCH EVOLUTIONARY
AS THEY ARE REVOLUTIONARY

The classic image of the entrepreneur is someone who suddenly gets a brilliant idea, as if a light went on in his or her head. For many women, however, accepting the mantle of the emerging entrepreneur may be far more helpful and closer to the mark. Businesses and markets evolve, just as people do. You don't need an absolutely clear idea of what your new business will be in order to launch your start-up, although you do need a strong sense of purpose, direction, and commitment to the cottage work style.

A CLEAR VISION IS OFTEN LESS IMPORTANT
THAN A SENSE OF PASSION

Your instincts are often the answers to questions you haven't given yourself time to ask. When you do what your heart tells you to do, things will fall into place and the next step you should take will become clear. So pursue your strongest impulse in a focused and energetic way and see where it leads you. If you persist, then the right idea will find you.

When casting about for new-business concepts, think about your outside interests. Whatever they are, there's probably a publication or organization dedicated to serving it (if not, you may have found your niche!). Use your own experience as a touchstone and explore the "pressure points" that are reshaping your life, your work, and your family commitments. It's more than likely that other people are experiencing these same demands. Find a way to meet them creatively and you may have the seeds of a successful business.

Learn as much as you can about the areas that intrigue you. When the drive to pursue these personal interests overwhelms your enthusiasm for your current line of work, it's probably time to move on.

INTENTION CREATES OPPORTUNITY

Put yourself out in the world, ask questions, do the next thing that comes to mind and hand, and eventually a pattern will emerge that will give you both drive and direction.

While it's perfectly OK not to have an overwhelmingly clear idea of where you're going, remember that forward motion is important. So keep forging ahead, despite the obstacles you encounter. If what you're doing works, it works. If not, then you've learned something valuable and moved that much closer to clarifying your goals.

MANAGING YOUR TIME

PROSCRASTINATION IS THE THIEF OF TIME

More than money, time is the most valuable commodity you have. Even if your ideas for a new business are only half formed, they may well be worth pursuing. Beware of time wasters. Leisurely phone chats, long, rambling lunches, poor organization, misplaced perfectionism, unfocused networking, and unnecessary meetings can all fritter away your hours and days and deflect your energy from client service, new business development, and marketing.

DON'T EXPECT THE COTTAGE LIFE TO GIVE YOU MORE FREE TIME

Your start-up will be far more demanding than you can imagine. Time will be at a premium, even more so than it is in a nine-to-five job, largely because you'll be doing all of the little things that people on your staff at work used to do—typing, filing, answering phone calls, whatever. Don't let these low-priority tasks be the ones you spend the lion's share of your time on. While forward motion is important, it's also easy to mistake motion for actual progress.

DON'T RELY ON HOME-BASED WORK TO MEET YOUR CHILD-CARE NEEDS

Many a cottage career is driven by the desire for greater time flexibility and the lack of adequate child care. But balancing the demands of work and family life often isn't any easier from your kitchen than it is from a corporate office. While you can start slowly,

structuring your business around your children's schedule and activities, at some point it will begin to demand more time and energy
from you. If and when it takes off, you may well have to seek outside
child care.

CLUSTER OR HIRE OUT TASKS YOU DON'T
LIKE OR DON'T DO WELL

This doesn't mean bringing in a horde of employees you can't
afford. Instead look for other small businesspeople who might want
to trade their expertise for yours, a concept called "clustering." Or
bite the bullet and pay an outside person to do your books, computer
graphics, or whatever else you're spinning your wheels trying to
complete. Remember, however, that it's *your* business. You can and
should have a general understanding of every aspect of its operation
before you turn portions over to an outside expert.

LOOK AT TASKS IN TERMS OF QUALITY RESULTS,
NOT TIME EXPENDED

What you control is less your time than the amount and quality
of the effort you're putting into the work you're doing. So make each
minute count and set clear, realistic goals for yourself. Know where
you want to go and you'll find both the time and creativity you need
to get there. Beware of saying yes to everything that comes
your way.

YOUR CLIENTS' TIMETABLE IS YOURS

Service is what your clients say it is. You're not the boss, your
client is—at least during the start-up days, when building your client
base is most critical. You have many masters. Yes, you make the
decisions as to when to start working and when to stop, how much
effort to devote to major projects and how much to new client acquisitions. At the same time, however, your clients' needs will drive
your day and determine your priorities. The key here is avoiding
the tendency to overservice a handful of clients at the expense of
your new business development and marketing. Sacrificing your
business needs to short-term client demands will be a losing proposition for everyone involved.

EXPECT TO SPEND AT LEAST SIX MONTHS FILLING THE PIPELINE

If you're in a service business, where growth depends on projects generated from outside clients, then you can easily find yourself coping with a feast-or-famine work flow. Managing your time effectively under these circumstances can be a major challenge. As a rule of thumb, you should expect to spend at least the first six months of your start-up getting organized, networking, and making contacts that eventually will result in new work.

ACTIONS HAVE CONSEQUENCES

What you put off today still needs to be done, and probably just when the dog's gotten into the dumpster or the baby won't sleep. Manage your time strategically, with an eye on both your mission and your bottom line. Use your downtime productively to recharge and regroup.

Money

PEOPLE NEVER, EVER HAVE ENOUGH WHEN THEY START OUT

Remember, you need enough to cover both your business expenses and day-to-day personal needs, and for many people this is overwhelming. On the other hand, plenty of businesses have started out of the back of pickup trucks and on the tops of kitchen tables. Be willing to accept a bare-bones existence when you're starting out and you'll make things easier for yourself.

EXPECT TO SPEND MORE MONEY THAN YOU HAD PLANNED

No matter how carefully you plan and how frugal you are, it's more than likely that you'll end up spending more money during your start-up than you intend to. Costs will go up, you'll make mistakes, a new tax or insurance bill will hit you. The best way to beat this problem is to accept it and build a contingency fund to help tide you over when you hit a spending snag.

GAIN CONTROL OF YOUR EXPENSES EARLY

Make every dollar count. The sooner you get a handle on your business and personal expenses, the more prepared you'll be to create a strategy for meeting them. When it comes to cash management, avoidance is one of the biggest dangers you'll face. If you find it hard to set up some basic systems for managing your cash flow, then find someone who can help you as quickly as possible.

DON'T SPEND A FORTUNE ON YOUR IMAGE

Be conservative financially, especially when it comes to image. Horror stories abound of new business owners who sank thousands into elaborate logos and brochures and all sorts of office equipment that ended up never being used. Start out with only the basics; keep everything simple. When you've been in business for a while, you'll know exactly what your needs are and how to meet them. Remember, clients and customers want services and products that meet their needs. They don't really care about whether or not your office is sleek and stylish or your computer has the latest bells and whistles. Professionalism depends on the results you produce, not on how or where you make them happen.

FINANCE YOUR BUSINESS IN A WAY
THAT MAKES YOU COMFORTABLE

Starting a business is a risky proposition to begin with, so why put yourself under additional stress by overextending yourself financially? Time and again, the same message emerged in my interviews when it came to money: start small, stay lean, substitute business savvy for spending, and build slowly. Whatever business you plan to enter, there is a way to fund it that meets your own comfort level. Take the time to find it and pursue it. It may mean delaying your start-up for six months or a year while you build a nest egg, or turning to friends and family for kick-off capital. It may mean teaming up with a seasoned business owner while you learn the ropes or searching out unconventional sources of venture capital. Whatever route you take, remember that your energy and creativity, not dollars, will drive your start-up's growth. As most seasoned entrepreneurs will tell you, in the end, money is the by-product of a successful business, not its engine.

BEWARE OF OLD SPENDING PATTERNS

When you're operating on a shoestring businesswise, it's vital that your personal spending habits reflect your start-up situation. You may have to think twice before going out to lunch or dinner with friends or before buying the little luxuries that used to make you feel better about yourself when things weren't going well at work. If your business needs and personal spending style are out of synch, then take steps to handle the mismatch as quickly as you can.

LET YOUR VENDORS WORK FOR YOU

Small businesses often have cash flow problems. Maintaining good relationships with vendors can help alleviate those problems and ensure the timely delivery of materials you might not have the cash to pay for. Vendors also can be a great source for client referrals. And if a project is appealing, they even may be willing to help underwrite it financially in order to tap into a new market or generate a new revenue stream. So be sure to see the vendors you work with as a valued part of your network.

KNOW WHAT MONEY MEANS TO YOU

To some people, money provides a meaure of freedom, or security, or self-worth. Others have a hard time focusing on financial problems or tend to undervalue their skills and services. Whatever your attitude, come to grips with it early, for it will have a great deal to do with how persistently you pursue your new-business goals. Take steps to identify your money style. Recognize that both your strengths and your weaknesses on the money front will be intensified when you are totally responsible for your financial future. Focus on separating your feelings of self-worth from your net worth. Come up with creative ways to pay yourself that don't involve money—give yourself the gift of time, renew your personal relationships, and volunteer your talents to help a cause you believe in. All of these steps can enrich your life and validate the cottage choice you've made.

BUSINESS PLAN

DO YOU NEED ONE?

Yes, it's vital. A written plan provides you with benchmarks and goals. It also provides the motivation you will need for the long haul. And it communicates to family, colleagues, and potential backers that you are seriously committed to beating the odds and making your business a success.

WHO SHOULD WRITE IT?

You should. Only you know the goals and values you aspire to. Your plan should include a mission statement—a short, concise statement of intent. If the business you want to start is still in the formative stages, then write down what you want to accomplish as clearly and precisely as you can. Give yourself a timetable for achieving those goals. Don't plan and plan and then not act!

EXPERT ADVICE

KNOW THE HELP YOU NEED

You need enough advice to avoid getting sued or hanging yourself. There are all sorts of "experts" out there, and there's no end to the amount of advice people are willing to impart for a fee. The information you need probably includes legal advice, accounting and tax advice, and management and marketing help. Usually an accountant and an attorney who specialize in small businesses are essential.

As for marketing and management expertise, any number of books and low-cost seminars are available on these topics. Before you hire a high-powered consultant with a fee to match, investigate lower-priced resources at local libraries and universities. The time to look for expensive expert advice is when you have a clear concept of the problems and challenges you face, and that point rarely comes before you've been immersed in your business for some considerable length of time.

MAKING CONTACTS

NETWORKING IS VITAL

You can't expect to thrive without it. Whether you see it as a burden or as a genuine pleasure, your connections to the outside world will be vital.

THINK OF EVERYONE YOU MEET AS A POTENTIAL CLIENT

Join all the professional organizations you can and attend their meetings. Help out on a committee or run for a board position. Take classes at the local university; teach if you're qualified. Do volunteer work for causes that matter to you. Work out at a gym that caters to businesspeople. Join your college or high school alumni association.

In other words, try not to look at networking as an onerous task that requires skills you may or may not have. Instead take advantage of the opportunities that present themselves every day to meet and talk to new people. Share your skills and your excitement about your new business. "Talk to people, talk to people, talk to people!" That's the best advice one entrepreneur said she had to offer.

LOOK FOR HELP OUTSIDE YOUR FIELD

Don't confine your networking to your own industry. Make it a point to reach out to people in other lines of work and investigate their strategies and successes. All too often, shop talk centers on common problems and commiseration instead of on the fresh viewpoints that inspire change. Be coachable; let people know that you're ready to listen and learn about what they have to offer.

SHARE YOUR SUCCESS

Everyone likes to hear a success story. Being part of one is even more satisfying. So keep the people you network with, especially those who've really helped you, up to date on what you're doing and any big wins you've had.

MANAGEMENT SKILLS

THE BIG THREE: PLANNING, MOTIVATING, DELEGATING

Planning means understanding present and future needs and putting aside the resources—time, money, energy—required to deal with them. It means being proactive, not reactive. Cottage businesses live or die on the vision entrepreneurs have of the future. To plan for the future means to give enough time to the things that keep a business afloat—marketing, soliciting for new clients, looking for new avenues of growth.

Motivation is a key element of cottage success. If you can't maintain an upbeat attitude about the effort required to keep your business going, then generating enthusiasm and a willingness to perform in others is going to be tough.

Your internal motivation comes from internal drive and attitude as well as the mission statement that embodies your goals and aspirations. This attitude is infectious; it's the key to getting the response you need from outside vendors, clients, and employees.

Delegation means handing off routine tasks to someone else so that you can focus on the aspects that truly require your attention. No one is an expert at everything. Know something about every aspect of your business so there won't be any surprises later, but delegate the tasks you truly hate or don't have time for to others. Concentrate on the 20 percent of the business that reflects your vision and personality, not the 80 percent that's necessary but routine.

FINDING AND WORKING FOR CLIENTS

FINDING CLIENTS TAKES TIME AND ENERGY

Soliciting for business is one of the most difficult demands of a business start-up. It means putting yourself in a position to be rejected, sometimes over and over again. This is where motivation and persistence come into play.

THERE IS NO SCARCITY OF BUSINESS

Even in tough economic times, there are over 250 million people in this country; in any given city and even in small towns, hundreds of businesses are represented. Plenty of people and plenty of businesses, and all you need is a piece of what's out there!

NO ONE EVER DEVOTES ENOUGH TIME
TO NEW CLIENT ACQUISITION

Even when business is rolling in, planning for the future and allocating the necessary resources to implement that plan must be central to day-to-day activities. Otherwise you will be at the mercy of cash flow and existing clients, whose timetables and payment cycles may not coincide with your needs.

DON'T UNDERPRICE AND OVERSERVE

Clients will be both the joy and the bane of your existence. You will be tempted to do everything for them, to provide service well in excess of the fees they are paying. In short, you'll probably fall in love with them. Yes, you need to provide the very best client service you can, but not to the detriment of marketing, networking, and planning. No one is well served when you're worried about what's going to happen once the project you're working on is completed. The chance to work with clients you like is a wonderful gift, but realize that enthusiasm and friendship must sometimes take a backseat to planning and effective time management.

MARKETING AND PROMOTION

MARKETING AND PROMOTION CAN SPELL
SUCCESS OR FAILURE

You must constantly reach out to the clients and customers you're interested in. Your goal? To create "top-of-mind awareness" so that you'll be the first person people think of when they need a product or service.

MARKETING AND PROMOTION TAKE MANY FORMS

Don't look to just the classic methods—advertising, direct mail, splashy brochures. Marketing takes other forms, too—telephone solicitation, news releases, special events, referral cards. Take the time to learn which methods will work best for you.

DON'T JUST HIRE AN ADVERTISING OR PR AGENCY

Even for expert marketers, doing promotional tasks on their own behalf can be a daunting prospect. This is one area where it often pays to get some expert advice. That advice can be expensive, however, so before you pay an outsider to do the work for you, take some classes at your local community college or an inexpensive seminar that focuses on small business promotion. You'll be surprised at the wide range of vehicles you can use to promote your business inexpensively and effectively. You even may discover that you have a real flair for promotion and that you enjoy it tremendously.

DEVELOPING A PERSONAL WORK STYLE

GIVE YOURSELF THE FREEDOM
TO CREATE A SATISFYING STYLE

When you're just starting out, your natural tendency will be to replicate the schedule you had at your last job. Even if you're not happy in a corporate setting, it still represents a familiar, comfortable structure. When you work for yourself, you have to develop both a new community and new ways to accomplish your goals. Take advantage of the opportunity to find your own rhythm and to shape your workday in a way that works best for you—within some clearly defined parameters. Make it a point to separate your personal and professional space and to create rituals that allow you to balance the two aspects of your life.

KNOW WHAT YOU MEAN BY ''CONTROL''

Some of the most common complaints people in corporate settings deal with concern control or lack of it—control of their time, budgets, work loads, and, most important, destinies. Yes, pursuit of the cottage life-style will enable you to control certain aspects of your work; you'll be able to take up the pen and draw the picture instead of fitting into someone else's game plan. Remember, however, that you aren't the boss, your business is. Or your clients are. They will have a huge say in how you control your time and resources. At the same time, the fact that you're operating in the cottage mode doesn't give your clients the right to infringe on your personal time unless it's absolutely necessary.

Managing Employees

BE SURE YOU REALLY NEED EXTRA PEOPLE BEFORE YOU HIRE THEM

Employees add a whole new level of responsibility and complexity to your business situation. Before taking on a full- or even part-time employee, look into other alternatives, such as contracting or clustering. Stay as small as you can for as long as you can—that's the advice many women entrepreneurs offer.

DON'T BE A MOTHER HEN OR A CONFESSOR—THAT'S NOT YOUR ROLE

Small business owners who were unhappy in their previous work situations often vow to make life easier for their own employees. This is a worthwhile goal but one that's almost impossible to realize. Getting caught up in your employees' lives and problems takes valuable energy away from your business. It is not your function.

BE REALISTIC ABOUT THE BENEFITS YOU CAN OFFER

Offer the best package you can, because you want to attract good people. But be careful not to jeopardize the financial health of your new enterprise for the sake of putting someone on salary and not commission, for example, if a commission makes more financial sense for you.

STAYING THE COURSE

REALIZE THAT STARTING A BUSINESS IS A GREAT ADVENTURE

Setting out on a new business venture is a lot like setting out to sea. As you leave port, the crowds cheer, the big whistle blows, there's a great feeling of purpose and excitement.

EVERY ADVENTURE SETTLES INTO ROUTINE; YOURS WILL TOO

That first flush of energy will wane as you settle down to the task of keeping the ship running and pointed in the right direction. No longer are you the focal point of tugboat captains and harbor traffic controllers; you become a little speck on the ocean, chugging along.

This is for many entrepreneurs the most dangerous time of all, when the excitement of setting out on a grand voyage has settled into a routine, when the first flush of enthusiasm wanes, and reality sets in.

Staying the course—staying true to your ultimate goals, staying true to yourself—is perhaps the greatest challenge you'll face in the transition to the cottage life. Tenacity in pursuit of the outcomes you hold most dear is the mark of the true entrepreneur.

YOUR ATTITUDE MAKES ALL THE DIFFERENCE

You can't change your genes, you can't change your personality, but you *can* change the way you face the challenges that come your way. Attitude may well be the element that separates success from failure. The spin you put on both setbacks and achievements is going to have everything to do with your ability to stay your course, despite the obstacles you'll face. So work hard to stay upbeat and to find the "secret motivator" that will help you regain your positive outlook when you hit an emotional stumbling block.

SOMETIMES IT WILL FEEL AS IF YOU'VE FALLEN INTO A BLACK HOLE

There comes a time, often within a few months of when you start out, when it will appear that everything is falling apart. Collections are slow; new business is trickling in or, worse, not appearing at all;

an assignment didn't turn out right or wasn't what the client wanted. A frightening experience, but one you'll come to value just the same.

IT'S NOT THE GOOD TIMES YOU LEARN FROM, BUT THE TOUGH ONES

Growth comes from adversity, from change, from mistakes. The point at which everything falls apart has been called the darkness before the dawn. Discipline yourself to make it through the tough times, with the knowledge that thousands have been there before you, and the outcome will be better than you ever dreamed possible.

DON'T DWELL ON YOUR FAILURES

Give your energy and concentration to what you're doing now, not to what went wrong yesterday and what's going to happen tomorrow. Try to stay "in the moment" as much as you can, letting the past go and the future unfold as it will.

KEEP YOURSELF "STRESS HARDY"

GIVE YOURSELF A BREAK

Both mentally and physically, that is. The cottage life will make great emotional and psychological demands of you, demands that can be met only if you're mentally and physically fit. So nurture yourself, and see the time that you give to personal renewal as an investment in your future health, wealth, and happiness.

EXERCISE TO BUILD YOUR STRENGTH AND EMOTIONAL STAMINA

There are a thousand reasons not to exercise but three very good ones why you should: you will look better, feel better, and perform better. Taking time out for fitness won't detract from the time you spend on business matters, it will make that time more productive.

EXERCISE YOUR MIND

Lack of balance is destructive. To focus on business to the complete exclusion of other interests is to become narrow in both mind and spirit. Read books and magazines that carry you far afield from your daily routines and demands. Socialize with your friends. Attend meetings. Go to the movies. Don't feel guilty because you spent a night or two watching TV. If you have an absolutely compelling need to do something other than your work, pay attention, for it may be nature's way of telling you to relax. Let your business enrich your family life, not endanger it.

DIVERSIONS MAY LEAD YOU IN EXCITING NEW DIRECTIONS

Things that divert your attention may provide the impetus and inspiration you need to broaden or even change the original mission of your business. As that business takes on a life of its own, you'll discover new skills and interests you never knew you had. Don't brush these aside or consider them distractions, for it's in these areas that growth can be most rewarding.

GIVE YOURSELF SOME QUIET TIME EACH DAY
TO RENEW AND RECHARGE

Set aside time for daily reflection, because it's during the quiet times that your instincts speak to you most strongly, and it's instinct that provides answers.

HAVE FAITH IN YOURSELF AND IN YOUR GOALS

It's been said that faith can move mountains; perhaps the particular problem facing you looks insurmountable, but there's always a way over or around it. Perspective is gained only with experience, but you'll never gain the wisdom of experience if you don't follow your dreams. And when those dreams are realized, be sure to share your success and strength with others on the road behind you. And then cast your eye toward the horizon once again and dream a bigger dream!

APPENDIX 1

The Trade-offs: What You'll Give Up if You Leave Your Job . . .

1. Your Corporate Identity and Status

If you've defined yourself largely in terms of your job and the status it conferred, then you may face a challenging period of readjustment as you move from giving up your corporate identity to building a professional identity—one that's based not on whom you work for, but on the skills you have to offer. Expect to experience feelings of abandonment and fragility for a while.

2. Day-to-Day Project Support

You may suffer from the "one-armed paperhanger syndrome" and be seen as a jill-of-all-trades, especially if you go into business as a solo practitioner. Be aware that you'll have to do everything, even the jobs you aren't good at and dislike the most, at least until you can afford to pay someone else to do them. Time wasters are a big problem; photocopying, faxing, mailing, and other unglamorous jobs can consume far more time than you anticipate.

3. Camaraderie

Probably the biggest single problem people who work on their own face—especially in home-based businesses—is isolation. When you give up your job, you're giving up much more than an office and a title; you're giving up the camaraderie and collegial atmosphere that helped make your work fun and rewarding. You're also giving up the "buzz" and synergy that teamwork may have offered.

4. Your Power Base and Insider's Status

As an executive, you had a built-in power base and insider's knowledge of your organization and its culture. When you leave, you surrender this insider's status along with everything else. In your new business, you may find yourself struggling to overcome the feeling of being on the outside looking in.

5. Your Financial Security and Momentum

There's a security and sanity in knowing when your next paycheck will arrive and the benefits you'll receive down the road. When you give them up, you're choosing to live on the edge financially, at least during your start-up stage. You also may be setting yourself back in terms of retirement and insurance. The result: undercapitalization and cash flow concerns.

. . . AND WHAT YOU STAND TO GAIN IF YOU START YOUR OWN BUSINESS

1. A New Self-Image and Professional Identity

One of the biggest benefits of starting a business is the boost it can give your self-image and the sense of freedom you'll experience. Your own venture also can give you a new perspective on your professional identity—the skills, talent, and experience you've acquired over the years and are now using to build your own base of operations and independent work style.

2. A Sense of Flexibility and Control

A major benefit entrepreneurs enjoy is the feeling of flexibility that having greater control over their time and work offers them. Yes, in the beginning, it may seem as if your business controls you, but you are still the captain of your fate and planner of your priorities. You shape your environment and set the goals.

3. A New Support System

Once you're no longer in an office surrounded by other people, one of your major challenges will be to create a new support system for yourself. Through networking, community service, associations, and loyal suppliers, you can begin to build a rewarding new business life and expand your horizons.

4. Self-Discovery and Personal Growth

The corporate identity you enjoyed as an employee afforded you an *external* power base. As you begin to craft a self-structured life, you will find yourself building an *internal* power base, one grounded in your growing self-confidence and the strength that comes from tapping new skills and capabilities.

5. Increased Financial Savvy and Earning Power

If there's one thing that being in business for yourself does, it forces you to come to terms with your deepest financial fears—and hopes. By compelling you to give up old patterns and understand your money style, your new venture can increase your creativity and financial savvy. Another incentive: your own business offers not only greater financial risks, but also greater financial rewards, than working for someone else.

Six Promising Trends for Female Entrepreneurs

1. The "Free-lance Economy" Redefines the Workplace

As corporate loyalty wanes, a new group of "migrant managers" geared to marketing their services across industries is emerging. As moonlighters, contract employees, and entrepreneurs, these business experts are helping to reshape work styles and expectations.

Once-secure employees who see themselves at risk are redefining their relationships with the companies they work for, transforming themselves from employees into free-lance professionals who sell their skills on the open market, moving from company to company. Some experts describe this shift as the rise of a "free-lance" or "contingent" economy. Middle managers in particular are repackaging themselves to appeal to different industries, networking, and taking interim project work to build their skills and broaden their experience. Some of these executives may moonlight, some may work on a short-term contract basis, and others are starting their own businesses. They are creating a new type of entrepreneur—a seasoned professional with a portfolio of marketable skills who has one foot in the corporate world and the other in the cottage door.

Women joining the ranks of the free-lance economy have received invaluable training from corporate America. As executives in middle management, many have expertise in budgeting, marketing, selling, hiring, and new product development. At this stage in their careers, they may have gained ten, twenty-five, or thirty years of business experience and have a solid foundation for launching and managing new ventures. As a result, the "experience gap" between men and women is rapidly closing—and women have a better chance than ever before to achieve entrepreneurial success by building on their corporate track records. In many cases, the corporations they once worked for are fueling the growth of the free-lance economy by taking advantage of the talent it offers. A study by one consulting company, the Wyatt Company, found that one-third of the country's thousand largest companies have increased their use of outside contractors since the late 1980s.

2. Home-based Businesses Gain Credibility and Clout

As the number of home-based businesses surges, the array of products, services, and other resources tailored to their needs has expanded dramatically. Today home business is big business.

By 1995, some experts predict that fifty million or more Americans will be performing all or some of their work at home. If this movement continues to grow at its current pace, by the time the year 2000 rolls around, more people will be working out of their apartments and houses than in offices and factories. Just as it once was in the nineteenth century, the cottage will become the focal point of the "new American workplace." As home-based businesses surge in numbers and profitability, they are gaining greater credibility and clout. Today some of the country's largest corporations— AT&T, American Express, and IBM among them—have decided that small businesses represent big dollars. As a result, office equipment companies are fighting for a piece of the home business market, phone companies are offering home-based entrepreneurs special services, and new computer software is being created to meet their needs.

The array of new resources and services for home-based entrepreneurs is expanding daily. With major corporate support, for example, *Home Office Computing* magazine recently sponsored a series of seminars around the country on new business start-ups. CompuServe, one of the country's largest on-line services, offers many programs tailored to small business, including an International Entrepreneur's Network, a consultants forum, a home-office forum, and public relations and marketing forums. As you'd expect, smaller players also are developing products and services for other small businesses. In the computer arena, for instance, a wide range of new user-friendly software designed to simplify proposal writing, direct mail promotions, record keeping, and other small business activities is now on the market. Even going global is now an option. GateWaze, a firm based in Manchester, Massachusetts, sells a software package called World Trader, designed to help small companies expand their reach by giving them access to export-marketing opportunities. Clearly the home business is no longer an exotic or isolated form of enterprise; it is rapidly becoming part of the mainstream of American economic life.

3. Technology Lowers the Barriers to Small Business Success

New advances in technology are eliminating the need for a fixed office, lowering the cost of doing business, and increasing professionalism, efficiency, and mobility.

No one, it seems, can talk about small business in the 1990s without talking about technology. And for good reason. Communications is the single most important tool a small business has, and new technology has made reaching and servicing clients and customers around the corner and round the globe easier than ever before. It's also lowered the barriers to entry in a host of service- and information-intensive industries, reducing start-up costs and making it possible for an entrepreneur to operate as efficiently as a Fortune 500 firm. Today, with some mix of the same basic equipment—a telephone, answering machine, fax, copier, computer, and a modem—many small businesses have everything they need to compete successfully with much larger firms, and at lower fees.

One exciting new technology trend is the growing number of electronic bulletin boards and data bases now available to small businesses. Through on-line services like CompuServe, GEnie, and Prodigy, entrepreneurs can access dozens of research data bases, attend classes, make travel arrangements, and contact experts and other business owners in scores of industries. Or by using electronic mail, a small business can instantly deliver press releases to editors across the country or barter for an exchange of equipment or professional expertise.

What's next on the technology horizon? Trend watchers are keeping their eyes on multimedia PCs, personal videophones, and the rise of a global network of "electronic cafes"—informal teleconferencing centers for telelearning, telework, and teleconsulting. These advances, like so many others, promise to virtually eliminate the need for fixed offices, allowing entrepreneurs to take ever greater advantage of the flexibility and mobility that are among their major assets. Whatever advances lie down the road, it's clear that technology is proving to be a powerful partner for small business.

4. Service Ventures Will Increase Through Niche Marketing

Female business owners enjoy a strong track record in service businesses. Creative entrepreneurs who can identify and explore niches in specialty markets will find abundant opportunities for start-up ventures and expansion during the 1990s.

Day-care centers are enjoying growing demand, but how about night-care centers? You may have hired a personal trainer to aerobicize your body into shape, but what about a "clutter consultant" to help you get your life in order? You may have heard of Outward Bound for teenagers, but now it's your mom's turn. How about a wilderness tour for seniors to Africa or an archaeological dig in Turkey? Welcome to the services sector, 1990s style!

As people feel more pressed for time, personal services catering to this need will be in greater demand than ever before. Little wonder, then, that today more than half of all self-employed women make their living by launching ventures geared to personal and business services. As American families and companies continue to change and redefine themselves, creative entrepreneurs who can identify and exploit niches in specialty markets will find the services sector wide open to them throughout the 1990s. This bodes well for female business owners, who traditionally have enjoyed a strong base in this arena. The relatively low overhead and ease of entry that fueled growth in the 1980s will continue to make start-up opportunities in the services sector extremely attractive, especially in dynamic industries like health care, human resources, direct marketing, environmental planning, information management, high technology, career counseling, and travel.

Technology, for example, isn't simply making it easier and cheaper to start home-based ventures, it also is spawning scores of new businesses. Women are starting electronic clipping services for graphic artists, consulting firms that guide small business owners through the growing maze of computer products, "shareware" services that electronically transmit software via telephone—the list goes on and on. The explosive growth of 900 number services is a case in point. Despite its once-shady reputation, the pay-per-call industry is spawning many new businesses by using new technology to satisfy consumers' demand for information on everything from skiing conditions and stock prices to parenting and health care.

5. Support Services for Female Entrepreneurs Are Multiplying

Many of the new resources springing up in support of cottage industries are geared to women. Specialized training programs, networking groups, and publications offer advice and support at all stages, from start-up through expansion.

The 1990s have been called the "golden age of the woman entrepreneur." The key reason for this expansive outlook is greater access and better information; women now have more support services available to them than ever before—from newsletters and magazines to networking groups and mentoring programs. Many of these resources are aimed at helping fledgling entrepreneurs survive the first one to three years of business ownership, while others focus on helping small businesses grow wisely and well. Most exciting of all, many successful female entrepreneurs, who've already lived through the ups and downs of a business start-up themselves, are reaching out to inspire and inform other women about the best ways to handle the challenges they'll face. This sharing of ideas, war stories, and success strategies is helping to demystify entrepreneurship as a work option. Outlined here are just a handful of examples; you'll find more resources in Appendix 3.

The SBA's Small Business Development Centers offer ongoing training to women around the country. For entrepreneurs whose businesses are poised for expansion, the SBA's Women's Network for Entrepreneurial Training (WNET) program offers one-on-one mentoring relationships with seasoned business owners, who share advice, resources, and support. EXCEL, a program offered by the National Association of Women Business Owners (NAWBO), with support from Deloitte & Touche, puts budding entrepreneurs in touch with successful businesswomen from NAWBO's local chapters. Through Avon's Women of Enterprise awards program, winners join a national network of role models who share their advice and experience at local conferences around the country.

There are also many small business self-help newsletters and publications. *ConneXions,* a newsletter geared to the special needs of home-based working mothers, is published by Caroline Hull from her home office in Manassas, Virginia. Barbara Brabec's quarterly, the *National Home Business Report,* her book *Homemade Money,* and other how-to guides generated from her home in Naperville, Illinois, all offer valuable help. *Executive Female* magazine features a special section called "Your Business: Starting It, Growing It" in each issue.

6. New Sources of Start-up Funding Are Emerging

Finding start-up dollars has always been a major challenge for small businesses. Today new sources of seed money are being developed to support the start-up stage of female-owned firms.

As more and more women make the decision to try their entrepreneurial wings, there is growing recognition that they face special challenges in securing seed financing. As the 1990s unfold, it appears that more avenues for securing start-up funds finally are becoming available to women.

The SBA, for example, now offers a Micro Loan Program, which targets businesses requiring $25,000 or less in start-up funds; today small business investment companies also are licensed by the SBA to offer seed capital. Through a special SBA demonstration loan program, a network of organizations across the country offers microloans and training to new or existing small businesses. One of the participants, WomenVenture of St. Paul, Minnesota, for example, provides a wide range of technical assistance programs and loans to in-state entrepreneurs. The SBA also sponsors conferences for women on marketing their products and services to the federal government and offers other financially related support.

Closer to home, some state and local governments are coming up with creative ways to support female entrepreneurs. The state of Illinois, for example, has started a program called Women's Financial Initiative, through which a coalition of banks, women's business groups, and small business advisors provide workshops and low-interest loans ranging from $2,500 to $500,000. By mid-1993 close to three hundred companies had received $3.5 million in loans.

As the 1990s unfold, an exciting new venture called Capital Rose is breaking new ground by launching a large-scale campaign to help women launch, finance, and expand their businesses. To underwrite the program, its founder, Rebecca Maddox, plans to raise a $40 million Capital Rose Perpetual Fund for female entrepreneurs (see Appendix 3).

HELPFUL PUBLICATIONS AND ORGANIZATIONS

Books

Adams, Jane. *Wake Up, Sleeping Beauty: How to Live Happily Ever After Right Now*. New York: William Morrow, 1990.

Albert, Susan Wittig. *Work of Her Own: How Women Create Success and Fulfillment Off the Traditional Career Track*. New York: Putnam/Tarcher, 1992.

Anderson, Nancy. *Work with Passion: How to Do What You Love for a Living*. New York: Carroll and Graf, 1984.

Applegate, Jane. *Succeeding in Small Business: The 101 Toughest Problems and How to Solve Them*. New York: NAL/Dutton (Plume Books), 1992.

Brabec, Barbara. *Homemade Money: How to Select, Start, Manage, Market, and Multiply the Profits of a Business at Home* (5th ed., February 1994). Cincinnati: Betterway Books/F&W Publications. In bookstores, or by mail from the author: Barbara Brabec Productions, P.O. Box 2137, Naperville, Ill. 60567.

Cook, Mel. *Home Business to Big Business: How to Launch Your Home Business and Make It a Success*. New York: Collier Books, 1992.

Davidson, Jeffrey, and Dean, Charles. *Cash Traps: Small Business Secrets for*

Reducing Costs and Improving Cash Flow. New York: John Wiley and Sons, 1992.

Drucker, Peter. *The New Realities.* New York: Harper and Row, 1989.

Edwards, Paul and Sarah. *The Best Home-Based Businesses for the Nineties.* Los Angeles: Jeremy P. Tarcher, a member of the Putnam Publishing Group, 1991.

————. *Making It on Your Own: Surviving and Thriving on the Ups and Downs of Being Self-Employed.* Los Angeles: Jeremy P. Tarcher, a member of the Putnam Publishing Group, 1991.

————. *Working from Home: Everything You Need to Know About Living and Working Under the Same Roof.* Los Angeles: Jeremy P. Tarcher, a member of the Putnam Publishing Group, 1990.

Gerber, Michael. *The E-Myth: Why Most Small Businesses Don't Work and What to Do About It.* New York: HarperCollins, 1990.

Godfrey, Joline. *Our Wildest Dreams: Women Entrepreneurs Making Money, Having Fun, Doing Good.* New York: HarperCollins, 1992.

Hallowell, Edward M., and Grace, William J., Jr. *What Are You Worth?* New York: Weidenfield and Nicolson, 1989.

Hawken, Paul. *Growing a Business.* New York: Simon and Schuster, 1987.

Helgesen, Sally. *The Female Advantage: Women's Ways of Leadership.* New York: Doubleday, 1990.

Hyatt, Carole. *Shifting Gears: Mastering Career Change.* New York: Simon and Schuster, 1990.

Kern, Coralee Smith. *How to Run Your Own Home Business.* Lincolnwood, Ill.: VGM Career Horizons/NTC Publishing Group (1-800-323-4900), 1990.

————. *Planning Your Own Home Business.* Lincolnwood, Ill.: VGM Career Horizons/NTC Publishing Group (1-800-323-4900), 1986.

Koltnow, Emily, and Drumas, Lynne S. *Congratulations! You've Been Fired: Sound Advice for Women Who've Been Terminated, Pink-Slipped, Downsized or Otherwise Unemployed.* New York: Fawcett, 1990.

Lieberman, Annette, and Lindner, Vicki. *Unbalanced Accounts: How Women Can Overcome Their Fear of Money.* New York: Penguin Books, 1987.

Mackoff, Barbara. *The Art of Self-Renewal: Balancing Pressure and Productivity On and Off the Job.* Los Angeles: Lowell House, 1992.

————. *What Mona Lisa Knew: A Woman's Guide to Getting Ahead in Business by Lightening Up.* Los Angeles: Lowell House, 1991.

————. *Leaving the Office Behind.* New York: Dell, 1984.

Pinson, Linda, and Jinnett, Jerry. *The Home-Based Entrepreneur: The Complete Guide to Working at Home.* Dover, N.H.: Upstart, 1989.

Roddick, Anita. *Body and Soul: Profits with Principles—the Amazing Story of Anita Roddick & the Body Shop.* New York: Crown, 1991.

Saltzman, Amy. *Down-Shifting: Reinventing Success on a Slower Track.* New York: HarperCollins, 1991.

Scott, Gini Graham. *Mind Power: Picture Your Way to Success in Business.* Englewood Cliffs, N.J.: Prentice-Hall, Inc., 1987.

Sinetar, Marsha. *Do What You Love, the Money Will Follow: Discovering Your Right Livelihood.* New York: Dell, 1987.

Magazines and Newsletters

Black Enterprise. Monthly newsstand magazine focusing on entrepreneurial success. For information, contact Earl Graves Publishing Company, 130 Fifth Avenue, New York, N.Y. 10011, or call 212-242-8000.

Bootstrappin Entrepreneur. A newsletter for new entrepreneurs with great ideas and limited funds. Also publishes *The Entrepreneur's Freebie Guide.* For subscription information, send a self-addressed, stamped envelope to: Suite B261-NAIW, 8726 South Sepulveda Boulevard, Los Angeles, Calif. 90045.

ConneXions: Networking for home-based mothers and professionals. A how-to newsletter published six times a year by Caroline Hull. Subscription: $21.95 per year. Contact: ConneXions, P.O. Box 1461, Manassas, Va. 22110, or call 703-791-6264.

Entrepreneur, the Small Business Authority. Monthly newsstand magazine with helpful articles, profiles, business updates, and technology trends. For subscription information, contact: Entrepreneur Group, 2392 Morse Avenue, Irvine, Calif. 92714, or call 1-800-421-2300 or 1-800-352-7449 (California only).

Executive Female. Published six times a year for members of the National Association for Female Executives (NAFE). Each issue features a special section, "Your Business: Starting It, Growing It," for entrepreneurs, focusing on strategies and success profiles. NAFE membership is $29 per year and includes a subscription to *Executive Female.* For information contact: NAFE, 127 West 24th Street, New York, N.Y. 10011, or call 1-800-634-NAFE.

Guerrilla Marketing Newsletter. Written by Jay Conrad Levinson, a marketing expert, the newsletter offers how-to advice, research updates, and new marketing techniques for small businesses. For subscription information, contact: Guerrilla Marketing Newsletter, P.O. Box 1336, Mill Valley, Calif. 94942.

Home Office Computing. Monthly newsstand magazine focusing on technology, small business trends, and marketing. For subscription information, contact: Home Office Computing, 730 Broadway, New York, N.Y. 10003, or call 1-800-288-7812.

Home Sweet Home. Quarterly publication focusing on small business ownership and advice on family-related concerns. For subscription information, contact: Home Sweet Home, East 201 Bourgault Road, Shelton, Wash. 98584. Sample back issue $6.30 ppd. Free brochure.

Inc. Monthly newsstand magazine focusing on "growing companies" but with helpful advice and profiles for small businesses. For information contact: Inc., 38 Commercial Wharf, Boston, Mass. 02110, or call 617-227-4700.

National Home Business Report. Quarterly companion to *Homemade Money,* edited and published by small business expert Barbara Brabec. Each issue focuses on home-business management and low-cost marketing strategies, and identifies helpful new resources and networking contacts. For subscription information, contact: Barbara Brabec Productions, P.O. Box 2137, Naperville, Ill. 60567. Subscription rate: $24 per year, U.S.; $28 per year, Canada. Sample back issue, $7.

Nation's Business. Monthly magazine focusing on general economic trends and issues published by the U.S. Chamber of Commerce. For subscription information, contact: Nation's Business, 1615 H Street NW, Washington, D.C. 20062, or call 1-800-638-6582.

"Small Business Success." Informative general how-to features and resource guide published by Pacific Bell Directory and cosponsored by the Small Business Administration. To obtain copies, contact: Pacific Bell Directory, 101 Spear Street, Communications Dept.–CWS5, Room 429, San Francisco, Calif. 94105, or call 1-800-848-8000.

Working Woman. Monthly newsstand magazine that often features entrepreneurial how-to articles and success stories. For subscription information, contact: Working Woman, 230 Park Avenue, New York, N.Y. 10169, or call 1-800-234-9675.

Your Company. A small business resource magazine published by American Express and sent at no charge to corporate cardmembers as a membership benefit. For information contact: Your Company, Custom Media Group, American Express Publishing Corporation, 1120 Avenue of the Americas, New York, N.Y. 10036.

Organizations and Associations

American Women's Economic Development Corporation. A nonprofit organization, AWED offers in-depth training programs, one-on-one counseling, conferences, publications, and other resources to both start-up and established female-owned businesses. For information contact: American Women's Economic Development Corporation, 71 Vanderbilt Avenue, Suite 320, New York, N.Y. 10169, or call 212-692-9100.

Association for Enterprise Opportunities. This organization can provide you with a list of microlenders in your region who supply seed capital and support funds. For information contact: Beverly Smith, 320 North Michigan Avenue, Suite 804, Chicago, Ill. 60601, or call 312-357-0177.

Association of Part-Time Professionals. This organization offers a newsletter, networking, resource information, and other how-to help to professionals operating small businesses on a part-time basis. For information contact: Association of Part-Time Professionals, Crescent Plaza, Suite 216, 7700 Leesburg Pike, Falls Church, Va. 22043, or call 703-734-7975.

Capital Rose. A multidimensional corporation dedicated to accelerating business success for women-owned businesses through access to financing, information, expertise, products, and services. The Capital Rose Perpetual Fund seeks $10.00 contributions from women business owners to create a $40 million fund to finance women-owned businesses. For information or to contribute to the fund, contact: Capital Rose Perpetual Fund, 175 Strafford Avenue, Suite One, Wayne, Pa. 19087, or call 215-687-1666.

Center for Entrepreneurial Management. A nonprofit organization that offers entrepreneurs a chance to network with peers and business experts several times a year. Dues range from $100 to $1,000. For information contact: Center for Entrepreneurial Management, 180 Varick Street, Penthouse, New York, N.Y. 10014, or call 212-633-0060.

CenterPoint in Aspen. A retreat program combining gentle day hikes, unstructured time for solitude, and networking opportunities, and facilitated discussions on topics ranging from personal vision statements, mentoring, and leadership to managing change and entrepreneurship. For information contact: CenterPoint in Aspen, 278 Oak Ridge Drive, Aspen, Colo. 81611, or call 303-920-2393.

Displaced Homemakers Network. If you have been a full-time homemaker and now must support yourself and your family because of divorce, separation, or other reasons, this organization can provide you with helpful advice and resources. Contact: Displaced Homemakers Network,

1625 K Street NW, Suite 600, Washington, D.C. 20006, or call 202-467-6346.

Mother's Home Business Network. This organization publishes a quarterly newsletter, *Homeworking Mothers*, and offers other publications and services. For information contact: Mother's Home Business Network, P.O. Box 423, East Meadow, N.Y. 11554, or call 516-997-7394.

National Association for Female Executives. NAFE offers a range of programs for both executive women and entrepreneurs, including access to its five hundred networks and special benefits for life and health insurance and low-interest loans. NAFE also publishes *Executive Female* magazine. For information contact: NAFE, 127 West 24th Street, New York, N.Y. 10011, or call 1-800-634-NAFE.

National Association for the Cottage Industry. An organization with over fifteen thousand members that collects information and conducts research on home-based business trends and issues. Founded by Coralee Smith Kern, an expert on home-based business, the association publishes a quarterly newsletter, the *Cottage Connection*, $45 per year. For information contact: National Association for the Cottage Industry, P.O. Box 14850, Chicago, Ill. 60614, or call 312-939-6490.

National Association for the Self-Employed. Offers a business hotline and benefits programs for an annual membership fee. For information contact: National Association for the Self-Employed, Membership Services, P.O. Box 612067, DFW Airport, Tex. 75261, or call 1-800-232-6273.

National Association of Black Women Entrepreneurs. This organization offers a range of support services and informational resources to its members. For information contact: National Association of Black Women Entrepreneurs, P.O. Box 1375, Detroit, Mich. 48231, or call 313-559-9255.

National Association of Private Enterprise. A nonprofit organization whose membership consists primarily of business owners with fewer than ten employees. Offers a range of benefits, including group health and life insurance, a business loan program, and consulting services. For information contact: National Association of Private Enterprise, 2501 Parkview Drive, Suite 550, Ft. Worth, Tex. 76102-5817, or call 1-800-223-NAPE.

National Association of Small Business Investment Companies. Venture capital for small start-up companies may be available through this network of private lenders licensed by the SBA. To receive a copy of "Venture Capital: Where to Find It," send a $10 check or money order to: National Association of Small Business Investment Companies, P.O. Box 2039, Merrifield, Va. 22116.

National Association of Women Business Owners. NAWBO offers programs, publications, research, legislative updates, and networking resources for members. National dues are $100 annually; local dues vary. For information contact: National Association for Women Business Owners, 600 Federal Street, Suite 400, Chicago, Ill. 60605, or call 312-922-0465.

National Association of Women's Business Advocates. This group tracks developments around the country supporting female entrepreneurs. For information contact: Melody Boshers, Ohio Department of Development, 77 South High Street, P.O. Box 1001, Columbus, Ohio 43255-0101.

National Business Association. A nonprofit organization with a membership base of over fifty thousand business owners. Membership includes a subscription to *National Business News,* special discounts on a wide range of products and services, and benefits ranging from medical and dental insurance to a credit union. For information contact: National Business Association, P.O. Box 870728, Dallas, Tex. 75287, or call 1-800-456-0440.

National Business Incubation Association. Incubators provide affordable office space and other support services for small start-up companies. For information on NBIA centers, send a self-addressed, stamped envelope to: NBIA, One President Street, Athens, Ohio 45701, or call 614-593-4331.

National Federation of Independent Business. The country's leading advocacy group for small business, with an active legislative awareness program. For information contact: National Federation of Independent Business, 600 Maryland Avenue SW, Suite 700, Washington, D.C. 20024, or call 202-554-9000.

National Self-Help Clearinghouse. An organization dedicated to providing support for the unemployed in transition. Publishes a quarterly newsletter and offers a list of support groups around the country. For information send a self-addressed, stamped envelope to: National Self-Help Clearinghouse, 25 West Forty-third Street, Room 620, New York, N.Y. 10036.

Office of Women's Business Ownership. Established by the SBA, OWBO offers a range of services, publications, and resources geared to female entrepreneurs. For information contact: Office of Women's Business Ownership, Small Business Administration, 409 Third Street SW, Sixth Floor, Washington, D.C. 20416, or call 202-205-6673.

SBA Answer Desk. Experts from the SBA's Office of Advocacy are available by phone Monday through Friday from 9:00 A.M. to 5:00 P.M. EST to handle questions related to your business or to government programs and resources. To contact, call: 1-800-827-5722.

KARIN ABARBANEL is available for:

- Conferences
- Workshops and seminars
- Individual and group consultations

For information, please contact:
Karin Abarbanel
39 Erwin Park Road
Montclair, NJ 07042
201-509-9592

The National Association for Female Executives, founded in 1972, is the nation's largest businesswomen's organization, with 250,000 members. NAFE helps women achieve career and financial success through education, networking, and public advocacy.

NAFE members are offered special insurance programs, low-interest loans, credit cards, a career data base, resume service, and travel discounts. Venture Capital Fund invests monies in business plans submitted by members that show high potential for return on investment. Perhaps the most popular feature of the organization is its bimonthly magazine, *Executive Female*. NAFE offers national and regional teleconferences in addition to local breakfasts and networking seminars.

The National Association for Female Executives is located at 127 West 24th Street, New York, N.Y. 10011. Or call toll-free, 1-800-634-NAFE.